*Joseph Conrad
and the
Fictions of Skepticism*

Mark A. Wollaeger

Joseph Conrad and the Fictions of Skepticism

Stanford University Press   Stanford, California   1990

Stanford University Press, Stanford, California
© 1990 by the Board of Trustees of the
Leland Stanford Junior University

Printed in the United States of America

CIP data are at the end of the book

Published with the assistance of the
Frederick W. Hilles Publication Fund
of Yale University

For Lon

Acknowledgments

I doubt I will be able to do justice to the many debts incurred in writing this book, but I'm delighted to give it a shot. As a Stanford undergraduate I was very fortunate to have had three eminent Conradians to consult: Albert Guerard, Thomas Moser, and Ian Watt. No doubt all have shaped my thought more than I know, but my greatest debt is to Ian Watt, whose advice and friendship over the years I have valued as much as his example as a scholar and thinker. Although he did not read this manuscript, his presence informs it. During my graduate career at Yale, this project began to take shape as a dissertation under the exemplary supervision of Martin Price, whose doubts about Conrad helped me define the nature of my own skeptical understanding. When I most needed some criticism and support at a critical stage of the dissertation, Jonathan Freedman made the former seem a friendly consequence of the latter. Hugh Baxter, the better philosopher, guided me through some thickets of abstraction, and numerous conversations with Lewis Klausner have helped me hone my ideas about Conrad. My colleagues Michael Cooke, Paul Fry, and Bob Stepto read the final dissertation manuscript and offered valuable suggestions and encouragement. Those graduate years were also made easier by my mother, who has always wanted to help.

In the fall of 1987, before beginning the next stage of revision, I tested my arguments on a talented group of students in a Yale Senior Seminar on Conrad, and the challenge of teaching contributed much to the development of these pages. Later I received useful commentary from Helen Tartar of Stanford University Press and the two anonymous readers she solicited. Thanks go also to Francesco Rognoni for his response to Chapter One, to David Hensley for some timely notes, to Alexandra Shelley for some proofreading, and to Mike Nabel for a late-night restoration of the path to my files. To the expert assistance of Susan

Williams, who weeded out numerous errors of fact and expression, I owe a great deal. Yale University generously supported my research with a Morse Fellowship for 1989–90 and with awards from the Griswold Research Fund. I thank also the staffs of Sterling Library, Cross Campus Library, and Beinecke Rare Book and Manuscript Library at Yale, the Olin Memorial Library at Wesleyan, and the Berg Collection at the New York Public Library.

Finishing may be as hard as beginning. In the last months of this project, several chapters benefited greatly from the keen editorial skills and generosity of Victor Luftig. And finally, with a sigh of relief, I thank my wife, to whom this book is dedicated, for her forbearance, support, and love.

M.A.W.

Contents

A Note to the Reader

Unless otherwise noted, all Conrad quotations are from *Joseph Conrad: Complete Works* (24 vols.; Garden City, N.Y.: Doubleday, Page, 1924). The pagination of this edition corresponds to Dent's *Collected Edition of the Works of Joseph Conrad* (London: J. M. Dent, 1946–55) and to the *Doubleday Complete Edition* of 1925. Quotations are identified by abbreviated title and page number.

AF	*Almayer's Folly*
C	*Chance*
HD	*Heart of Darkness* (in the Doubleday *Youth* volume)
LE	*Last Essays*
LJ	*Lord Jim*
N	*Nostromo*
NLL	*Notes on Life and Letters*
NN	*The Nigger of the "Narcissus"*
P	Preface to *The Nigger of the "Narcissus"*
PR	*A Personal Record*
R	*The Rescue*
SA	*The Secret Agent*
SL	*The Shadow Line*
SS	*A Set of Six*
T	*Typhoon*
TH	*Tales of Hearsay*
TU	*Tales of Unrest*
UWE	*Under Western Eyes*
V	*Victory*

In addition, three other works cited frequently have been abbreviated for convenience:

LL	Jean-Aubry, ed., *Joseph Conrad: Life and Letters*
THN	Hume, *A Treatise of Human Nature*
WWR	Schopenhauer, *The World as Will and Representation* (trans. Payne)

Preface

"You want more scepticism at the very foundation of your work. Scepticism, the tonic of minds, the tonic of life, the agent of truth,—the way of art and salvation."
　　　　　　　　　　　　　　　　—Conrad to Galsworthy

In 1907 a review in the London *Sunday Times* complained that *The Secret Agent* "absolutely defies all laws of construction." Not content with "wilfulness of treatment, Mr. Conrad encourages himself in obscurities of style. His book is almost as stiff reading as a dissertation on metaphysics."[1] The terms are apt, but the reviewer's description of the philosophical in Conrad could be improved by saying that *The Secret Agent* reads like the left-handed creation of someone who might produce a philosophical treatise with the right. In this book I aim to uncover Conrad's "laws of construction" by analyzing the part each hand plays in the production of Conrad's texts.

While *The Secret Agent* may be Conrad's likeliest target for such a review, Conrad's readers are familiar with the experience of wanting to account for his strange "obscurities": the uneasy conjunction of hypnotic pictorialism and philosophical abstraction; the irregular counterpointing of violent action and restless meditation; the tendency of sentences and stories alike to run on past natural stopping points; the investment in solidarity doubled by an obsession with solitude. Conrad's critics have often turned to biographical explanations, discussing Conrad's divided nature as a "sea dreamer"—the man of action blessed (or cursed) with an artist's imagination—or his ambivalent allegiance to the revolutionary will of his father and the conservative restraint of his uncle. I undertake a different kind of accounting by arguing that Conrad's most important writing participates in a tradition of philosophical skepticism that extends from Descartes to the present. Expressed, forestalled, mitigated, and suppressed, Conrad's epistemological and moral skepticism provides the terms for re-thinking the peculiar relation between philosophy and literary form in his writing and, more broadly, for reconsidering what it means to call any novel "philosophical."

As Conrad knew well, participation in a tradition—whether philosophical, literary, or maritime—not only empowers but constrains, and Conrad's interest as a skeptic is heightened by the degree to which he resists the insights proffered by his own skepticism. Skepticism arises as a logical consequence of rigor-ous empiricism, and Conrad the skeptic was drawn also to the stance of the Romantic seer who yearns to achieve knowledge beyond the horizons of empiricism. Conrad's well-known state-ment in the Preface to *The Nigger of the "Narcissus"* that his aim is "to make you *see*" (*P* 147) derives simultaneously from the pri-macy of perception in the empirical tradition and the visionary response to the epistemological limitations of that tradition. From this dialogue of opposing attitudes emerges the "fictions" of my title. The word is intended to refer both to the skeptical "foundation" of Conrad's novels and to the fictive dimension of the philosophical tradition.

It is not new, of course, to think of Conrad as a skeptic,[2] but skepticism itself has become a new subject in recent years. By returning to Conrad with a more rigorous understanding of skepticism as a genuine philosophical issue, I claim to shed new light on familiar matters as well as to open new lines of inquiry. Too often the word *skepticism* when applied to Conrad and other early modernists slides into a diffuse sense of social detachment and a reluctance to believe in the existence of ascertainable truths. Such usage implies the practical skepticism of Montaigne rather than the philosophical skepticism of Descartes.[3] More in-terested in the Cartesian tradition, I invoke skepticism as a many-faceted concept whose significance expands as it is used to explore the varied formal and intellectual intricacies of Conrad's fiction. Among the issues freshly argued here in the context of authorial skepticism are Conrad's thematics of coercion, isola-tion, and betrayal; the complicated relations among author, nar-rator, and character; and the logic of Conradian romance, com-edy, and tragedy. Specific formal characteristics are also understood in relation to the articulation of Conrad's skepticism. The distinctive features of his chronological dislocations and his presentation of character, for instance, both express and resist the pull toward a more radical skepticism.

To establish important features of the skeptical tradition, I return to classic texts of modern philosophy, chiefly those of Descartes and Hume, in order to highlight certain novelistic components of philosophical skepticism. Not simply literary ornaments, the recurrent narrative situations, tropes, and themes of skepticism are constitutive features of a discourse that can be traced forward from Descartes to such contemporary philosophers as Hilary Putnam and Stanley Cavell. Skepticism derives from the Greek *skepsis*, meaning inquiry or examination, and in this study close readings of Conrad's short stories, novels, and letters locate him within a continuing line of skeptical inquiry. This tradition has shown sustained interest in, among other things, the relation of sensory impressions to knowledge, the problem of other minds, definitions of the self, problems of individual agency, and the persistence of the sacred. Taking up this last topic, philosophical skepticism brings new urgency and interest to the potentially tired matter of thinking through the disappearance of God in modern literature.

To model the antiskeptical axis of Conrad's thought I turn to his favorite philosopher, Schopenhauer, whose philosophical idealism provides a model for the will to transcendence imaged in Conrad's language. The visionary pressure to see through to something more real or true, whether located in Marlow as narrator or Razumov as character, compensates for the diminished potential for efficacious action in Conrad's canon and produces both his persistent imagery of ghosts and the charged verbal patterning of his descriptions. Schopenhauer's dualistic idealism offers a paradigm for the implicit metaphysics of such language, and his theory of aesthetic contemplation models the visionary features of Conrad's characteristic narrative situations.

Narrative fiction rightfully lays claim to the province of philosophy, according to some modern novelists. "If you want to be a philosopher," wrote Camus, "write novels."[4] According to D. H. Lawrence, "it was the greatest pity in the world, when philosophy and fiction got split. . . . [T]he novel went sloppy, and philosophy went abstract-dry. The two should come together again—in the novel."[5] Yet Conrad was not a philosophical novelist in the way Camus or even Lawrence was. Rather than espouse an identifiable doctrine, Conrad, like Swift, distrusted system builders or "projectors," believing that the dreamer of a comprehensive system was likely to lose touch with reality by becoming imprisoned within his or her own new structure of thought. Radical skepticism, in which reason subverts itself, may be considered the antithesis of the systematic, but Conrad did not turn from the (false) consolations of system to the deconstructive power of unmitigated skepticism.[6] Conrad's evasive suspension between philosophical disavowal and declaration irritated E. M. Forster, who complained that Conrad "is always promising to make some general philosophical statement about the universe, and then refraining with a gruff disclaimer."[7] But philosophy (*pace* Forster and Alasdair MacIntyre) should not be restricted to the doctrinal or systematic, and the idea of Conrad as a philosophical novelist needs to be rethought.

Robert Penn Warren pointed out long ago that Conrad's fiction shares in the impulse that is basic to philosophical speculation: "The philosophical novelist, or poet, is one for whom the documentation of the world is constantly striving to rise to the level of generalization about values, for whom the image strives to rise to symbol, for whom images always fall into a dialectical configuration, for whom the urgency of experience, no matter how vividly and strongly experience may enchant, is the urgency to know the meaning of experience."[8] Conrad projects in narrative form the hunger for meaning that Schopenhauer describes as originating in "a *wonder or astonishment* about the world and our own existence" (*WWR* II: 170).[9] In Conrad's words, the artist responds to "the enigmatical spectacle" of life and "speaks to our capacity for delight and wonder" (*P* 145). For philosopher and novelist alike, life is a summons to interpretation. Warren's fine formulation errs only in the word *dialectical*, for in Conrad contradictions and oppositions do not evolve into a progressive sequence of thought. Because Conrad's countervailing attitudes are engaged not dialectically but dialogically, in chapters that focus on narrative structure I make use of Bakhtin's poetics of dialogue. In Chapter One I discuss in some detail the Bakhtinian model of dialogue in relation to authorial skepticism; here I want to distinguish Conrad's philosophical novel from Dostoevsky's (as presented by Bakhtin), as well as from what Bakhtin refers to dismissively as "philosophy in the form of a novel."[10]

For Bakhtin, the virtue of Dostoevsky is that the polyphony of his novels resists the dialectical unity of the traditional philosophical novel, which ultimately subordinates refractory intellectual complications to the monological or unified design of the author. What differentiates Conrad, as well as my approach to him, is that he does not conduct a particular philosophical argument through the interplay of authorial and characteral perspectives: explicit discourse *on* skepticism is subsumed by an encompassing discourse *of* skepticism. Whereas Dostoevsky strategically deploys perspectives on redemption and restraint in *The Brothers Karamazov*, Conrad's skepticism is not, and cannot be, parceled out as a set of irreconcilable hypotheses embodied by author and character. By its very nature skepticism is not susceptible to narrative expression in this fashion given that, far from constituting a particular conceptual arena, skepticism is engaged in a sustained interrogation of the very categories that permit rational discussion to begin. Rather than simply offering commentary on skepticism, then, the narrative, descriptive, and generic modes of Conrad's fiction *enact* the operations of skepticism as a perpetual assessment of "our constructions of the world."[11] Often it is the tension between philosophical assertion and fictional embodiment that distinguishes Conrad's texts. In *Nostromo*, for instance, the narrator castigates Decoud for his skepticism, even as the paired fates of Decoud and Nostromo enact contrasting versions of the relation between self and other as construed in the skeptical tradition. Betrayal of self and other, an obsessive theme in Conrad's canon, can be understood as an inevitable response to the threat of radical skepticism. The "philosophy" of Conrad's fiction is constituted by such literary performances of the discourse of skepticism.

A philosophical approach to Conrad yields other benefits as well. F. R. Leavis notwithstanding, the uniqueness of Conrad's multifarious literary and cultural inheritance makes it difficult to locate him securely in the dominant tradition of the British novel. Yet my sense of the philosophical qualities of Conrad's fiction links him to other late-nineteenth- and early-twentieth-century novelists—notably Hardy, Forster, and Woolf—all of whom share in the increasing philosophical burden of the modern novel by tending toward the enactment of the very philosophical issues that are discussed within their pages.[12] In Chapter One I sketch some of the historical contexts that account for such affinities between Conrad and his contemporaries, and in Chapter Two I analyze the appeal of Schopenhauer to the early modernist period. Elsewhere I largely bracket the importance of the cultural and historical moment in order to pursue a more concentrated interest in the relation between philosophy and literary form. No doubt work remains to be done on the social and political contexts of skepticism in this period, and at a later date I plan to pursue connections among anarchism, skepticism, and modern political fictions.

My argument here is informed throughout by the work of Stanley Cavell, largely because he, along with Saul Kripke in more mainstream philosophy, has done the most to restore legitimacy to skepticism as an authentic philosophical problem.[13] When handled maladroitly, epistemology and skepticism can uncomfortably resemble adolescent indulgence. (How do I *know* that our world is not a single cell in the fingernail of some giant creature in another universe? that I'm not dreaming this?) But Cavell and others have shown that the issues raised can be real ones and that the fundamental questions posed by skepticism have to do with acknowledgment and the nature of the ordinary. Accordingly, questions about belief and the rational, pain and suffering, individuality and community, long concerns of humanism generally, become more sharply focused as issues of skepticism. By accepting and ramifying Hume's understanding of skepticism as a part of ordinary existence, contemporary thinking about skepticism has the effect of situating it within the genre most committed to everyday life: the novel, particularly the modern novel.

Since the articulation of skepticism in Conrad's corpus changes, my approach also casts new light on the shape of his career. For the purposes of analysis, moreover, different philosophers occupy the foreground at different moments. The continuity of concerns in the skeptical tradition has encouraged me to adopt a

Conradian dislocation by examining Schopenhauer, Hume, and Descartes (in that order) as models for Conrad's skeptical and antiskeptical attitudes. The introductory chapter ranges over various writers in order to establish the concept of the Conradian "shelter." Schopenhauer then presides over my analysis in Chapters Two and Three, where I feature the visionary intensity of the early short stories and "Heart of Darkness" (1899–1900); in *Tales of Unrest* (1898), especially, the language of metaphysical speculation spills over into a religious impulse that resists the disintegrating effect of Conrad's skepticism. The next two chapters take up those philosophers of skepticism that Kant and Schopenhauer claimed to have refuted: in Chapter Four I use Hume to model the authorial skepticism that in *Lord Jim* (1900) contests the continuing visionary strain of the earlier fiction; and in Chapter Five I turn to Descartes's ideal of pure rationality and its attendant "demon" of radical skepticism in order to analyze the ways in which Romantic vision is more stringently chastened by irony in *Nostromo* (1904) and *The Secret Agent* (1907). As skepticism emerges as a dominant influence on Conrad's narrative method and the status of character, the speculations of both Hume and Descartes model a "technique of trouble"[14] that nearly vanishes in Conrad's later work, where various "sheltering conceptions," particularly romance, come to suppress skepticism and permit the construction of fictional worlds in which resolutions can be found and continuities affirmed. Chapter Six touches on *Chance* (1913), *Victory* (1915), and lesser works before focusing more intently on *Under Western Eyes* (1911). In this last great fiction of skepticism, Conrad's continuing interest in political power finds its most subtly effective expression.

Conrad's fiction is filled with the danger of seduction: women entice men into fatal commitments; "the call of an idea," in the words of *Lord Jim*, enthralls those who would be its master; both Conrad and his narrators incline toward the seduction of the aesthetic. The danger I face corresponds to the second of these sirens: having had an idea about the explanatory power of authorial skepticism, I may flirt with the danger of letting the idea have me. I try, however, to remain skeptical about my own skepticism.

Joseph Conrad
and the
Fictions of Skepticism

It is when we try to grapple with another man's intimate need that we perceive how incomprehensible, wavering, and misty are the beings that share with us the sight of the stars and the warmth of the sun. It is as if loneliness were a hard and absolute condition of existence; the envelope of flesh and blood on which our eyes are fixed melts before the outstretched hand, and there remains only the capricious, unconsolable, and elusive spirit that no eye can follow, no hand can grasp.

—Lord Jim

. . . now I know in part; but then shall I know even as also I am known.   —1 Corinthians 13:12

Chapter One

Skepticism and the Sheltered Retreat

In a characteristically authoritative moment, the reader of *Middlemarch* (1872) is schooled in a principle of life: "Scepticism, as we know, can never be thoroughly applied, else life would come to a standstill: something we must believe in and do, and whatever that something may be called, it is virtually our own judgment, even when it seems like the most slavish reliance on another."[1] At the turn of the century, when Conrad began to publish his most important writing, the magisterial calm with which George Eliot lays down the limits of skepticism was no longer tenable; in *Lord Jim* (1900) her confident "we" becomes Marlow's beleaguered attempt to conjure a consensus in the repeated claim that Jim is "one of us." Other moments in the passage anticipate Conradian crises of belief in more specific terms. Life at a skeptical "standstill" describes the predicament of Martin Decoud in *Nostromo* (1904), marooned on an island, dying of skepticism; and the prospect of judgment degraded to "slavish reliance on others"—the last refuge of weary belief—shadows forth the character who fails to rescue Decoud: Nostromo. While belief circumscribes skepticism with relative ease in Eliot, in Conrad skepticism often becomes radical, belief only a ghost hovering at the borders of perception.

Sheltering Conceptions

Conrad's declared commitment to the imperative of proper conduct—to duty, fidelity, and honor—tends to align him with traditional Victorian standards. He also inherited a sense of chivalric commitment from his Polish ancestry: "the world . . . rests on a few very simple ideas," Conrad wrote in a gesture of willed affirmation. "It rests notably . . . on the idea of Fidelity."[2] Yet a swing toward skepticism could also produce a different sentiment: "Faith is a myth and beliefs shift like mists on the shore."[3]

Left unchecked, skepticism characteristically calls forth modes of consolation, and in Conrad's best work skepticism remains continually at odds with the various forms of refuge afforded by his recurrent trope of the sheltered retreat. In this Conrad resembles all skeptics, who, having turned reason against itself, recognize the need to set limits to skeptical inquiry. As T. H. Huxley remarks of Descartes, "No man of common sense when he pulls down his house for the purpose of rebuilding it, fails to provide himself with some shelter while the work is in progress."[4] Conrad's most powerful expression of this idea appears in *Lord Jim*, where Marlow feels forced to seek refuge in what he calls, with some defensive irony, a "sheltering conception of light and order" (*LJ* 313). The trope recurs throughout the skeptical tradition, and Conrad's versions include authority, tradition, and "the idea of fidelity." The most important sheltering conception for Conrad the novelist is fiction itself; but, like the ramshackle house of *Almayer's Folly* (1895), Conradian shelters no longer stand as strong as Eliot's.

Huxley's maxim implies that philosophers too require a house of fiction. It is accordingly no surprise to find that one contemporary philosopher claiming to refute Cartesian skepticism appears to echo (no doubt unknowingly) Conrad's well-known letter about a machine that has fabricated our existence. Conrad to Graham in 1897:

[The machine] evolved itself (I am severely scientific) out of a chaos of scraps of iron and behold!—it knits. . . . And the most withering thought is that the infamous thing has made itself; made itself without thought, without conscience, without foresight, without eyes, without heart. . . .

It knits us in and it knits us out. It has knitted time space, pain, death, corruption, despair and all the illusions—and nothing matters.[5]

Compare Hilary Putnam, who in 1981 is responding to the updated, technological version of Descartes's hypothetical "*malin génie*," the evil genius, who, usurping the power Descartes prefers to attribute to God, controls our faculties of perception and knowledge. Putnam's philosophical narrative combines the creepiness of Descartes's lonely speculations with the hokum of a horror film in which human beings are "brains in vats" tended by an "evil scientist":

Perhaps there is no evil scientist, perhaps (though this is absurd) the universe just happens to consist of automatic machinery tending a vat full of brains and nervous systems.

. . . [L]et us suppose that the automatic machinery is programmed to give us all a *collective* hallucination. . . . [L]et us specify that [it] is supposed to have come into existence by some kind of cosmic chance or coincidence (or, perhaps, to have always existed). In this hypothetical world, the automatic machinery itself is supposed to have no intelligent creator-designers.[6]

Conrad's metaphysical nightmare (and fable of technology?) is for Putnam only an enabling hypothesis, but the repetition reflects a larger body of concerns shared by the discourse of skepticism. For Conrad, Descartes's philosophical exploration of the possibility that life may be but a dream, or maybe a demonic practical joke, was a deeply felt metaphor for the nature of existence.[7] Fear of helplessness is common to nightmares and philosophical skepticism, though the latter typically has the dubious distinction of thinking through the loss of personal agency with greater rigor. Fiction making, a form of fantasy more rigorous than dreams, may itself constitute an attempt to reclaim the power to inspire Putnam's "collective hallucination," for one of the defining features of the novel (now exploited more widely by film) is the power to absorb us into a world not of our own making. Spinning a world out of his or her own imagination, the novelist becomes, from this perspective, a valorized instance of Descartes's evil genius. Whereas Putnam notes the absurdity of his hypothesis in order to keep a saner eye on what must be the real, Conrad evokes the felt absurdity of modern life, which was expressed more radically by his contemporary Alfred Jarry and later disseminated in its most influential form by Camus's "The Myth of Sisyphus" (1942). All these writers rediscover Hume's insight that uncurtailed skepticism leads to conclusions that are as irrefutable as they are absurd, and all spin fictions that provide shelter from a skepticism that threatens to become more extreme.

The rhetoric of "threat," or, to use Hume's word, "malady" (*THN* 218), is appropriate to skepticism since it spreads, like a computer virus, through contact alone. Consider two responses to *Lord Jim*, one from a contemporary review, the other from a critic prominent now; each in its own way brings into focus a problem of agency that recalls Conrad's knitting machine. From *The Critic*, May 1901:

Imagine a fat, furry spider with green head and shining points for eyes, busily at work, some dewy morning, on a marvellous web,—and you have the plot of *Lord Jim*. It spins itself away, out of nothing, with side tracks leading, apparently, nowhere, and cross tracks that start back and begin anew and end once more—sometimes on the verge of nowhere, and sometimes in the centre of the plot itself;—and all with an air of irresponsible intentness and a businesslike run at the end that sets the structure trembling on gossamer threads.[8]

The grotesquerie of Conrad *qua* spider seems at first gratuitous. (Why a *green* head, after all? Fat, perhaps, from a diet of unwary readers.) Yet further reflection reveals the metaphor as a response to the felt absence of a traditional author. Emphasis falls on what the reviewer evidently considers the text's sheer oddness but most insistently on the "nothing" and "nowhere" from which it seems to have sprung. Seduced by its own metaphor, the review (appropriately, it is unsigned) fills in the absence of the author with a "furry spider." Fredric Jameson describes the advent of a new kind of replacement, less extravagant but equally inhuman:

Certainly the first half of *Lord Jim* is one of the most breathtaking exercises in nonstop textual production that our literature has to show, a self-generating sequence of sentences for which narrative and narrator are mere pretexts, the realization of a mechanism of well-nigh random narrative free association, in which the aleatory and seemingly uncontrollable, unverifiable generation of new detail and new anecdotal material out of the old—all the while filling in the exposition, so that it ends up presenting the narrative content as exhaustively as any representational aesthetic—obeys a logic of its own, as yet unidentified in this text taken by itself, but which in the hindsight of the emergent textual aesthetic of our own time we can clearly see to be textuality born fully grown.[9]

The spider has died leaving behind the web. Born at the expense of the author, "textuality" also spins itself out of nothing, though the idea of a single spinner has been superseded by a more advanced form of "mechanism" and "production." Obeying a logic of its own, the self-generating text is as independent of individual agency as is Conrad's knitting machine. One of

Jameson's hypotheses in particular reproduces the skepticism of Conrad's metaphysical fantasy: "the literary 'character' is no more substantive than the Lacanian ego," Jameson suggests; "it is to be seen rather as an 'effect of system' than as a full representational identity in its own right."[10] In *Under Western Eyes* Conrad both entertains and resists the idea that ideology effectively usurps the autonomous identity of the individual; elsewhere he explores without fully accepting the meaning expressed in the once-popular poststructuralist slogan, "Language speaks us."[11] Poststructuralism and postmodernism alike embrace the skepticism with which Conrad struggles.

Conrad's novels, it follows, defend against skepticism even as they express it. A relatively benign version of the world viewed from the perspective of a mitigated skepticism might be Jim's aestheticized vision from the hospital before signing on to the *Patna*. When powers of evaluation are suspended, sensory impressions take on a hallucinatory quality: "Jim looked every day over the thickets of gardens, beyond the roofs of the town, over the fronds of palms growing on the shore . . . at the roadstead dotted by garlanded islets, lighted by festal sunshine, its ships like toys, its brilliant activity resembling a holiday pageant" (*LJ* 12). Emptied of meaning, the scene becomes mildly unreal: activity has become mere spectacle, instruments of international commerce only toys. (There may also be a hint of protective regression in Jim's perception of the ships.) Yet the language of the passage neatly discriminates between elements, and the scene itself has an air of sedentary order. Such descriptions actually *arrest* the disintegrating effect of a more severe skepticism by claiming, in effect, that this is what *is*—the world prior to the intervention of conventional categories of understanding. Perception itself, then, can function as a shelter. Radical skepticism, however, annihilates the evidence of the senses and opens a void where otherwise one might at least see "the streets full of jumbled bits of colour like a damaged kaleidoscope" (*LJ* 157).

A tempered skepticism also emerges in Marlow's meditations on the apparent binding power of what many would simply call patriotism. Searching for the proper formulation, he calls it "the spirit that dwells within the land," "the demand of some such truth or some such illusion—I don't care how you call it, there is so little difference, and the difference means so little" (*LJ* 222). Although Marlow's juggling of terms presents a clear target for the parodist,[12] his seemingly facile reversal arises from an anxious desire to lock "truth" and "illusion" into a stable opposition. Jim is the locus of that anxiety, for though he appears to be an exemplary sailor ("I would have trusted the deck to that youngster on the strength of a single glance"), his jump from the *Patna* betrays that image. In a classic crisis of radical skepticism, "depths of horror" open up under Marlow's fascinated gaze as he contemplates Jim's threat to the "fixed standard of conduct" (*LJ* 45, 50). Marlow's sense that the loss of a "sovereign power" has exposed the fragility of the forms of order on which he most depends may be taken as a synecdoche for Conrad's concern with the grounds of belief.

Conrad's letters reveal that he, like Marlow, frequently suffered through crises of belief. His letter to David Meldrum while blocked in his composition of *Lord Jim* and *The Rescue* is characteristic: "while I am thus powerless to produce my imagination is extremely active: whole paragraphs, whole pages, whole chapters pass through my mind. Everything is there. . . . [E]verything but the belief, the conviction, the only thing needed to make me put pen to paper."[13] Conrad could also be flippant about the problems posed by skepticism in a letter to R. B. Cunninghame Graham: "It is impossible to know anything tho' it is possible to believe a thing or two."[14] Possible, but not easy.

"Prince Roman" (1911), a story about Conrad's early memories of a Polish national hero, exemplifies in measured tones the problematic that finds more fevered expression in the early fiction. Describing their unyielding stand, the narrator proclaims the valor of Polish revolutionaries besieged by Russian soldiers: "The religion of undying hope resembles the mad cult of despair, of death, of annihilation. The difference lies in the moral motive springing from the secret needs and the unexpressed aspirations of the believers. It is only to vain men that all is vanity; and all is deception only to those who have never been sincere with themselves" (*TH* 48). One often has the sensation in Conrad of overhearing only one side of an ongoing debate in which a tendency toward rhetorical excess suggests an exasperated effort to end the conflict. Although Conrad wrote to Edward Garnett that Poles are "used to go to battle without illusions,"[15] Conrad himself was tormented by the possibility that such courage might simply substitute one illusion for another. Belief overcomes skepticism in "Prince Roman," but because the terms of commitment contain the means of their own undoing, we sense that if it does not in this story, the voice of skepticism eventually will respond.

Simply suspect that few men in the conduct of their public lives can be "sincere with themselves" or simply give voice to aspirations that are safer when "unexpressed," and the "moral motive" that divides hope from death and despair begins to erode. An ironic perspective on the patriotic nobility of "Prince Roman" appears in *Nostromo*, where the ultimate vanity of Nostromo's civic loyalty and the cynicism of Martin Decoud's failed commitment to Sulaco contrast sharply with Prince Roman's hopeless fidelity to the lost cause of Polish nationalism. The contrast derives in part from a counterpointing of past and present, for Conrad, like many modern writers, frequently rejects the immediate past in favor of a remoter time that is presented as purer or more authentic; Poland sometimes becomes that touchstone. In a later book, *A Personal Record* (1912), Conrad listens more intently to his idealized Polish past: "I catch myself in hours of solitude and retrospect meeting arguments and charges made thirty-five years ago by voices now for ever still; finding things to say that an assailed boy could not have found, simply because of the mysteriousness of his impulses to himself" (*PR* 121). Although Conrad's complicated ambivalences will ultimately take us beyond national and historical issues, such matters require further attention here.[16]

Framing Skepticism: Contesting Contexts

Conrad was born into an age of doubt, and the climate of opinion became increasingly skeptical as the century drew to an end. In England, as Walter Houghton has written, Victorians were "uncertain about what theory to accept or what faculty of the mind to rely on; but it never occurred to them to doubt their capacity to arrive at truth." After 1870, however, with the growing influence of scientific and historical attitudes, as well as the modern disciplines of sociology, anthropology, and psychology, "faith in the existence of ultimate truths" and in the mind's ability to apprehend them was seriously undermined by a deeply skeptical relativism.[17] Joyce's Gabriel Conroy, remarking in his after-dinner speech that "we live in a thought-tormented age," manages to trivialize what had become a common diagnosis of a contemporary cultural problem. Although Conrad did not set foot in England until 1878, his childhood in Poland could only have deepened the emotional effect of the intellectual and ethical crises that were by no means restricted to the Victorian frame of mind. Poland was always in close touch with currents of thought in England and Europe, and the premature deaths of Conrad's mother and father owing to their involvement in Poland's revolutionary nationalism no doubt contributed to his sense of the dangerous instability of human enterprises in general.[18]

Jostling for space, Conrad's cultural, scientific, and philosophical interests tend to make one hear, to borrow from *Under Western Eyes*, "the murmur of abstract ideas" even when they are not explicitly at issue (*UWE* 294). Though not formally trained in the new academic disciplines, Conrad's letters reveal familiarity with contemporary science unusual for a literary man, and his experiences in his journey up the Congo and in the eastern seas deepened his suspicion that "universal truths" may be products of culture. Given the diversity of Conrad's own intellectual and cultural background, it would be surprising if the collision of cultures examined in "Heart of Darkness" did not generate far more than a narrative of colonial subjection.

Since the Renaissance the discovery of "savages" apparently superior in their moral sense has cast doubt on ethical theories centered in the assumptions of European civilization. But with the colonial explorations of the late nineteenth century the moral drawn by Conrad and others began to shift from the wonder of the "noble savage" to the horror of the savage European.[19] Though early on "Heart of Darkness" accords with the ideological critiques of the "civilizing" project that had become common in the socialist and anarchist literature of the previous decade,[20] in the second and third sections the narrative focus begins to shift, and with considerably more abstract "secondary notions" coming to the foreground, Marlow's increasing emphasis on sensation and perception begins to dissolve political history into more subjective scraps of data.[21]

The subjectification of Marlow's narrative reflects the primacy of sensory experience in the empirical tradition generally as well as the "vehement and passionate interest in the relation of general principles to irreducible and stubborn facts" that characterizes the modern scientific perspective.[22] While most of Conrad's characters enter into this broad problematic in their struggles to establish a meaningful relationship between principled belief and intrusive facts, Conrad's interest in science also can assume more particularized expression, as in his use of Lombroso (as mediated by Max Nordau) and contemporary physics in *The Secret Agent*.[23] Stevie's abnormality and the diagnoses of Ossipon are indebted to the former, while the latter is used to intensify the grotesque incongruity of Winnie's emotional anguish over Stevie's death and the stark indifference of matter: "The veiled sound [of her husband's voice] filled the small room with its moderate volume, well adapted to the modest nature of the wish. The waves of air of the proper length, propagated in accordance with correct mathematical formula, flowed around all the inanimate things in the room, lapped against Mrs. Verloc's head as if it had been a head of stone" (*SA* 260). Unlike the lighter tone of *Victory* ("The world of finance is a mysterious world in which, incredible as the fact may appear, evaporation precedes liquidation"—*V* 3), the physics of comedy in this extended representation of catatonia works to grimmer effect by reducing Winnie to mere matter.

If in *The Secret Agent* the laws of physics are invoked to express psychological states—or, as the case may be, the absence of psychological interiority—the discoveries of modern science sometimes became points of departure for Conrad's metaphysical speculations. In the early fiction Conrad's abrupt transitions between abstraction and visual immediacy, expressed stylistically in his frequent pairing of sensory and abstract adjectives, are symptomatic of his yearning for something beyond the material world. "Facts! They demanded facts from him, as if facts could explain anything!" (*LJ* 29): it is easy to find evidence for Conrad's share in Jim's impatience on the witness stand. Excerpted below, Conrad's long letter to Edward Garnett about having seen Neil

Munro's "backbone and . . . ribs" by means of the new technology of the x-ray exemplifies his speculative leanings even when starting from a purely empirical perspective:

> The secret of the universe is in the existence of horizontal waves whose varied vibrations are at the bottom of all states of consciousness. If the waves were vertical the universe would be different. This is a truism. But, don't you see, there is nothing in the world to prevent the simultaneous existence of vertical waves, of waves at any angles; in fact there are mathematical reasons for believing that such waves do exist. Therefore it follows that two universes may exist in the same place and in the same time—and not only two universes but an infinity of different universes—if by universe we mean a set of states of consciousness. And, note, *all* (the universes) composed of the same matter, matter, *all matter* being only that thing of inconceivable tenuity through which the various vibrations of waves (electricity, heat, sound, light etc.) are propagated, thus giving birth to our sensations—then emotions—then thought. Is that so?[24]

Garnett presumably could not answer this question, and one is reminded that metaphysical speculation, like radical skepticism, sometimes resembles familiar adolescent forms of self-indulgence—fantasy on the one hand, despair on the other. (This does not, of course, make the experience of such thoughts any less serious or authentic.) Conrad's "scientific" projection of a parallel universe resembles a short tale by his acquaintance H. G. Wells, "The Plattner Story" (1896), in which a young chemistry teacher is blown into "the Fourth Dimension" by some "greenish powder."[25] (Green, it happens, is also the powder of choice for the Professor in *The Secret Agent*.) The letter also has some affinities with the metaphysical vocabulary of Conrad's descriptive language in *Tales of Unrest*, also published in 1898. Although Conrad later collaborated on a piece of science fiction, *The Inheritors* (1901), with Ford Madox Ford, the novel's brief visionary moments (inspired early on by a female visitor from the fourth dimension) do not use the conventions of Wells's "scientific romance" as a pretext for metaphysical speculation but only as a vehicle for some rather obvious political satire.

Elsewhere, particularly in the early work, Conrad's reluctance to abandon his faith in transcendent truths produces an impatience with the limitations of empiricism and a desire to pierce through material fact to an absolute realm beyond. The letter to Garnett begins characteristically with scientific fact before moving on to metaphysical speculation—only to return to a radically materialistic epistemology of the path from pure sensation to thought. This equally intense investment in the empirical and the ideal represents a literary as well as a philosophical problem. Late in his career Conrad wrote to Sidney Colvin: "[A]ll my concern has been with the 'ideal' value of things, events, and people. . . . Whatever dramatic and narrative gifts I may have are always, instinctively, used with that object—to get at, to bring forth *les valeurs idéales*."[26] In *Lord Jim* Conrad's interest in the relationship between the ideal and the empirical appears as an interrogation of the ethical status of his intensely visual fictions. Visionary aspirations abate in later work, but one model for a way out of the dead end of empiricism earlier on can be found in the philosophical idealism of Schopenhauer, who posits a penetrating mode of cognizance capable of generating the moments of vision Virginia Woolf recognized as a defining feature of Conrad's fiction.[27] As in Schopenhauer, empiricist and idealist modes of understanding in Conrad compete for supremacy, and, until the less compromising skepticism of *The Secret Agent*, the boundaries of skeptical empiricism are challenged by appeals to transcendence.

Visionary moments also suggest the influence of Walter Pater, who was very likely the most important voice of skepticism Conrad found in the English literary tradition. Conrad may echo Pater in his letters, and they clearly share a concern with solipsism; their deepest affinities, however, lie in a common inheritance from Hume. In his famous conclusion to *Studies in the Renaissance*, according to one critic, "Pater wrote his version of Hume," and Hume's reflections on skepticism in *A Treatise of Human Nature* offer striking parallels to the skeptical turns of consciousness in Conrad's fiction.[28] Hume posits a "naturalism" that counters what contemporary critical discourse has come to call an *aporia* (Marlow's "depths of horror") by rejecting a frame of mind that places too much "strain" on consciousness (*THN* 183, 185–86). Marlow experiences an analogously "naturalistic" foreclosure of skeptical insight in *Lord Jim*, and elsewhere in Conrad we find various forms of less instinctive consolation. An investment in tradition, for instance, represents a logical bulwark against skepticism, for if informed judgments are impossible and all knowledge a chimera, one might as well adhere to a tradition or an arbitrary code of conduct in order to define, in Stein's words, "a way to live." Thus the intensity of Conrad's commitment to the value of continuity, as revealed in his essay "Tradition" (1918) and in his late novel *The Shadow Line* (1917), where a young captain settling into his first command sits in the captain's chair, gazes at himself in the mirror, and, with naive self-assurance soon dispelled by the narrative, feels deep satisfaction at becoming part of "a dynasty" that encompasses him "in the blessed simplicity of its traditional point of view" (*SL* 53).

Yet modes of consolation, such as the reliance on tradition, can raise new problems. Pushed to an extreme, the "blessed simplicity" sought in traditional order can become hostility toward consciousness itself. Consider Conrad's objection to Graham's idea of bestowing an education on Singleton, a man praised in *The Nigger of the "Narcissus"* for having "steered with care" during a storm that nearly destroys the ship and crew:[29] "Is he to study Platonism or Pyrrhonism or the philosophy of the gentle Emerson? . . . Would you seriously . . . cultivate in that unconscious man the power to think. Then he would become conscious—and much smaller—and very unhappy. Now he is simple and great like an elemental force."[30] The letter represents an extreme version of Conrad's antipathy toward those who would automatically elevate consciousness and intelligence over moral responsibility. Yet it also inadvertently reveals the danger that an overreaction to skeptical consciousness can issue in dehumanization (man as "an elemental force") or authoritarianism (the simplicity of "dynasty").

Difficulties lie at the other extreme as well. Pushing against the limits to skepticism defined by Hume's naturalism, Conrad sometimes returns to a position reminiscent of the *First Meditation*, in which Descartes formulates a vision of uncompromised Pyrrhonism in order to set up his refutation in the *Second Meditation*. Although Descartes aimed to conquer skepticism by establishing beyond doubt the reality of the *cogito* (from which he then claimed to derive a range of objective truths, including the existence of God), his solution fails on several counts. Either one can challenge, for instance, the bridge between one's subjective conviction of the reality of the self and transsubjective truths, or one can question the grounds of the *cogito* itself. In *A Treatise of Human Nature* Hume ultimately rejects the complete skepticism of the *First Meditation*, but he nevertheless takes up the critique of the *cogito* in his description of the self as "nothing but a bundle or collection of different perceptions, which succeed each other with an inconceivable rapidity, and are in a perpetual flux and movement" (*THN* 252). Although Conrad is inclined to entertain the skepticism of the *First Meditation* and to worry over the dissolution of the self theorized by Hume, he also tends to seek consolation in dogmatism on one hand and despair on the other. (For despair, too, dispenses with troublesome questions.) Between dogmatism and despair lies a quest for stability that accepts epistemological limitations and makes do with what can be established short of absolute certainty. While this is the way of pragmatism, positivism, and modern science, it is not an accommodation Conrad allowed himself to accept on a permanent basis. The hunger for the absolute always returns, as does the vision of the abyss opened by total skepticism.

Despite the assumed anti-intellectualism of the letter to Graham, if Singleton must not become a Pyrrhonist, Conrad himself often wrote as one. Indeed, Conrad's writing sometimes duplicates in form and content many of the issues that extend through the tradition of philosophical skepticism from Descartes to the present. The dissolving identities of Conrad's characters project in fictional form Hume's dismantling of the stable Cartesian *cogito* as a nexus of shifting relations and perceptions. Descartes's philosophical fantasy of a *malin génie*, or evil genius, already at work in Conrad's knitting machine, surfaces again in *Nostromo* and *The Secret Agent* as a tension between characters and the unseen forces that seem to determine their actions. In *The Secret Agent* Conrad also picks up, in comic form, the classic philosophical formulation of the problem of other minds as the question of whether one could know if an apparently human other were actually an automaton.

Huxley, reflecting the particular urgency "other minds" took on in the late nineteenth century, traces the mechanistic model back to Descartes in "On the Hypothesis That Animals Are Automata, and Its History" (1874). Despite the title, the real burden of Huxley's essay lies in the possible application of the idea to human consciousness, and he selects as his chief medical example the case of a French sergeant wounded in the battle of Bazeilles. Trauma to the officer's parietal bone (one of two large bones that together form the sides and top of the skull) has caused "periodical disturbances of the functions of the brain," and Huxley wonders if, during the French sergeant's abnormal states, "consciousness [is] utterly absent, the man being reduced to an insensible mechanism?"[31] No doubt it is a happy coincidence that in *Lord Jim* the first to board the abandoned *Patna*—a stolid soul who bears "an old wound, beginning a little below the temple and going out of sight under the short grey hair at the side of his head" and who speaks with "the passionless and definite phraseology a machine would use" (*LJ* 140, 159)—is a lieutenant in the French merchant marine. (After all, why would Conrad promote Huxley's lower-ranking invalid?) What's important for my purposes is the shared use of Cartesian tropes of the mechanical in contexts quite removed from the tropes of mechanization found later in literature critical of England's increasingly technocratic society. Lawrentian symbolism, for instance, is tied more closely to Taylorization, Futurism, and the general rationalization of society than to the philosophical skepticism explored by Conrad and Huxley.

Philosophizing presupposes a desire for community, and "the wish and search for community are the wish and search for reason."[32] Conrad was committed to the idea of community, but when the dream of reason becomes the self-canceling operations of radical skepticism, the search for community, like Marlow's desire to hear Kurtz's voice, can end only in disappointment. Acutely sensitive to all that can undermine moral reasoning, Conrad views skepticism as antithetical to ethics in *The Secret Agent*, where Stevie is described as "no sceptic, but a moral creature" (*SA* 172). A skeptic himself, Conrad nevertheless remained consciously devoted to a moral perspective on life and literature. When he left the sea for life as an author, writing became the locus of Conrad's effort to preserve a sense of community despite his subversive intuition of the ease with which communities dissolve. Much of the force in Conrad's declared aim of "making" the reader "see" derives from his desire to establish an immediate connection with the audience: if author and reader can, in every sense of the word, "see" together, they join in a community of understanding. This investment in the shelter of community underlies every Conradian affirmation.

The Aesthetics of Morality and the Quest for the Absolute

Yet the power of fiction to represent and invoke community, as Conrad was all too aware, does not offer an unproblematic refuge from the corrosion of skepticism. Some of the forces of discontinuity that disrupt Conrad's novels are located within characters as a kind of anarchic individualism or surge of irrational motivation (reminding us that Conrad was a contemporary of Freud); but the most pervasive agent of discontinuity is authorial skepticism, and authorship does not easily provide the kind of reassurance Conrad claimed to find in the maritime tradition. Looking back on his departure from life at sea, in *A Personal Record* Conrad reasserts the value of the maritime code in an effort to establish a sense of continuity between two seemingly discontinuous periods of his life: "I have carried my notion of good service from my earlier into my later existence. I, who have never sought in the written word anything else but a form of the Beautiful—I have carried over that article of creed from the decks of ships to the more circumscribed space of my desk, and by that act, I suppose, I have become permanently imperfect in the eyes of the ineffable company of pure esthetes" (*PR* xix). Hoping to reconcile the claims of the aesthetic and the moral in his new vocation, Conrad brings forward the ideal of good service as a third term mediating between ethical commitment and an aestheticism lacking moral value.[33] Throughout *A Personal Record* Conrad insists that his career as a writer be considered analogous to his earlier vocation: each offers the ordering principles as well as the constraints of working within a tradition, and each is fundamentally an ethical activity. Yet Conrad's arguments betray an anxiety that the ethics of writing may not be so easily defensible.

While the Preface to *The Nigger of the "Narcissus"* abjures rigid classifications of literary modes such as realism, romanticism, or naturalism, as an alternative to these it harkens to the encouraging whisper of "Art for Art itself" (*P* 147). Conrad does not wish to endorse the *fin de siècle* project of scandalizing bourgeois morality (though *The Secret Agent* may be read as an attempt to do just that), and in *A Personal Record* he eloquently rejects the common meaning of the slogan—a decadent disregard for moral values—in an extended tribute to Pater's valorization of aesthetic consciousness as an inherently ethical activity of the mind:

The ethical view of the universe involves us at last in so many cruel and absurd contradictions, where the last vestiges of faith, hope, charity, and even of reason itself, seem ready to perish, that I have come to suspect that the aim of creation cannot be ethical at all. I would fondly believe that its object is purely spectacular: a spectacle for awe, love, adoration, or hate, if you like, but in this view—and in this view alone—never for despair! Those visions, delicious or poignant, are a moral end in themselves. . . . And the unwearied self-forgetful attention to every phase of the living universe reflected in our consciousness may be our appointed task on this earth. A task in which fate has perhaps engaged nothing of us except our conscience, gifted with a voice in order to bear true testimony to the visible wonder, the haunting terror, the infinite passion and the illimitable serenity; to the supreme law and the abiding mystery of the sublime spectacle. (*PR* 92)

There are many things worthy of note here. First, we may notice in passing the lingering Victorian quality of Conrad's hesitation (however mocking or ironic) over the rejection of the ethical aim of the universe. Second, if the "spectacular" view of the universe shelters one from despair, the gloom and pessimism of much of Conrad's fiction testify to his inability to sustain such a vision. (Conrad's pleasure in Bertrand Russell's romantic essay "A Free Man's Worship" [1903] no doubt lay partly in Russell's assertion that following the ascendancy of scientific materialism, "the soul's habitation" must henceforth be safely built "on the firm foundation of unyielding despair."[34]) However difficult to achieve in practice, the concept of good service in "A Familiar Preface" posits the possibility of achieving Conrad's stated ideal of fusing the moral and the aesthetic by cultivating a "self-forgetful" consciousness of "every phase of the living universe." Thus Conrad's repeated use of "fidelity" to refer to both an ethical norm and a mimetic ideal.

Still, one is frequently struck by the way in which the aesthetic and the ethical tend to part company in Conrad. In a 1904 book review Conrad praised W. H. Hudson's *Green Mansions* for being "steeped in that pure love of the external beauty of things" (*LE* 136), and in Conrad's own fiction the intensity of his love of beauty for its own sake finds expression in prolonged descriptive passages that remain untouched by his equally strong investment in the symbolic. Most of "The Lagoon," as Conrad himself acknowledged, consists of extended descriptions of the natural scene, and *The Rescue* (1920) contains a tremendous number of passages that luxuriate in their power to evoke an intensely visualized scene:

> He snatched nervously at the long glass and directed it at the dark stockade. The sun had sunk behind the forests leaving the contour of the tree-tops outlined by a thread of gold under a band of delicate green lying across the lower sky. Higher up a faint crimson glow faded into the darkened blue overhead. The shades of the evening deepened over the lagoon, clung to the sides of the *Emma* and to the forms of the further shore. Lingard laid the glass down. (*R* 299)

The contrast between Lingard's agitation and the serenity of nature may contribute to the charged atmosphere, but the sensual rhythm of the passage mainly expresses a love of color and form. Conrad's highly developed visual imagination frequently found expression in the pictorial, and Lingard's prismatic sunset no doubt provided the author with a moment of escape from the narrative difficulties that delayed the completion of *The Rescue* for over twenty years. In these visual tableaux Conrad may well have found the same value Marlow finds in "the exquisite grace and beauty" of Stein's gardens while in retreat from Jewel's angry mourning: "I remember staying to look at it for a long time, as one would linger within reach of a consoling whisper" (*LJ* 351). Elicited by Jim's decision to abandon his lover rather than betray his ideal of conduct, Jewel's grief drives Marlow to the refuge of beauty—the consolation of a steady stare. While Conrad's narratives typically trace the consequences of moral choice, the seduction of the aesthetic often defers the moment when vision must become action.

Sometimes an anodyne to doubt, contemplation may also invite skepticism, and the moment of skeptical vision is not always a welcome one. Many of these visions, remaining uneasily poised between religious revelation and the fully aestheticized epiphanies of Joyce, recognize, only to agonize over, the terrible emptiness left by the departure of the sacred. In *Lord Jim* Marlow denounces the skeptic consciousness that may result from such insight, but only after musing at length about the puzzle presented by Jim: "Hang ideas! They are tramps, vagabonds, knocking at the back-door of your mind, each taking a little of your substance, each carrying away some crumb of that belief in a few simple notions you must cling to if you want to live decently and would like to die easy!" (*LJ* 43). Belief becomes an aristocratic privilege, the right to defend one's door against less fortunate doubters. Marlow can also provide a kind of visionary affirmation, as in his momentary perception of Jim's "imperishable reality" during his discussion with Stein: "I saw it vividly, as though in our progress through the lofty silent rooms amongst fleeting gleams of light and the sudden revelations . . . we had approached nearer to absolute Truth" (*LJ* 216). This potentially self-canceling duality, the affirmation and negation offered by imaginative vision, underlies many of the most intensely imagined moments in Conrad's fiction, and it distinguishes his visionary mode from the more sanguine aestheticism of Pater.

The intensity of Conrad's conflicting skeptical and visionary impulses pushes him to extremes. Martin Decoud's skepticism ends in suicide; Prince Roman's commitment nearly elevates him to sainthood. Yet the word "commitment" ultimately seems inadequate to Conrad's hunger for absolute values: while the loss of what Marlow calls a "sovereign power" clearly has political, moral, and literary significance, it also betokens a religious impulse that has received scant attention in Conrad studies. Failure to recognize Conrad's religious yearning has resulted in attempts to see him as an existentialist, but such arguments typically do more to reveal Conrad's *resistance* to the metaphysical emptiness of existential thought.[35] In his letters Conrad denounces Christian mythology and is quick to call himself an atheist, but his religious impulse is not channeled into a wholly conscious conviction or bound to a particular religious institution; rational assertion diverges from emotional investment.

The religious impulse issues as a kind of negative theology,

and in many ways Conrad's imagination, like Joyce's more resolutely secularized vision, is profoundly Catholic. This is not surprising; to this day the Catholic church in Poland, as in Ireland,
extends its influence throughout the cultural life of the nation.
Conrad is not as close to Joyce, however, as he is to Stephen Dedalus; despite his heterodoxy, Stephen shies away from com-
munion because he fears "the chemical action which would be
set up in [his] soul by a false homage to a symbol behind which
are massed twenty centuries of authority and veneration."[36] Fear
of a sovereign power takes refuge in the name of chemistry and
history. The Catholic quality of Conrad's imagination also appears in the various Dantesque visions allotted to Marlow. At
Stein's, for instance, Marlow conjures a scene of damnation
when, turning inward and away from his host's oracular romanticism, he sees "the great plain on which men wander amongst
graves and pitfalls . . . circled with a bright edge as if surrounded by an abyss full of flames" (*LJ* 215). When Conrad insists
to Graham that "there is no morality, no knowledge and no
hope,"[37] that skeptical claim coexists uneasily with what in
"Prince Roman" is called the "religion of undying hope." The os-
cillation between such extremes occurs between works, within
individual texts, and within individual characters. Conrad's
yearning for the absolute may be compared with Winnie Verloc's
nostalgia for a happier time: "The memory of the early romance . . . survived, tenacious, like the image of a glimpsed
ideal" (*SA* 275).

A residual Christian sense of the absolute sometimes inheres
in Conrad's frequent tropes of incarnation; sometimes the theological resonance is lost in a more diffuse sense of the soul-body
distinction as a figure for the concealed significance of visible
forms.[38] Whether presented ironically or mystically, language of
incarnation and disembodiment tropes the fall from wholeness
into division that so often is Conrad's theme. In an idealized response to skepticism, the romance conventions of Patusan allow
Jim to incarnate for a time the heroic ideal he could only read
about in the first half of the novel. Later Marlow's surmise about
Jim's fatal encounter with Gentleman Brown suggests Biblical ty-
pology—"They met, I should think, not very far from the place,
perhaps on the very spot, where Jim took . . . the leap that

landed him into the life of Patusan" (*LJ* 379–80)—and so amplifies the religious connotations of Jim's death, an incarnation undone: "he passes from my eyes like a disembodied spirit astray
amongst the passions of this earth" (*LJ* 416). Irony consistently
denies the spirit in *The Secret Agent*, whose most benevolent character, Stevie, is dismembered in a botched attempt to carry out
the intentions of another. Where slippage between intention and
action is a constant concern, the Professor's dream of a "perfect
detonator"—one that would lessen, presumably, the twenty-
second lag between compression and explosion—represents a
fantasy of closing the gap between act and disembodied thought
opened by skepticism. In the murder of Verloc, Winnie perfectly
realizes her concentrated intention—furious revenge—and her
moment of inspiration reads like an instance of incarnation: knife
in hand, Winnie approaches her husband "as if the homeless
soul of Stevie had flown for shelter straight to the breast of his
sister, guardian, and protector" (*SA* 262). Jim's death, unlike Verloc's murder or Winnie's suicide, carries the further implication
of a loss of linguistic perfection: until, shot by Doramin, Jim falls
dead "with his hand over his lips," his word in Patusan is "the
one truth of every passing day" (*LJ* 226, 416). After Jim dies, the
equivocations of Marlow's narration, straining toward the "soul"
of a constancy no longer in the world, can only gesture toward
the perfect silence of Jim's consummation.

Skepticism as Style and Structure

Conrad's style is cognate with his narrative structure, for what
apposition is to syntax, analogy is to narrative form. Setting aside
Conrad's use of analogy for later consideration,[39] here I want to
look briefly at the way skepticism informs Conrad's stylistic practices before analyzing in greater detail how Bakhtin's idea of dialogic structure illuminates the relation between narrative form
and the operations of skepticism.

In its hesitancies, ellipses, and repetitions, the style of Marlow's narration marks a fall away from the impossible omniscience of a sovereign power—impossible because to Conrad too
(not just from our historical retrospect) the idea of a reliably omniscient narrator must have seemed a doomed effort to banish a

multitude of unreliable ones. Even apart from Marlow's prolixity, Conrad's expansive style is governed by appositions and adjectives, with each new phrase doubling back to reinterpret the previous one in a vain attempt to expand the sentence into the "full utterance" that "through all our stammerings," Marlow claims, is "our only and abiding intention" (*LJ* 225). Take even a relatively simple instance from the first chapter of *Victory*: "His most frequent visitors were shadows, the shadows of clouds, relieving the monotony of the inanimate, brooding sunshine of the tropics" (*V* 4). The expansion of "shadows" into a prepositional phrase and the decision to make the sunshine "brood" provide understated examples of two rhetorical habits: first, a will to elaboration that, held in check here, often produces long, undulating sentences whose continuity of rhythm only partially conceals the countersuggestion that a definitive formulation might never be reached, that the closure achieved is an effect of rhythm alone;[40] second, the pathetic fallacy, whose device is bared, as the Russian Formalists say, in the rapid reversal of "sunshine" that "broods" as soon as it is labeled "inanimate." The "pathos" of Ruskin's coinage derives from his intuition that dead nature cannot be revived, and Conrad's recurrent use of the trope (Jim sees "a fierce purpose in the gale"; "the wasting edge of the cloudbank" in *Nostromo* "always strives for, but seldom wins, the middle of the gulf") remains nostalgically invested in the possibility of discovering a form of significant permanence amid the deliquescence of skepticism.

Bestowing the pleasure of arrested attention within the incessant instability of skepticism, contemplation of "the sublime spectacle" is crucial to Conrad's narrative poetics. Though eloquent in his conscious commitment to action, Conrad frequently avoids representing action in the narrative present. At the same time, his troubled belief in the value of action prompts him to preserve a place for it in the past, where completed narrative becomes an occasion for reflection.[41] Thus Marlow's retrospective narration transforms the stuff of adventure stories into brooding explorations of truth and value. With the attenuation of action as plot, the activity of representation itself, focused in the gaze of the narrator, becomes as much the locus of ethical value as the problems of conduct the narrator records. The modernizing effect of Marlow's mediation can be gauged by reading "Heart of Darkness" alongside a more Victorian rendering of very similar materials in Robert Louis Stevenson's *The Beach of Falesá* (1893). Producing a poetry of recollected action and an ethics of words, Conrad is frequently drawn to the kind of question implicit in Marlow's role in *Lord Jim*: does the very attempt to narrate Jim's story constitute a betrayal of Jim's life?

Questions of this sort typically lead to more. Vexed by Jim's compulsive behavior, Marlow asks Stein if anything is "good" for Jim's affliction. "Strictly speaking," Stein replies, "the question is not how to get cured, but how to live" (*LJ* 212). Conrad, like Stein, indulges in neither cures nor resolutions: no dialectical syntheses, only a continuing dialogue.[42] The radically opposed claims of the individual and the community, for instance, are never fully settled. At one moment the solidarity of the craft may establish an adequate code of conduct for the individual—or, in Marlow's more imperative words, "Woe to the stragglers! We exist only in so far as we hang together" (*LJ* 223). In "The Return" (1898), however, we are made to sense the deadening homogeneity of society in the "kinship" of anonymous commuters whose "stare" is "concentrated and empty, satisfied and unthinking" (*TU* 119).[43] Rather than a dialectical model, then, Bakhtin's dialogical poetics better suits Conrad's narrative projection of skepticism and its discontents.

Bakhtin opposes the "dialogic" or "polyphonic" novel, in which the perspectives of individual characters remain fundamentally autonomous, to the "monologic," in which a single consciousness, usually associated with the discourse of the author, dominates the design of the novel.[44] In one sense, the polyphonic dimension of Conrad's fiction exists as a defensive response *to* skepticism. Skeptic questioning of the reality of other minds ultimately ends in solipsistic self-enclosure and so seals the mind in silence or endless converse with itself. Conrad's definition of the novel speaks directly to that danger: "What is a novel," he writes in *A Personal Record*, "if not a conviction of our fellow-men's existence strong enough to take upon itself a form of imagined life clearer than reality?" (*PR* 15). In another sense, skepticism itself, by refusing to foreclose on any line of inquiry, may resist the monologic by opposing other voices or perspectives to the potential dogmatism of a single point of view. Beyond the otherness intrinsic to the novel form, then, Conrad also tempers the possibility of subjective self-enclosure through his characteristic fictional structures: the dialogical juxtaposition of analogous characters and situations in *Nostromo* and *The Secret Agent*, Marlow's propensity for subordinate narrators in *Lord Jim* and *Chance*, and the conjuring of audiences within the text through a variety of narrative frames.

Yet the virtue of skepticism can also become disabling. As skepticism becomes more radical and inclusive, it may threaten to collapse into a monological discourse in several ways. Short of solipsism, when the mind becomes concentrated intently on itself, the result may be total disablement, as with Martin Decoud, or the monomania that animates so many of Conrad's characters, from the Professor to Charles Gould. A truly polyphonic novel would juxtapose such characters against a range of more engaged figures, privileging none, including the perspective of the narrator, over any other. In Conrad, however, the desire to assail such characters for their failings sometimes produces what Bakhtin calls an "authorial 'surplus,'" "an all-encompassing field of vision . . . that is fundamentally inaccessible to the consciousness of the characters."[45] In Bakhtin's implicit hierarchy of value (though not in Conrad's), an author's surplus awareness necessarily indicates less than ideal novelistic structure, and *The Secret Agent* demonstrates how authorial omniscience can indeed come to weigh on characters, as if the relation between the narrator's overbearing discourse and that of the characters were to dramatize Foucault's description of the burdensome materiality of language.[46] The monological grip of the author may also be tightened by moral skepticism, which, in its most radical form, dismantles all values and construes other people as objects to be manipulated. Denying autonomy to other minds, such an attitude translates into fiction as battles between characters to control each other, and—a response to authorial surplus—as the rebellion of characters against the ways in which the narrator or other characters define them.

Authorial skepticism thus plays a complex role within the opposed models of dialogical and monological fiction. Most broadly, skepticism can motivate the play of autonomous per-

spectives that constitutes the polyphonic novel. It may also pro-
voke an opposing pull toward authority (as in "the blessed simplicity" of a "traditional point of view") in the form of a monological suppression of competing perspectives. The interplay between
monological and dialogical modes in Conrad may be gauged in
the contrast between the savage irony at the expense of wholly
objectified characters in "An Outpost of Progress" and Marlow's
rendering of the colonial experience in "Heart of Darkness."

Claiming Knowledge: Marlow and "An Outpost of Progress"

Without the dramatized mediation supplied by an involved
narrator, Conrad is frequently drawn toward a more monological
mode. In "Heart of Darkness" Conrad's skepticism issues as
Marlow's suspension between possible meanings (what does
"the horror" mean, anyway?); in "An Outpost of Progress" the
author seeks relief from troubling ambiguities and ambivalences
(such as those produced by his loyalty to the *British* cause for
progress) in the shelter of authority.

The overbearing quality of the presiding consciousness in "An
Outpost of Progress" derives initially from the narrator's omniscience and the characters' limitation; the former sees what the
latter cannot.[47] Such a relation between narrator and character is
common enough, but we also sense that Conrad has built into
the story an absolute distinction between what Kayerts and Carlier can know and what the narrator knows. The lack of "all independent thought" in these characters is attributed to society,
which, "under pain of death," has forbidden them "all initiative,
all departure from routine." We are not surprised, then, to read
that, like Descartes's animals, "they could only live on condition
of being machines" (*TU* 91). But as the story advances we are
forced to acknowledge that the engineer of these machines is not
some abstraction called "society" but the author himself.

Kayerts's thwarted movement toward greater awareness provides a telling example. Having accidently killed Carlier in an ab-
surdly degrading fight over the sugar rations, Kayerts "seemed
to have broken loose from himself altogether. His old thoughts,
convictions, likes and dislikes, things he respected and things he
abhorred, appeared in their true light at last! Appeared contemptible and childish, false and ridiculous. He reveled in his

new wisdom while he sat by the man he had killed." The story could take several directions at this point. Kayerts's "new wisdom" could embrace an understanding of his own folly, his own exploitation at the hands of the trading company, or the value of the companion he has slain. Instead Kayerts "argued with himself about all things under heaven with that kind of wrong-headed lucidity which may be observed in some lunatics" (*TU* 114–15). Under the influence of Maupassant, Conrad is so seduced by irony that he transforms the promise of revelation into lunacy, and Kayerts's ascension to "the highest wisdom" results only in the attempt "to imagine himself dead" (*TU* 115). In the morning, hearing the call of "progress" in the whistle of the approaching steamer, Kayerts hangs himself, and the last sentences of the story linger over his corpse: "he seemed to be standing rigidly at attention, but with one cheek playfully posed on the shoulder. And, irreverently, he was putting out a swollen tongue at his Managing Director." It is difficult to believe that this playful irreverence belongs to Kayerts rather than to Conrad, for Conrad has never given us reason to believe Kayerts capable of such a rebellious gesture. (Such rebellion becomes central, however, in *Nostromo*.) While the plot indicts the heavily ironized call of progress, Kayerts is sacrificed less to civilization than to the ironic pressure of a monological perspective.

Standing smugly aloof from the fatuous behavior of Carlier and Kayerts, the narrator lays implicit claim to an authoritative perspective by virtue of having been there himself: "One must have lived on such diet to discover what ghastly trouble the necessity of swallowing one's food may become" (*TU* 109). Asserting that he knows what the reader cannot, the narrator's stance resembles Marlow's attitude toward ordinary people just after his return from the Congo: "they were intruders whose knowledge of life was to me an irritating pretence, because I felt so sure they could not possibly know the things I knew. Their bearing . . . was offensive to me like the outrageous flauntings of folly in the face of a danger it is unable to comprehend. I had no particular desire to enlighten them" (*HD* 152). Remarking that he was "not very well at that time," Marlow licenses us to imagine that an earlier narration of his story, as opposed to the one recorded in the novella, might have been dominated by the coercive irony of "An Outpost of Progress." But Marlow recovers from the illness that remains with the narrator of the earlier story: though he occasionally scorns his listeners for their presumed complacency, ultimately Marlow hands his interpretive authority over to them: " 'Of course in this you fellows see more than I could then. You see me, whom you know . . .' " (*HD* 83). The narrative situation presents a scene of dialogue: the presence of a frame narrator defines Marlow's perspective as one among many, and even though Marlow's voice dominates the novella, his discourse seems "to shape itself in opposition to the anticipated objections of an imagined interlocutor."[48] In consequence, the authority of having "been there" does not, as it does in "An Outpost of Progress," establish an authoritarian perspective that dominates and objectifies the materials of the narrative. Although "An Outpost of Progress" suffers from the authorial surplus of its narrator, Conrad later makes a virtue of what Bakhtin would consider a defect, especially, as I will show in Chapter Five, in the structure of ironic coercion that characterizes *The Secret Agent*.

Coping

Neither the dialogic expression nor the monologic forestalling of skepticism alone can contain the threat of a skeptical dissolution of meaning. However much Conrad's novels may affirm human connectedness by providing "a conviction of our fellowmen's existence," the sheltering conception of fiction cannot render that conviction inviolable. Conrad writes in *A Personal Record* of being interrupted in his study by a general's daughter:

The whole world of Costaguana (the country, you may remember, of my seaboard tale), men, women, headlands, houses, mountains, town, *campo* (there was not a single brick, stone, or grain of sand of its soil I had not placed in position with my own hands); all the history, geography, politics, finance; the wealth of Charles Gould's silver-mine, and the splendour of the magnificent Capataz de Cargadores, whose name, cried out in the night (Dr. Monygham heard it pass over his head—in Linda Viola's voice), dominated even after death the dark gulf containing his conquests of treasure and love—all that had come down crashing about my ears. I felt I could never pick up the pieces. (*PR* 100)

Writing eight years later, Conrad virtually quotes from the last sentence of *Nostromo*, thus transforming old fragments into a new whole while at the same time underscoring the fact that, the general's daughter notwithstanding, the book got finished after all. Though Conrad clearly delights in recreating the momentarily failed creation of the past, the confident gesture of retrospection simultaneously acknowledges that the walls may come tumbling down again. All writers know the experience, but the skeptic knows it best, "the awful disenchantment of a mind realising suddenly the futility of an enormous task" (*PR* 101).

Conrad to Graham: "Half the words we use have no meaning whatever and of the other half each man understands each word after the fashion of his own folly."[49] Conrad to Galsworthy: "Scepticism, the tonic of minds, the tonic of life, the agent of truth,—the way of art and salvation."[50] Bridging the gap between doubt and act, the challenging body of work Conrad left behind testifies to his ability to turn weakness into strength.

Chapter Two

Early Stories and the Ghosts of Belief

*Whilst science . . . is with every end it attains again and again
directed farther, and can never find an ultimate goal or complete
satisfaction . . . art, on the contrary, is everywhere at its
goal. For it plucks the object of its contemplation from the
stream of the world's course, and holds it isolated before it.*
      —*The World as Will and Representation*

*To snatch in a moment of courage, from the remorseless rush of
time, a passing phase of life, is only the beginning of the task.
The task approached in tenderness and faith is to hold up
unquestioningly, without choice and without fear, the rescued
fragment before all eyes and in the light of a sincere mood.*
      —Preface to *The Nigger of the "Narcissus"*

Lying beyond the limits of empiricism, the transcendent in Conrad's early stories resists and tempers the more full-blown skepticism that later emerges in "Heart of Darkness" and *Lord Jim*.
The sense of an "elsewhere," reached only in moments of vision,
may resemble the Schopenhauerian will—a locus of blindly striving energy—or it may be reconstrued as a repository of absolute
value. The ambiguity in Conrad has an analogue in Schopenhauer, the philosophical idealist. T. H. Huxley, writing of Descartes, observed that "of the two paths opened up to us in the
'Discourse on Method,' the one leads, by way of Berkeley and
Hume, to Kant and Idealism; while the other leads, by way of De
La Mettrie and Priestley, to modern physiology and Materialism."[1] The second path leads also to my discussion in Chapter
Five, which takes up Conrad's materialism and Cartesian notions
of the mechanical in a reading of *Nostromo* and *The Secret Agent*.
Here I want to remain on the post-Kantian extension of the first
path by analyzing problems of belief in Conrad's early short
stories in the context of Schopenhauer's philosophical idealism.

Reading the two writers as mutually illuminating locates each within evolving ideas of transcendence that are characteristic of post-Romantic literary and intellectual history.

In Conrad problems of belief have a way of becoming problems of faith; in Schopenhauer metaphysics nearly tumbles into theology. Hostile toward organized religion, especially Christianity, Conrad shows himself in his writing to be neither a serene fideist nor a peaceful skeptic. The ancient skeptic aimed for a state of tranquillity or "freedom from disturbance" called *ataraxia*.[2] Falling far short of the skeptic's nirvana, Conrad struggles instead with a residual sense of the holy that summons a countervailing skepticism of virtually punitive force. In the early fiction skepticism sometimes appears explicitly as a response to religious belief ("The Idiots") or the supernatural ("The Black Mate"); sometimes the dialogue between skeptic and antiskeptic voices registers in confrontations between characters, sometimes in the way narrators seem to haunt the ghost-ridden tales they tell. The psychological in these stories, particularly Conrad's obsessive concern with guilt, tends to shade into the metaphysical, the metaphysical into the religious.[3] Schopenhauer's antiskeptical side issues through his concept of aesthetic contemplation, a privileged mode of vision that penetrates beyond phenomena to noumena or will. As Conrad's shadowy "elsewhere," like Schopenhauer's noumena, begins to slip into a sense of the numinous, each writer exhibits a species of religious feeling characteristic of what I will describe as negative theology.

Conrad, Schopenhauer, and the Metaphysics of Belief

Schopenhauer articulates a division between phenomena and noumena—between what is perceived and what is independent of perception—in terms that shed light on the visionary aspirations of Conrad's contemplative narrators.[4] In the Preface to the first edition of *The World as Will and Representation*, Schopenhauer states that what he has to impart "is a single thought": the world should be understood under two aspects, as representation and as will. The world as representation corresponds to the world of phenomena and presupposes a perceiving subject. Hence the famous first sentence of Schopenhauer's masterwork: "The world is my idea."[5] While such a world has been enough for many, Schopenhauer also posits another, the world as will, which is the ground of the world as representation. The will is "that of which all representation, all object, is the phenomenon. . . . It is the innermost essence, the kernel, of every particular thing and also of the whole" (*WWR* I: 110). Fundamentally irrational, the will is an aimless energy that objectifies itself on all levels of reality, from the inorganic to the human.[6] By presenting the world in terms of a radical dichotomy, Schopenhauer insists on the limitations of human knowledge. Only the will is "real"; but because will exists beyond ordinary understanding, reality—always elsewhere—is profoundly and irremediably mysterious. As Conrad, writing to Graham, once put it, "we, living, are out of life—utterly out of it."[7] Yet both writers remain suspended between idealist and empirical understandings of reality: even as they insist, like orthodox empiricists, on the primacy of perception, each finds ways to subvert his own strictures on the consequent limitations of knowledge.

Schopenhauer's dualistic idealism may well have provided a model for similar metaphysical divisions in Conrad, and the English reception of Germany's foremost analyst of illusion (before Freud) helps to clarify his place in Conrad's thought. Although *The World as Will and Representation* (1819) was long in reaching a wide audience in England, after decades of neglect Schopenhauer became so popular that Josiah Royce could declare in a university lecture in the early 1880s that "the name of Schopenhauer is better known to most general readers, in our day, than is that of any other modern Continental metaphysician, except Kant."[8] Ford Madox Ford's father, Franz Hueffer, specialized in Schopenhauer and, in 1873, even founded a magazine devoted to him, *The New Quarterly*. Since Schopenhauer anticipated a remarkable number of developments in nineteenth-century thought, it is hard to trace precisely his influence on Conrad, and the task becomes trickier given the variety of sources from which Conrad could have learned of him. The pervasive struggle for survival in Conrad may echo Schopenhauer's description of the world as "a permanent battlefield" (*WWR* I: 265); but it is equally reminiscent of Herbert Spencer's popularization of Darwin in "the survival of the fittest." Yet even when the influence may not be direct, Schopenhauer's presence is unmistakable well before he surfaces explicitly in *Victory* (1915).[9]

John Galsworthy wrote in 1927 that "of philosophy [Conrad] had read a good deal. . . . Schopenhauer used to give him satisfaction twenty years and more ago."[10] It is easy to see why Conrad would have found pleasure in Schopenhauer. While one may not easily imagine Schopenhauer laughing, a slight nudge brings out the potentially mordant humor in his pessimism. In the following quotation from *The World as Will and Representation*, a little imaginative license allows one to hear a scene missing from *The Secret Agent*: "just as we know our walking to be only a constantly prevented falling, so is the life of our body only a constantly prevented dying, an ever-deferred death" (*WWR* I: 311). A last stumbling step deferred to the moment of death: Vladimir could have used this aphorism to dress down Verloc for permitting Stevie to walk alone in the grounds of Greenwich Observatory.[11] Conrad also sees people as windup puppets winding down in the kinetic comedy of "The Duel" (1907), where the imperative of defending one's honor achieves its parodic apotheosis in the comically repeated encounters between Lieutenants Feraud and D'Hubert, "insane artists" pursuing "a private contest" during the "universal carnage" of the Napoleonic Wars (*SS* 165). Though beautiful, the 1977 film *The Duelists* utterly misses the ironic excess of the story. Conrad and Schopenhauer alike are connoisseurs of futility.

No doubt Conrad was drawn as well to the lucidity of Schopenhauer's prose. Writing to Hugh Clifford, Conrad extolled the power of the right word "to *present* the very thing you wish to hold up before the mental vision" of the reader.[12] Schopenhauer, reacting against Hegel's opaque abstraction and convoluted syntax, modeled his style on David Hume's, and the Haldane and Kemp translation (1883–86), which Conrad would have read, preserves much of the vivid immediacy of the original German. When Schopenhauer evokes the poetry latent in his sense of metaphysical interconnection, one analogy summons another, and the rhythm of elaboration competes with the demands of argument:

And if we consider them attentively, if we observe the strong and unceasing impulse with which the waters hurry to the ocean, the persistency with which the magnet turns ever to the north pole, the readiness with which iron flies to the magnet, the eagerness with which the electric poles seek to be re-united, and which, just like human desire, is increased by obstacles. . . . [I]f we observe all this, I say, it will require no great effort of the imagination to recognize, even at so great a distance, our own nature.[13]

Ruskin might have described this pervasive animism as pathetic fallacy on a cosmic scale. Or, to reverse the flow of the analogy, the force that through the green fuse drives the flower drives everything else too. Conrad's prose seems attuned to the Schopenhauerian will in nature, and in the early Malayan novels his odd descriptions of writhing plants read almost as parodies of Schopenhauer's characterization of "mere vegetation" as "blindly urging force" (*WWR* I: 117):

[A]ll around them in a ring of luxuriant vegetation bathed in the warm air charged with strong and harsh perfumes, the intense work of tropical nature went on: plants shooting upward, entwined, interlaced in inextricable confusion, climbing madly and brutally over each other in the terrible silence of a desperate struggle towards the life-giving sunshine above—as if struck with sudden horror at the seething mass of corruption below, at the death and decay from which they sprang. (*AF* 71)

The hypothetical analogy dangling at the end of the sentence repeats in a more obsessive form the rhetorical pattern of Schopenhauer's evocation of the will: the human and the natural reflect each other, revealing a frightening underworld of mad energies. Clearly Conrad also brings his own private agonies to the passage. As the lovers Dain and Nina paddle through this animated scene, one feels that if Schopenhauer had not existed, Conrad would have invented him.[14]

While Schopenhauer's influence on Conrad's fiction has received a good deal of scholarly attention, their remarks on art reveal more important affinities.[15] In the epigraphs to this chapter, Conrad seems in explicit dialogue with Schopenhauer, and the most famous of Conrad's declarations, "My task . . . is, above all, to make you *see*," has clear antecedents in several passages in *The World as Will and Representation*. Explaining his concept of aesthetic contemplation, for instance, Schopenhauer emphasizes the artist's technical ability to let us see "the essential" in things "with his eyes" (*WWR* I: 195).[16] Schopenhauer insists on the primacy of perception and, in a characteristic metaphor, evokes his vision of the "essential"—that is, the will—that subtends the multiplicity of visible phenomena: "Just as a magic lantern shows many different pictures, but it is only one and the same flame that makes them all visible, so in all the many different phenomena which together fill the world or supplant one another as successive events, it is only the *one will* that appears, and everything is its visibility, its objectivity" (*WWR* I: 153).[17] In the Preface to *The Nigger of the "Narcissus"* Conrad's language picks up Schopenhauer's evocations of the will as the "essential" singleness within the multiplicity of shifting phenomena:

[A]rt itself may be defined as a single-minded attempt to render the highest kind of justice to the visible universe, by bringing to light the truth, manifold and one, underlying its every aspect. It is an attempt to find in its forms, in its colours, in its light, in its shadows, in the aspects of matter and in the facts of life, what of each is fundamental, what is enduring and essential—their one illuminating and convincing quality—the very truth of their existence. (*P* 145)

Conrad goes on to praise music as the ideal art, and although this judgment has been traced back to Pater's well-known saying that *"All art constantly aspires towards the condition of music,"*[18] it was Schopenhauer who first popularized the idea that music possesses a privileged access to metaphysical truths. For both Conrad and Schopenhauer art is partly a release from the tyranny of ordinary perception, partly a rescuing of knowledge from the flow of time.[19]

Conrad's early indebtedness to Schopenhauer, particularly in the Preface, is not surprising in light of the power Schopenhauer attributes to art in *The World as Will and Representation*. The Preface was Conrad's first attempt to state publicly his understanding of the art of the novelist, and he wished to justify the enterprise in his own eyes as well as his readers'. While the early nineteenth century saw a general tendency to reassert the value of art against the loss of prestige it had suffered in the seventeenth and eighteenth centuries, even in this context Schopenhauer's claims for art are large, especially the idea that art is a form of knowledge that penetrates to the essence of life. In the Preface Conrad

also asserts that art is a form of knowledge superior to philosophy and science. Although the scientist and thinker "speak au-
thoritatively to our common sense," Conrad asserts a critical difference in a one-sentence paragraph: "It is otherwise with the artist." Not only is the artist's appeal made "to our less obvious
capacities": it is "less loud, more profound. . . . [I]ts effect en-
dures for ever" (*P* 145). The "otherwise" of art points back to
Schopenhauer, whose theory of aesthetic contemplation, in Ian
Watt's words, "had long before done to philosophy what Pater,
following the Romantics and Matthew Arnold, did to religion—
undermined its claims to be man's supreme source of truth, and
put those of art in its place."[20] But Conrad badly needed reassurance about the capacity of art to substitute for religion and philosophy.

Having begun his second career as a professional writer relatively late (his mid-thirties), Conrad did indeed feel with Schopenhauer "the warlike conditions of existence" (*P* 145), and the
art of fiction seemed a poor weapon to bring to the battle. Struggling to support his family, Conrad was troubled by more than
deep anxiety about his economic hardships. His correspondence also reflects profound insecurity about his ability to write
and, consequently, about his decision to pursue a literary
career.[21] Anxious for support in every sense, Conrad was drawn
in the early novels to the artistic authority of Flaubert, the ex-
emplar of the novelist as artist. In the power Schopenhauer attributes to art Conrad would have found another authoritative
spokesman for the value of his new life as an artist, this time in
the discipline of philosophy.[22] At his most confident, as in the
Preface, Conrad was able to see his own fiction as fulfilling the
marriage between philosophy and art that Schopenhauer as-
cribed to music.

Other affinities between Schopenhauer and Conrad transcend
the particular relationship between them. Though Schopenhauer has been linked to several developments in *fin de siècle* art,
such as aestheticism and French symbolism, his belated popularity may also be attributed to his pivotal role in the history of
subjectivity.[23] The special appeal of Schopenhauer for the emerging modernist sensibility makes sense in light of the Janus-faced
nature of his dualistic idealism, which looks back, admittedly

with revisionary eyes, to the neoclassical identification of nature with reason, and forward to the modernist understanding of meaning as a purely human construct. Schopenhauer's departures from Kantian idealism help to specify the double connection with neoclassicism and literary modernism.[24]

Since "noumenal" derives from the Greek for "reason," Kant, like all previous philosophers, associated the word with the rational. But Schopenhauer aimed to overturn tradition by antithetically defining the noumenal as the irrational. Schopenhauer also transformed Kant's concept of phenomenal reality by construing Kant's knowing subject—an elusive, transcendental abstraction—as a corporeal individual, sense organs and all. Unlike Kant, then, Schopenhauer's idealism is tempered by an empirical bias: constructed by the human mind, the perceived world possesses significance even as that significance is subtended by the underlying chaos of the will. Positing the will as an ultimate source of meaning remains a fundamentally neoclassical gesture, yet Schopenhauer simultaneously claims that this ground for sense is itself senseless.[25]

Transposing the philosophical to the literary, we may say that Schopenhauer posits, *avant la lettre*, T. S. Eliot's "immense panorama of futility and anarchy"[26] as noumenal reality, and he anticipates the modernist quest for systems of order by making the phenomenal world available to the individual consciousness as an ordered whole.

The illusory coherence of phenomena thus takes on something like the contingent status of the artistic ordering of reality in high modernism. However chaotic, the will restores to the world the possibility of a fullness of meaning by assuming a primary connectedness within and between all levels of existence. Achieving that plenitude, however, remains an ideal eternally beyond reach. In Georg Simmel's words, "Schopenhauer's philosophy is the absolute philosophical expression" of the "inner condition" of the post-Christian European: "an empty urge for a goal which has become inaccessible."[27]

As the Preface implies, Conrad too shows signs of nostalgia for "the truth, manifold and one" once thought to underlie every aspect of "the visible universe" (*P* 145). Yet neither Conrad nor Schopenhauer is consistent in his projection of a transcendent realm. Schopenhauer's positing of the will as the one truth of manifold phenomena involves a fundamental equivocation, and Conrad's fiction also embodies an equivocal attitude toward the transcendent.

The ambiguity in Schopenhauer arises in his theory of music, which implicitly reconceives the blind hunger of the will by describing it as the epitome of truth as beauty.[28] Art, for Schopenhauer, offers privileged access to knowledge because aesthetic contemplation pierces through the world as representation to what he calls (misleadingly) "Platonic Ideas," the irreducible forms from which all others derive. But it is otherwise with music, which is "by no means like the other arts, namely a copy of the Ideas, but a *copy of the will itself*" (*WWR* I: 257). Music is thus empowered to transcend the epistemological limits already expanded by aesthetic contemplation. Schopenhauer wants to account for the nonmimetic nature of most music and to explain why its effect seems more powerfully immediate than in the other arts. But can the claim that music allows *direct access* to the will accommodate the beauty of music? A "copy of the will itself" ought to reveal the chaotic energy underlying the veil of the visible. What resonates beyond the world as representation: the music of the spheres, or the cacophony of the will's endless war with itself?

Schopenhauer's philosophical system does not stand or fall on this ambiguity; over the years more fundamental critiques have threatened transcendental idealism, not to mention the very project of writing a metaphysics. But when considered in relation to Conrad the issue gains significance. And so an interpretation of Schopenhauer's ambiguous presentation of the will must await inquiry into an analogously divided attitude toward the transcendent in Conrad.

Haunting the World: 'Tales of Unrest' and the Noumenal

The hauntings and shadowy presences of Conrad's early stories can easily be psychologized as visible signs of the author's obsessive investment in guilt. Yet these ghosts also trace the contours of a problem of belief that derives from Conrad's skeptical fascination with the apparent power of absent causes.[29] Many

ghost stories suspend the reader between supernatural and naturalistic modes of explanation;[30] what is at stake in Conrad is the
nature of faith in a world dominated by skepticism, and his
hauntings are complicated by the gradual emergence of tropes
that posit the existence of an elsewhere analogous to Schopenhauer's world as will. The status of this transcendent realm is always in doubt, its instability seeming only a vagueness of attitude in some stories but a powerful principle of structure in others. Absences that register as ghostly presences, these equivocal
representations offer access to Conrad's internal dialogue about
the claims of belief.

In what may be considered the first story Conrad ever wrote,
"The Black Mate," questions of transcendence and belief already
begin to assume the dialogical form characteristic of the later
fiction.[31] "The Black Mate" is presented explicitly (though de-
viously) as a ghost story: "As this is really meant to be the record
of a spiritualistic experience . . . there is no use in recording the
other events of the passage out" (*TH* 97). With a "passion of credulity," Captain Johns believes wholeheartedly in the spirit
world, but his first mate, Winston Bunter, ridicules and resents
Johns's obnoxious proselytizing. But when Bunter injures himself at sea in a fall down the poop ladder and his jet-black hair
begins mysteriously to turn white, he tells Captain Johns that his
new look was caused by the shock of having seen an apparition.
Gloating, the captain comes to believe that the ghost must have
appeared to avenge a murder Bunter committed long before. In
later stories, such as "Karain," ghosts *will* reevoke the guilt of
past transgressions, but here the reader eventually learns that
Bunter concocted the ghost story simply to disguise his age: his
bottles of black hair dye had broken in a storm, and Captain
Johns was known to refuse to sign on older sailors. Since Bunter's story works (Johns never sees through it), readers who miss
Conrad's many clues are at least temporarily grouped with the
credulous captain as the butt of the joke.

But an oddly excessive resentment toward Johns in the denouement, which continues past what seems a natural stopping
point, suggests that however comic, the story touches on some
important issues for Conrad. "You are punished for your incredulity, Mr. Bunter," says Johns (*TH* 110), referring to the sup-

posed apparition. Bunter in turn wants to punish Johns—for his credulity. The violence of Bunter's desire for revenge—he carries on about Johns "with a fury that frightened his wife" (*TH* 117)—implies a need to expunge any trace of Johns from his mind, and in the end the skeptical author of ghost stories has vanquished his credulous foe: Captain Johns, befuddled, is home in retirement, with "devils on the brain" (*TH* 120). And so what appears at first to be a conversion narrative about an "unbelieving scoffer laid low" (*TH* 109) becomes a comic dialogue in which a duped zealot—belief appearing here in the degraded form of superstition—is overborne by vengeful skepticism.

Although the story is not one of Conrad's best, it anticipates in a less complicated form many features of the later fiction. The link between the supernatural and skepticism will reemerge in *Nostromo*; the thematics of coercion and violence come to dominate *The Secret Agent*. Conrad also returns to "The Black Mate" in his last great work, *The Shadow Line* (1917), in which various details of the earlier story—the breaking bottles, for instance—are redeployed within an initiation narrative that again stages an opposition between supernatural and naturalistic explanation. Reversing the roles of mate and captain while taking up the latter's first-person perspective, the narrative articulates a late version of Conrad's *malin génie*, here represented in the belief of the fever-mad mate (shared in unguarded moments by the narrator) that the deceased former captain, buried at sea, is preventing their safe passage. Notwithstanding contemporary readers who thought it a ghost story, *The Shadow Line* does not aim to invite such confusion as much as it bears witness to Conrad's conflicted investment in forms of ironized mysticism as a response to anxieties about agency and control.[32] The narrator in "The Black Mate," unlike the captain of *The Shadow Line*, is not fully developed as a character, but by encompassing within his own discourse the competing voices of skepticism and belief, he looks forward to Marlow, whose probing intelligence opens to investigation the energies held in check by the comic resolution of the earlier tale.

In Conrad's first volume of short stories, *Tales of Unrest*, the connection between skepticism and the ghosts of belief begins to emerge more distinctly. Each story, R. A. Gekoski has pointed out, centers "on a character who, safe in a clearly defined understanding of life's regularities and values, is confronted with an experience so traumatic that it destroys belief, and opens up a vista of a universe implacable and terrifying."[33] Within the turbulence produced by the destruction of belief, I would add, there arises invariably a host of phantoms, and this hauntedness evokes Conrad's skeptical suspension between conflicting attitudes toward transcendence. Before turning to detailed analyses of "Karain" and "The Return," I will use brief readings of "The Lagoon" and "The Idiots" to bring out the sense in which the very idea of haunting and being haunted is intrinsic to Conrad's discourse of skepticism.

The narrative structure of "The Lagoon" is very simple: an old acquaintance, identified only as "the white man," stops for the night at Arsat's hut; he learns that Arsat's lover, Diamelen, is very ill; Arsat tells the story of having rescued her at the expense of his brother's life; Diamelen dies; the narrator continues on his way. Though immobilizing guilt dominates the buildup to Arsat's confession, there is little reason to think that the narration itself has had any effect, cathartic or otherwise, on the Malayan Arsat or the white narrator. Race *seems* to be important here, if only because insistent allusions to the ghostly are explicitly linked to Arsat's being shunned by his fellow Malays, who fear him because they believe that, like a white man, "he is not afraid to live amongst the spirits that haunt the places abandoned by mankind" (*TU* 190). Once drawn, however, the racial distinction between those who do and those who do not believe in spirits never again comes into play. Compared with the distinctive presence of Conrad's later narrators, the narrative voice here seems almost absent, itself one of the ghosts in this haunted story. The elusiveness of the narrator's attitude recalls the equivocation in Conrad's treatment of the supernatural in "The Black Mate," where incompatible attitudes assume form in discrete characters. Unsatisfactory in many ways, "The Lagoon" offers no resolution of the question of belief focused in Diamelen's death: is it retribution for the death of Arsat's brother or only a consequence of tropical disease? The narrative simply stops with a perfunctory reference to "a world of illusions," but neither the narrator nor Conrad decides which world is illusory—Arsat's or the white man's.

Conrad returns to problems of belief in a more complicated form in "The Idiots," where the comic effect of the dialogic opposition between Bunter and the captain in "The Black Mate" is recast as tragic fatality. Jean-Pierre Bacadou, a young farmer without religious conviction, marries a Catholic girl, Susan, who soon gives birth to retarded male twins, and later to another boy, also an idiot. Willing to try anything to secure a sound heir, Jean-Pierre suppresses his skepticism and begins to attend his wife's church. When his prayers, joined with Susan's, fail and another idiot is born, this time a girl, Jean-Pierre's anger and resentment build to the point that his (sexual?) assault forces Susan to kill him. The focus then shifts abruptly to Susan, who flees from the house in the belief that she is pursued by Jean-Pierre's ghost. As she runs in terror along the beach, only one man among a group of seaweed gatherers, Millot, has the courage to follow her. The rest believe that *she* is a ghost and should be let alone, but "Millot feared nothing, having," like Jean-Pierre, "no religion" (*TU* 80). In pursuit, Millot tells himself one story, "As if there were such things as ghosts! Bah! . . . But it was curious. Who the devil was she?", while Susan screams out quite another: "How many times must I kill you—you blasphemer! Satan sends you here" (*TU* 83–84). Though their thoughts seem almost to meet in the language of damnation, the verbal echo proves wholly fortuitous, and the incompatibility of her belief and his skepticism soon produces a fatal misunderstanding. "Come . . . I am perfectly alive," calls Millot, but Susan, trying in terror to evade the man she thinks is her dead husband, falls from a raised roadway to her death. The true causes of Susan's death are thus absent but determining: Jean-Pierre, who appears in the spectral yet living figure of Millot, and the authority of the Church, whose Royalist designs on his Republican property only add fuel to Jean-Pierre's furious resentment.

Since "The Idiots" picks up the theme of guilt that runs through "The Black Mate" and "The Lagoon," one might argue that ghosts in these stories solve a problem of representation by bringing into the realm of the visible psychological realities that

otherwise would lie outside it. But if the supernatural enters
Conrad's fiction only "to make us *see*" the determining power of
guilt, how do we account for the distinction in "The Lagoon" between natives' and white men's attitudes toward the supernatural? The narration there is limited to the white man's point of
view, and when the narrator attributes one description of the setting—the night as "a shadowy country of inhuman strife, a
battle-field of phantoms" (*TU* 193)—to a "fleeting and powerful
disturbance of [the white man's] being," that disturbance seems
to result from the white man's sympathetic participation in Arsat's belief in the presence of evil spirits. Imagination allows not
only the white man but the story itself to hover uneasily between
two worlds.

The skeptical tradition suggests a further perspective on Conrad's obsession with ghosts. In one of the many letters he wrote
in the 1890s lamenting an inability to actualize the world of his
imagination, Conrad's frustration produces a strange yet expli-
cable self-portrait: "my very being seems faded and thin like
the ghost of a blonde and sentimental woman, haunting romantic ruins pervaded by rats."[34] Exploiting the conventions of
Gothic romance, Conrad's characteristically extravagant mock-
ery also aligns him with Emerson as a writer compelled to live
the life of skepticism. Stanley Cavell has shown how Emerson
extends Descartes's speculations about thought as proof of the
cogito to the point that, if thought ceases, "the skeptical possibility is realized—that I do not exist, that I as it were haunt
the world."[35] A few years before presenting himself as blonde,
helpless, and feminized before the task at hand, Conrad, again
blocked, wrote to Poradowska—as plaintive, admittedly, as he
was philosophical: "I don't even think; therefore I don't exist
(according to Descartes)." In luxuriant self-pity Conrad goes on
to implore Poradowska to rescue him from a state of depressed
inactivity in which he imagines himself as a broken, discarded
doll: "I feel as if I were in a corner, spine broken, nose in the
dust."[36] Guiltily haunting the world as a writer who is not writing, Conrad also experiences his body as the absolute horizon of
existence.

The blocked writer's twin self-representations—as ghost and
marionette—are linked by the discourse of skepticism. For one

corollary to exploring the absurd yet at certain moments pressing possibility of one's own ghostly nonexistence may be the suspicion that self-authoring through thought—one implication of Descartes's argument from the *cogito*—serves to mask the equally absurd yet troubling fear that the self is wholly authored by forces external to it.[37] This metaphysical nightmare points back to Conrad's knitting machine and forward to his sustained interest in determinism as played out in *Nostromo*, *The Secret Agent*, and *Under Western Eyes*. As in Conrad's letters, transmigrating souls in these novels will again, with surprising frequency, leave bodies untenanted. In this chapter, however, I want to remain with the metaphysics of belief implicit in the hauntings and hauntedness of the early stories.

In "Karain"—essentially a retelling of "The Lagoon"—the moment of vision that "disturbs" the narrator of that story dilates, and the resulting scene transforms the ambiguous representation of guilt in "The Idiots" and "The Lagoon" into a searching investigation of the pressures of the "unseen." In its anticipation of Conrad's more mature art, and as the best of the early short stories, "Karain," together with the far less impressive "The Return," warrants extended attention here. In "Karain" the skeptic's guilty sense of haunting the world combines with fears of malign manipulation to shape a narrative keenly in touch with the skeptical turn of mind.

"Karain": Cultural Collision and the Ghosts of Belief

"Karain" employs the most complex narrative strategy Conrad had yet attempted.[38] For several years the unnamed narrator and two shipmates, Hollis and Jackson, have been sailing to an isolated Malayan community to deliver smuggled arms to Karain, the chieftain of three villages. To the traders Karain epitomizes heroic leadership, and they come to think of him as a respected friend. But suddenly, on their final trip, Karain swims out to the visiting ship virtually incapacitated by fear. Through an entire night Karain, like Arsat, tells the white men the story of a betrayal many years before; but unlike Arsat's tale, Karain's narration establishes significant connections with its frame. Promising to help his closest friend, Pata Matara, avenge a family disgrace, Karain had agreed to track down and kill Pata Matara's sister and her lover. Over the years of pursuit Karain gradually became entranced by the image of the beautiful woman and, having insensibly transferred his allegiance, shot Pata Matara just as he sprang to stab his sister. Haunted by the ghost of his murdered friend, Karain later found peace only in the company of an old shaman, "who could command ghosts and send evil spirits against enemies" (*TU* 16). The sheltering power of the shaman represents a retreat to authority as an anodyne to self-doubt, and as such his relationship with Karain anticipates analogous father-son relationships throughout Conrad: Marlow and Jim, MacWhirr and Jukes, Nostromo and Giorgio Viola, to name only a few. With the death of Karain's wizard, however, a few days before the final visit of the white men the haunting has begun anew, causing Karain to hide in solitude before escaping to the ship for protection.

After Karain ends his narration, only Hollis can rise to Karain's demands for either asylum in Europe, the "land of unbelief, where the dead do not speak," or a charm imbued with the power of the white man's imperviousness. Hollis creates an amulet from some ribbons, a piece of a woman's leather glove, and a jubilee sixpence. Karain is especially impressed by the image of Queen Victoria on the coin, and, his belief having invested the coin with meaning, the charm works: he returns to his people with restored confidence and authority.

But like "The Black Mate" (and the typical Conradian sentence), the story continues past its natural stopping point to a chance meeting seven years later between the narrator and Jackson. The memory of Karain has remained with Jackson, but Jackson, who still muses about the reality of Karain's haunting, has been more deeply affected than the narrator. Under the influence of Karain's story, Jackson is troubled by a new awareness of the unseen, and London phenomena come to seem far more phantasmal than the illusion of Karain's heroism ever did. Although the narrator ends with an ironic remark at the expense of Jackson's restructuring of consciousness, Jackson's new way of seeing is worthy of more consideration than it generally receives.

Though intermittent, the comic tone of "Karain" has distracted critics from exploring the breakdown of culturally enforced modes of understanding at the end of the story. Peering at his own reflection in a storefront window, Jackson wonders hesitantly "whether the thing was so, you know . . . whether it really happened to him" (*TU* 54). Astonished, the narrator tells him to look at the surrounding London scenery, as if that should be answer enough to his doubts about the nature of the real. Three long descriptive paragraphs of nearly hallucinatory intensity follow:

A watery gleam of sunshine flashed from the west and went out between two long lines of walls; and then the broken confusion of roofs, the chimney-stacks, the gold letters sprawling over the fronts of houses, the sombre polish of windows. . . . [A] line of yellow boards with blue letters on them approached us slowly, tossing on high behind one another like some queer wreckage adrift upon a river of hats. . . . A clumsy string of red, yellow, and green omnibuses rolled swaying, monstrous and gaudy . . . a ragged old man with a face of despair yelled horribly in the mud the name of a paper; while far off, amongst the tossing heads of horses, the dull flash of harnesses, the jumble of lustrous panels and roofs of carriages, we could see a policeman, helmeted and dark, stretching out a rigid arm at the crossing of the streets. (*TU* 54–55)

Although the quotation, which draws from all three paragraphs, amounts to only one-third of the original, it is true to the sense of unreality projected there. The perception of language within the passage—"gold letters sprawling over the fronts of houses," "yellow boards with blue letters on them . . . some queer wreckage adrift"—anticipates in its self-consciousness the lettered sandwich boards that wander through *Ulysses*; the sheer accumulation of isolated sensory impressions amplifies the force of the descriptions of "language adrift" within the passage and redirects our attention to the phantasmagoric dislocation of the writing itself. The figure of a seemingly petrified policeman that ends the montage coincides with a more general absence of authority in the description: contrary to the narrator's intentions, the words seem not to represent an actual scene at all but rather to call attention to their own status as writing. The verbal texture of disjunctive images displaces the illusion of representation.

The closing paragraphs of "Karain" look back to the opening pages, in which the narrator introduces the reader to an exotic fictional locale through a virtual invocation to the evocative re-

sources of language. Carefully framing the narrative, Conrad locates these resources in a newspaper, the same form of writing
hawked by the "ragged old man" who calls out in the sequence
of images that ends the story:[39]

I am sure that the few [who remember Karain] are not yet so dim-eyed
as to miss in the befogged respectability of their newspapers the intelligence of various native risings in the Eastern Archipelago. Sunshine
gleams between the lines of those short paragraphs—sunshine and the
glitter of the sea. A strange name wakes up memories; the printed words
scent the smoky atmosphere of to-day faintly, with the subtle and penetrating perfume as of land breezes breathing through the starlight of
bygone nights; a signal fire gleams like a jewel on the high brow of a
sombre cliff; great trees, the advanced sentries of immense forests, stand
watchful and still over sleeping stretches of open water; a line of white
surf thunders on an empty beach, the shallow water foams on the reefs;
and green islets scattered through the calm of noonday lie upon the level
of a polished sea, like a handful of emeralds on a buckler of steel. (*TU* 3)

Although these images may also seem disjunctive, as a totality
this montage is more coherent than the later one. We sense the
gradual creation of literary illusion, the coalescing of elements
into a representational whole. This prose invocation solicits the
imagination to close the gap between the verbal and the real by
making us see in a way Jackson no longer can. The narrator continues in this descriptive mode for several pages gradually introducing the main characters, but the vividness of the writing
should not distract us from its implication in the theme that culminates in Jackson's closing puzzlement.

   Emerging from the dialogue of assertion and counterassertion
between Jackson and the narrator, the complications in "Karain"
masquerade as light entertainment. For this reason Lawrence
Graver's interpretation is especially interesting because, while
recognizing both the complexity and the wry comedy, he simply
asserts, against a great deal of evidence, that the former is not
important: "Although it is possible to point to some larger Conradian ironies hidden behind the humor and to say that Conrad
is having his little jest at the expense of the English as well as the
Malays, these are not the main impressions of the story. We remember Victoria and her jubilee, not the suggestions of dark and
horrible voids, or Jackson's musings on appearance and reality."[40]

"Impressions," as Graver implies, depend on those parts of the story one remembers. But memory always reconstructs the text according to some principle of order, whether implicit or explicit, and Graver takes at face value Conrad's remark to Graham that there is something "magazine'ish" about "Karain."[41] Consequently, although Conrad begins with a "serious" story, Graver says, he "deliberately takes the edge off by using a slick, humorous ending to evade the full complexities of his theme."[42]

Though evasive by temperament, Conrad in "Karain" is less so than his critics. To respond within Graver's assumptions (and with the same kind of evidence, Conrad's stated intentions), I certainly agree that some of Conrad's stories are "magazinish." Conrad himself once described "The Lagoon" to Edward Garnett as "a tricky thing with the usual forests rivers-stars-wind sunrise, and so on—and lots of second hand Conradese in it."[43] Against Graver one could cite the author's note to *Tales of Unrest*, where Conrad writes that although the "*motif*[s]" of "The Lagoon" and "Karain" are "almost identical," "the idea at the back is very different" (*TU* ix–x). Yet whatever the line of argument, authorial intentions can never be recovered from a text with complete confidence, and Conrad's explicit commentary on his own work is notoriously unreliable.[44] Neither Conrad's dubious self-evaluation nor Graver's reading should permit the dismissal of so many "serious" passages or "hidden" ironies.

Graver describes the opening paragraphs of "Karain" as "charming," and I single out the word only to note its connection to the "charm" Hollis bestows on Karain. Hollis wants to make Karain believe in its power, just as the opening of the story aims to persuade the reader of the reality of the visible universe it describes. But by the end of the story, when the narrator turns to the London scene, a profound skepticism has put in question both the reality of the visible and the power of language to represent it. The difference appears distinctly in one of the sentences I omitted from the description that ends the story: "Over all, a narrow ragged strip of smoky sky wound about between the high roofs, extended and motionless, like a soiled streamer flying above the rout of a mob" (*TU* 54–55). Even as the simile vividly evokes a concrete image, it diverges from the immediate "reality" of the scene by insisting that we perceive it under the aspect of something blatantly artificial. "Yes; I see it," muses Jackson, "But I'll be hanged if it is yet as real to me as . . . as the other thing . . . say, Karain's story" (*TU* 55). In *Lord Jim*, where Marlow's skeptical crises constitute the most intensely imagined moments of the novel, the mental dislocation brought on by world-consuming skepticism will return as a more sharply focused narrative concern.

If the contrast between the beginning and end of "Karain" is not so distinct as the foregoing quotations might imply, that is only because many passages in between also articulate a sharp dislocation between "reality" and the representable world. Early on the narrator repeatedly evokes Karain's heroic stature as a form of dramatic spectacle: "Day after day he appeared before us, incomparably faithful to the illusions of the stage, and at sunset the night descended upon him quickly, like a falling curtain." And nightfall in Karain's village has a distinctly Schopenhauerian quality: "sounds ceased, men slept, forms vanished—and the reality of the universe alone remained—a marvellous thing of darkness and glimmers" (*TU* 9). The narrator also describes the daylight pole of the opposition: "the scenic landscape . . . intruded upon the reality of our lives by its motionless fantasy of outline and colour" (*TU* 10). Conrad's frequent evocations of an excessive intensity of the visible, as when the sun shines "violently upon the undulating surface of the land" in "The Idiots" (*TU* 56), often suggest the illusory quality of the world as representation,[45] and in "Karain" the hidden reality of the universe becomes apparent only when the world of forms disappears into an encompassing darkness.[46]

These descriptions belong to a narrator who is consistently unwilling to pursue the implications of his own words, and the author's more discerning perspective becomes clear at several key junctures. Characterizing Karain's efforts to organize his armies (for battles he later wins), the narrator manages within a few sentences to exemplify a full range of racial condescension.[47] Although the racism has been attributed to Conrad, it has also been pointed out that Hollis, who seems to show most insight into Karain's problem, has a point of view closer to Conrad's own.[48] When Karain resents the narrator's condescending consolation, the latter becomes privy to a new realization: "It was amazing.

To him his life—that cruel mirage of love and peace—seemed as real, as undeniable, as theirs would be to any saint, philosopher, or fool of us all" (*TU* 44).[49] Though rebuked by Hollis for his platitudinous insensitivity, the narrator nevertheless resists the recognition that Karain is as human as himself, just as he ultimately ignores everything that conflicts with his established construction of the world. He prefers, like the vaguely Western narrator of "The Lagoon," to attribute his more unusual impressions to moments of imaginative vision, which he can then dismiss as mere fancy. In this he remains blind to the further significance of the central fact that it is Karain's imaginative transformation of the coin that restores his equilibrium.

The narrator's resistance to unsettling redefinitions of the real becomes most apparent in the reflective silence following Karain's narration: "it seemed full of noiseless phantoms, of things sorrowful, shadowy, and mute, in whose invisible presence the firm, pulsating beat of the two ship's chronometers ticking off steadily the seconds of Greenwich Time seemed to me a protection and a relief" (*TU* 40). While "Karain" may anticipate Conrad's more sophisticated representations of the moral effect of storytelling on an inscribed audience,[50] the narrator's full response has as much to do with metaphysics as with ethics: he cannot allow the perception of irrational forces to invade the refuge of rational civilization represented by Greenwich standard time. The felt presence of absent causes must be categorized and dismissed as superstition in order to preserve the sheltered retreat afforded by the spatialized regularity of time.

Later, however, while contemplating Karain's terror, the narrator gains sudden insight into this shadowy realm when, in a moment of sublime vision, the boundaries defined by "superstition" break down.

And it seemed to me, during that moment of waiting, that the cabin of the schooner was becoming filled with a stir invisible and living as of subtle breaths. All the ghosts driven out of the unbelieving West by men who pretend to be wise and alone and at peace—all the homeless ghosts of an unbelieving world—appeared suddenly round the figure of Hollis bending over the box; all the exiled and charming shades of loved women; all the beautiful and tender ghosts of ideals, remembered, forgotten, cherished, execrated; all the cast-out and reproachful ghosts of

friends admired, trusted, traduced, betrayed, left dead by the way—
they all seemed to come from the inhospitable regions of the earth to
crowd into the gloomy cabin, as though it had been a refuge and, in all
the unbelieving world, the only place of avenging belief. . . . It lasted a
second—all disappeared. (*TU* 48–49)

The dialogue between skepticism and belief assumes narrative
form as a romance of exile and return. Just as Johns rages against
the skeptical incredulity of Bunter (and vice versa), so here
ghosts seek relief in "avenging belief." They arise to populate a
world made barren by the banishing of value to a realm that can
be understood only as something unreal, ghostly. (Recalling
Jackson's sense of the unreality of the London scene, and Schopenhauer's redefinition of the noumena, we may note that from
the vantage of either realm the other seems ghostly.) In his moment of vision the narrator perceives Hollis as Karain's new shaman, who, by conjuring the "tender ghosts of ideals," puts in
question the adequacy of the world of chronometers the narrator
normally inhabits. Envisioning in Hollis an artist-magician capable of redeeming a world of vanishing values, it is now the narrator who, in the suddenly expanded range of his imagination,
momentarily approaches Conrad. The narrator's transient insight recalls Conrad's own divided attitude toward the realm of
the formless, which both threatens the stability of consciousness
and gives shelter to the ideal.[51]

We have already seen that Conrad, lacking inspiration, sees
himself as spectral, haunting the ruins of what he cannot restore.
Inspired, he sees, like the narrator of "Karain," into the realm inhabited by "the charming shades of loved women"; having done
so, he gains access to the "tender ghosts of ideals." For Conrad,
James (whom he addressed as "*cher maître*") epitomized the
writer capable of capturing the spectral in his language: "Exquisite Shades with live hearts, and clothed in the wonderful gar-
ment of your prose."[52] The praise of James's characters implies
the terms of Conrad's ideal: the skeptic artist, himself haunting
the world, also has the power to haunt the world with ghosts of
his own creation.

When Conrad wants to summon shades, the tokens of expression, like Hollis's sixpence, require a spell. The underlying association between coins, words, and imaginative transformation

is repeated in the Preface, where the artist hopes that "that light of magic suggestiveness may be brought to play for an evanescent instant over the commonplace surface of words: of the old, old words, worn thin, defaced by ages of careless usage" (*P* 146). But simply making us see through artistic enchantment is not enough. For, to return to the Colvin letter, Conrad felt that his true subject was

> . . . the "ideal" value of things, events, and people. That and nothing else. The humorous, the pathetic, the passionate, the sentimental *aspects* came in of themselves—*mais en vérité c'est les valeurs idéales des faits et gestes humains qui se sont imposés à mon activité artistique.*
>
> Whatever dramatic and narrative gifts I may have are always, instinctively, used with that object—to get at, to bring forth *les valeurs idéales.*[53]

Even here the sense that absent values must be conjured from another world registers in the use of French, which surfaces in Conrad's English as an emissary from elsewhere. Compare Conrad's figurative language in characterizing his first reading of Flaubert: "I was somewhere at sea. . . . It was another life which I remember with misty tenderness, as a transmigrated soul might be supposed by a miracle to remember its previous envelope."[54] The skeptically decentered subject nostalgically invests the past, here associated with Flaubert as predecessor, with a value already fading into ghostliness; and the space between "envelopes," the disembodiedness prior to the next incarnation, becomes the unhappy emblem of the difficulty of representing that which eludes the world as representation.

When Jackson seems to peer beyond representation at the end of "Karain," the narrator decides in the concluding line that Jackson "had been too long away from home." Although "Karain" can be read as a therapeutic shuttling from home to home, a form of "cross-cultural purgation" in which Karain seeks refuge in England just as Lord Jim will try to make a new life in Patusan,[55] more striking is the way in which the psychology of guilt is shadowed by Conrad's interest in the respective metaphysical shelters constructed by "natives" and "white men." The narrative holds in suspension a complex set of conflicting attitudes toward the question of what lies in the mysterious "elsewhere" beyond the empirical. Jackson slides from one pole of understanding to another; the narrator remains steadily skeptical (with the one exception). More flexible than either, Hollis manages to inhabit both understandings at once, "as a transmigrated soul might be supposed by a miracle to remember its previous envelope." In the center of the story remains Karain, whose drama of guilt and atonement pivots on terrifying swings between belief and unbelief. In this light the Malayan setting itself, with the white men moored in a kind of liminal space offshore, can be seen as a metaphor for a radically different understanding of the world, an understanding Marlow would struggle with, though in a somewhat different form, in "Heart of Darkness."

First Conrad would continue to draw the philosophical out of the psychological in "The Return" (1897), a story he wrote as a break from "Karain." Though "The Return," the longest story in *Tales of Unrest*, never leaves the London home of the Herveys, Alvan Hervey nevertheless follows Jackson in calling into question the visible as a final source of knowledge. In this sense the story anticipates Conrad's interrogation of the visual dimension of his fiction in the Stein discussion of *Lord Jim*; and it will lead us, via Hervey's visionary moments, back to the ambiguous conjunction of skepticism and transcendence in Schopenhauer.

Skepticism as Theology: "The Return" of Schopenhauer

"The Return" brings into focus the central ambiguity (or equivocation) in Conrad's projection of a world beyond experience, and it does so in the unlikely context of a failing marriage.[56] The story begins with Hervey's discovery that his wife has left him for another man. She returns within minutes, however, and Hervey eventually ends the story by walking out on *her*, never to return. Beyond the melodrama, the real story takes place in the language characterizing Hervey's response to his abandonment and in Conrad's confused attitude toward those emotions. Since Conrad appears unaware of the extent to which Hervey's anxieties may dramatize his own, the inherent difficulty of distinguishing between voices in free indirect discourse becomes complicated further by a blurring of boundaries between author and narrator. The story's wild inconsistencies of tone and attitude have been read as symptoms of Conrad's inability to write about sex, but much of the strangeness derives from the incongruous intrusion of a rhetoric of other worlds into the Herveys' marital problems.[57]

Beyond unwitting parodies of the Jamesian moment of moral awakening, Conrad's effort to imitate *cher maître* in "The Return" also brings out an explicitly metaphysical urge that overrides James's more insistently psychological orientation. Alvan Hervey experiences two central epiphanies, but around these cluster an array of further revelations, all couched in the rhetoric of the microcosm. The description of the couple's confrontation is typical: "He walked at her, raging, as if blind; during these three quick strides he lost touch of the material world and was whirled interminably through a kind of empty universe made up of nothing but fury and anguish, till he came suddenly upon her face—very close to his" (*TU* 144–45). As the story strains toward a nearly continuous sense of an opening out into other worlds, moments of vision give way to one another with startling frequency:

[H]e had a vision, a vision quick and distinct as a dream: the vision of everything he had thought indestructible and safe in the world crashing down about him. (*TU* 130)

A dark curtain seemed to rise before him, and for less than a second he looked upon the mysterious universe of moral suffering. (*TU* 133)

[H]e was made aware that some essential part of himself had in a flash returned into his body, returned finally from a fierce and lamentable region, from the dwelling-place of unveiled hearts. (*TU* 140)

[W]hen he stood up he was penetrated by an irresistible belief in an enigma, by the conviction that within his reach and passing away from him was the very secret of existence. (*TU* 176)

Although these are among many passages intended to characterize Hervey's emotional shock, the felt presence of the enigmatic "secret of existence" pushes the discourse into a higher level of abstraction, prefiguring both the more controlled metaphysical speculations of "Heart of Darkness" and the more relentlessly abstract language of *The Secret Agent*. Citing the familiar examples of "west and east, London and the Congo, Switzerland and Russia," Tony Tanner has described a characteristic

Conradian strategy as "the ironic juxtaposition of . . . opposed realms."[58] To Tanner's cultural formulation we can add another. Like most stories in *Tales of Unrest*, "The Return" asks us to see psychological and emotional conflicts under the aspect of the metaphysical: one world always exists in opposition to another.

But what kind of elsewhere does the story ultimately project? Hervey's twin revelations range from the vision of "man's tragic isolation" when Mrs. Hervey leaves to the "vision of Love and Faith" when she returns.[59] His last glimpse of another world is distinctly Schopenhauerian: "He was saddened by an impersonal sorrow, by a vast melancholy as of all mankind longing for what cannot be attained" (*TU* 179). This realm of eternally frustrated desire, where one drifts, according to Schopenhauer, between boredom and despair, is also represented as a form of haunting: "He believed the shadow of [that vision] had been with him as long as he could remember; that invisible presence had ruled his life" (*TU* 180–81). Near the story's climax Hervey's new awareness carries him "on the track of the enigma, out of the world of senses into the region of feeling" (*TU* 177). Since conflicted fears of intimacy unsettle most of Conrad's characters, the "region of feeling" typically constitutes a threat to postures of secure defensiveness. In "The Return," however, the promise of renewed vigor in Hervey's life suddenly dispels Schopenhauerian pessimism and recalls instead the narrator's vision of ideal values in "Karain": "That touch of grace . . . flung open for him the portals of beyond, and in contemplating there the certitude immaterial and precious he forgot all the meaningless accidents of existence" (*TU* 177). Since everything connected with Hervey's wife comes to seem "like a mist of facts thickening between him and the vision of love and faith," he chooses finally to abandon both his mausoleum-like house and his wife, who is associated all too often with a "woman of marble, composed and blind on the high pedestal" in the hallway (*TU* 178, 182). The language of the scene suggests that Hervey's departure tropes an escape from "the world of senses," an achievement unavailable to the wife as statue but not to the husband as "seer" (*TU* 178).

"The Return" thus recapitulates and intensifies the divided attitude toward the transcendent found in "Karain." Taken together, these stories suggest that the Conradian world as will carries both positive and negative charges. On one hand, there is the perception of an intolerable truth that must be repressed. In "The Return" the penetrating vision sees into our ineluctable isolation in a world where relationships are the only ground of value. (In "Heart of Darkness" Marlow's lie to Kurtz's Intended will pick up and raise to principle Hervey's tentative conclusion that "deception should begin at home"—*TU* 170.) On the other hand, Hervey also sees into a world where salvation *can* be found in love: "there can be no life without faith—faith in a human heart" (*TU* 177). The suspicion that such a statement in Conrad can only be ironic must be tempered by the general consideration that Conrad's irony often defends against the attraction of sentimentality and by the particular consideration that Axel Heyst later speaks virtually the same words without irony at the climax of *Victory*.

And so beyond the visible world, in the words of "Karain" and "The Return," lie *both* the "tender ghosts of ideals" and a "mysterious universe of moral suffering." Imaginative vision in these stories presents radically opposed versions of transcendence, and imagination itself, which can give access to either, is both valued and feared. The ambivalence corresponds to Conrad's own: without denying its importance to his art, Conrad usually relied less on imagination than on memory to supply his fundamental narrative materials, and he was inclined, in the words of *Lord Jim*, to regard imagination as "the father of all terrors" (*LJ* 11). Marlow's response to Kurtz's final utterance can be seen as emblematic: "it had the appalling face of a glimpsed truth—the strange commingling of desire and hate" (*HD* 151). In this context the repetition of the word "bind" in the Preface takes on a more complex urgency: the artist hopes that the "vision" of art will "awaken in the hearts of the beholders that feeling of unavoidable solidarity . . . which binds men to each other and all mankind to the visible world" (*P* 147).[60] The art that binds us to the visible universe may be either a blessing or a curse. Perhaps, Conrad suggests, we need to huddle together in the shelter of the visible to avoid seeing the terrors of the "unseen." Or is the visible only a mesmerizing spectacle keeping us from truths more profound and (like the shades of sentimental women) more beautiful?

The ambiguity returns us to Schopenhauer, whose theory of

music invited a similar question. What is it that lies behind the world as representation: the cacophony of the will's blindly striving energy, or the beauty of a nineteenth-century version of *concordia discours*? Although the unexpectedly harmonious music Schopenhauer imagines beyond the world as representation eventually came to be heard as Wagner, from another perspective it has affinities with the heavenly choir. Metaphysics has been described as coy theology, and in both Conrad and Schopenhauer the metaphysical impulse threatens to spill over into a religious one. Schopenhauer anticipates the charge that he is writing a covert theology and confronts it directly; Conrad does not.[61]

Conrad's visions beyond the ordinary are forced on resistant characters with a violence that resembles the more overt association of the sacred with shattered complacency in the work of Flannery O'Connor.[62] Less orthodox (but also quite Catholic), Conrad repeatedly returns to a sense of the transcendent that verges on the religious: the noumenal shades into the numinous. To refer to the numinous is to invoke Rudolf Otto's *The Idea of the Holy*, where the word was first used to isolate the *feeling* of the sacred that exists in excess of its conventional ethical content.[63] And, to be sure, the sacred in these stories enters more as the sheer power of otherness than as a sanction for morality. Those less sympathetic to Romanticism might dismiss these qualities as "spilt religion,"[64] but I prefer to think of "the place of avenging belief" in its battle with Conrad's pervasive skepticism as a form of negative theology.

The simplest definition of negative theology is "the defining of God in terms of what he is not, as when God is described in words like 'immortal,' 'immutable,' 'infinite,' 'unbounded,' 'impassive,' and the like."[65] My usage, however, is intended to bring out the sense in which the negative theology of *Tales of Unrest* tends to become "negative" twice over. Given that the nature of the unseen is more often diabolical than divine, the ineffable evoked through negation may itself be negative. Absence need not be evil, but Conrad's readiness to gesture toward something beyond phenomena cannot conceal the fear that the absolute otherness of the holy may prove merely destructive, that the shattering of the ordinary may issue in ruins rather than renewal.

In Schopenhauer and Conrad alike, as in the emerging modernist sensibility that sustained them, the claims of skepticism are contested by the consolations of transcendence. Schopenhauer constructs a metaphysical system designed to destroy the neoclassic centrality of reason, yet the equivocal omnipresence of the will ultimately ratifies belief in the unified coherence of the world. In Conrad visionary experience would seem to catalyze world-consuming skepticism, yet a nostalgic investment in the recovery of lost immanence prevents skepticism from becoming nihilism. Here I diverge sharply from Hillis Miller, who claims that "the special place of Joseph Conrad in English Literature lies in the fact that in him the nihilism covertly dominant in modern culture is brought to the surface and shown for what it is."[66] Like Schopenhauer, Conrad *resists* the radical skepticism Miller accepts as a given, for his discourse of skepticism includes a discourse of reaction that counters the very insights skepticism proffers. In its moments of greatest intensity that reaction strains toward a sense of the holy. With this dialogic of dissolution and recuperation Conrad lays the groundwork for less conflicted versions of the aesthetic ordering of reality later carried out in the narratives of high modernism.

The resurgent romanticism that characterizes Conrad's early stories does not persist in this form throughout his career. As authorial skepticism assumes new forms, the Schopenhauerian model of aesthetic contemplation recedes in importance. In *Lord Jim* the tension between ordinary life and a world elsewhere will be literalized in the unstable boundaries between Patusan as trading post and Patusan as romance; the ambivalence there is ultimately projected as narrative in the transformation of Jim's idyll into Hervey's "mysterious universe of moral suffering." In the more static narratives of the early period, including "Heart of Darkness," Conrad's divided attitude toward the transcendent emerges in the language of vision I have been tracing in *Tales of Unrest*. What remains crucial to any moment in Conrad's career is an understanding of the ways in which a particular fiction articulates authorial skepticism.

In the following chapter Conrad's skeptical suspension between what I have called the noumenal and the numinous provides the terms for a reading of Gothic and melodramatic modes in his most celebrated story, "Heart of Darkness."

Chapter Three

"Heart of Darkness": Visionary Skepticism

"Inconceivable," "impenetrable," and "inscrutable": Marlow's favorite adjectives in "Heart of Darkness" fill out the lexicon of negative theology discussed in the previous chapter. The argument advanced there, that Conrad's attitude toward the irrational can be understood as a version of the Schopenhauerian will *and* as a covert quest for the divine, brings us now to consideration of two literary modes associated with the sacred: the Gothic and the melodramatic. Between them these modes reproduce the divided attitude toward the noumenal I have been tracing in Conrad and Schopenhauer: the Gothic tradition brings out a sense of the lurking malevolence of Schopenhauer's metaphysical will, and melodrama attempts to recover the consolation of morality in a world losing touch with the assurance of an ethical order. The Gothicism of Marlow's path toward Kurtz culminates in paired scenes of melodrama: the climactic encounter with Kurtz and the interview with the Intended.

The urgency of Marlow's narration on board the *Nellie*—he plunges into it without warning, "the speech that cannot be silenced" (*HD* 97)—bespeaks his need to be purged of thoughts he still finds disturbing: ". . . No, it is impossible; it is impossible to convey the life-sensation of any given epoch of one's existence— that which makes its truth, its meaning—its subtle and penetrating essence. It is impossible. We live, as we dream— alone. . . ." (*HD* 82).[1] The skeptical implications of this passage reverberate throughout Conrad's canon. Marlow earlier gives voice to a more measured skepticism in his subversion of the frame narrator's naive celebration of "the great spirit of the past" on the Thames (*HD* 47); but from "Heart of Darkness" forward until the affirmations of the later romances, skepticism continually threatens to become more radical and inclusive. Since *Lord*

Jim will introduce more complex instances of the skeptical crises
that both generate and threaten Marlow's discourse, I will defer
full discussion of radical skepticism to later chapters and focus
here on the problematics of transcendence that elicit the countervailing operations of skepticism characteristic of the later fiction.

Melodrama, Gothic, and the Numinous

Conrad's melodramatic tendencies have often been singled out
for criticism, less so his Gothic.² Yet, given the relative optimism
and pessimism of the two traditions, we can see that Conrad criticism itself has developed along broadly melodramatic and
Gothic lines. Although Hillis Miller recognizes that man's confrontation with "a spiritual power external to himself . . . offers
the possibility of an escape from subjectivism," his emphasis falls
on the darker vision of what he considers Conrad's nihilism.³
Thus the characteristically Gothic description of Conrad's art:
"By a return, through language, to the heart of darkness, the
writer affirms himself as the power which breaks down the fron-
tier between man and the darkness, and makes the darkness enter for a moment the daylight world. Writing is a dangerous hovering between two realms which are incompatible."⁴ For readings
more inclined to focus on the triumphant drama of morality one
turns to Ian Watt, who recognizes the potential nihilism of Conrad's vision, yet emphasizes his effort to respond: "Alienation, of
course, but how do we get out of it?"⁵

The analogy with Schopenhauer allows us to define a middle
ground, for the irrationality of the metaphysical will may be considered a melodramatic-philosophical ground for a Conradian
Gothic. The melodrama of Schopenhauer's philosophy lies in the
relation between his ethics and his theory of the will. Although
virtue generally overcomes evil in melodrama, in Schopenhauer
the amorality of the metaphysical will always triumphs, for the
will has only itself to battle. Yet by introducing the possibility that
the individual somehow can cease to will through an act of will—
the achievement of resignation—Schopenhauer, against all
odds, restores the possibility of a marginally happy ending, not
to mention an ethical system cognate with the stoic resignation

of Christian humanism.[6] The question of spiritual value and the sacred in the Gothic and melodramatic traditions thus provides a logical point of departure for my reading of skepticism and the numinous in "Heart of Darkness."

The Gothic revival of the 1790s has long been recognized as a response in part to the loss of the sacred in an age dominated by scientific rationalism.[7] With the decline of religion, humankind's primitive fear of a divine power greater than itself found expression in the ghosts, demons, and supernatural grotesqueries of Gothic fiction. "Gothic novels arose out of a quest for the numinous," according to Devendra Varma. "They are characterized by an awestruck apprehension of Divine immanence penetrating diurnal reality."[8] Yet the evident romanticism of the Gothic resurgence of irrational energies did not reveal a reassuring immanence of the divine in nature as much as the demonic within the apparently angelic. Hence the tales of sexual abandon and perversion within monasteries and the preoccupation with the crumbling walls of ruined abbeys—objective correlatives for the decay of religious order.[9] But the decadence also betokened a nostalgia for the other-worldly experience of the sacred. Varma continues:

The consequent "renaissance of wonder" created a world of imaginative conjurings in which the Divine was not a theorem but a mystery filled with dread. The phantoms that prowl along the corridors of the haunted castle would have no more power to awe than the rats behind fluttering tapestries, did they not bear token of a realm that is revealed only to man's mystical apperception, his source of all absolute spiritual values.[10]

This is Otto's *mysterium tremendum*, the felt presence of the *origin* of spiritual value without the rational apprehension of the values themselves.[11]

The melodramatic tradition, according to Peter Brooks, also seeks to resacralize the world but is "less directly interested in the reassertion of the numinous for its own sake than in its ethical corollaries." "Melodrama starts from and expresses the anxiety brought by a frightening new world in which the traditional patterns of moral order no longer provide the necessary social glue. It plays out the force of that anxiety with the apparent triumph of villainy, and it dissipates it with the eventual victory of virtue."[12] Just as Gothic writers seek to rediscover what Varma calls the "source of all absolute spiritual values," so authors of melodrama aim to pierce to "the moral occult": "the domain of spiritual forces and imperatives that is not clearly visible within reality, but which they believe . . . demands to be uncovered, registered, articulated." Looking back at the momentary "disturbance" of being in "The Lagoon," or Hollis's more sustained vision in "Karain," we can identify versions of the moral occult Brooks locates in melodrama. Melodrama, Brooks continues, tends "to diverge from the Gothic novel in its optimism, its claim that the moral imagination can open up the angelic spheres as well as the demonic depths and can allay the threat of moral chaos." Thus, in Otto's terms the melodramatic restores to the numinous the traditional ethical value of the holy.

The ghosts that emerge in Conrad with the sudden intuition of a world beyond conventional perception suggest an immediate link to the Gothic. One book on the Gothic tradition even begins with a reference to the frame narrator's description of Marlow's mode of narration in "Heart of Darkness":[13] "to him the meaning of an episode was not inside like a kernel but outside, enveloping the tale which brought it out only as a glow brings out a haze, in the likeness of one of these misty halos that sometimes are made visible by the spectral illumination of moonshine" (*HD* 48).[14] Effectively evoking the story's ambiguity, the description nevertheless misleads to the extent that it fails to acknowledge the narrative investment in penetrating to a truth Marlow imagines *within* the heart of darkness, and Marlow's conflicted impatience with surface phenomena on his journey to the "Inner Station" can be assimilated to the melodramatic mode. Describing melodrama as "a mode of excess" typical of the moral imagination, Brooks deepens and broadens the concept to include a characteristic pressure placed on the surface of reality in order to penetrate to a more spiritual realm.[15] For Marlow the defeat of all human intentions in the heart of darkness intensifies the desire to pierce to occulted moral values. But when Marlow's sense that a veil has been lifted offers him visions he would prefer not to have, we are returned again to the divided attitude toward the transcendent in *Tales of Unrest*.

Description and the Surface of Truth

The language of Conrad's descriptions in "Heart of Darkness" frequently seems to refer beyond the immediate scene, though it is not clear to what. The more florid of these passages have been condemned in the well-known critique of F. R. Leavis, who complained about Conrad's "adjectival insistence" in "Heart of Darkness": "The insistence betrays the absence, the willed 'intensity' the nullity. He is intent on making a virtue out of not knowing what he means."[16] No doubt Conrad is sometimes guilty of rhetorical excess, and not every passage in "Heart of Darkness" can be defended. But here he stands accused (and for Leavis, at least, convicted) of knowing no more than Marlow, whose words Leavis quotes in order to demonstrate Conrad's epistemological shortcomings. Separating the perspectives of Conrad and his narrators is usually a complicated affair, but the failure even to try prevents Leavis from seeing that in Marlow Conrad dramatizes a gradual recognition and acceptance of the limits of human knowledge and, consequently, of what can be represented in Marlow's discourse.[17]

But Leavis is right to call our attention to the verbal excess that characterizes "Heart of Darkness." As Marlow's language strains toward definitive meanings, his words sometimes accumulate without effect; hence Leavis's irritated awareness of the stream of adjectives such as "inconceivable," "unspeakable," "inscrutable." But the effort to evoke the ineffable by describing what it is not sometimes amounts to more than an acknowledgment that language is an imperfect tool. Like the language of mysticism, Marlow's discourse often finds rapture in its inadequacy and consummation in the release into silence. Words become gestures, and they gesture toward a presence that resists verbal articulation.[18] They constitute, in short, a negative theology. The desire to overcome verbal limitations by gesturing even more emphatically derives from a conviction analogous to Schopenhauer's motive for positing the world as will: the belief that the world as representation—whether it be a hippo sunning itself on a riverbank or the "pale plumpness" shaking hands with Marlow in Brussels—does not encompass the whole of reality. Beyond representation lies the Gothic threat of the numinous and the melodramatic appeal of the moral occult.

These dimly perceived realms are usually expressed through variations of the trope of the container and the thing contained: the surface conceals depths; the outside, an inside. While backed against his beached steamer by the garrulous brickmaker, Marlow wonders "whether the stillness on the face of the immensity looking at us two were meant as an appeal or as a menace": "The moon had spread over everything a thin layer of silver—over the rank grass, over the mud, upon the wall of matted vegetation standing higher than the wall of a temple, over the great river I could see through a sombre gap glittering, glittering, as it flowed broadly by without a murmur. All this was great, expectant, mute" (*HD* 81). Nature overshadows the temple, and Marlow responds to the sinister hint of the wholly other by trying to put a face on it. But the projection only refigures his alienation from the inhuman scene as an incomplete humanity: "I felt how big, how confoundedly big, was that thing that couldn't talk, and perhaps was deaf as well. What was in there?" The oppositions of inner/outer and surface/depth continue throughout the narrative, and Marlow's occasional glimpses beyond the enigmas and opacities of outer or surface reality only intensify the ambiguity about what is concealed.

Marlow distinguishes explicitly between a "surface-truth" and "an inner truth." The former he associates most directly with the immediate tasks of preserving the security of one's existence: "I had to watch the steering, and circumvent those snags, and get the tin-pot along by hook or by crook. There was surface-truth enough in these things to save a wiser man" (*HD* 97). The wiser man is apparently endangered by his own wisdom, which hinders him from finding solace in the distraction offered by Marlow's "superficial" duties: "when you have to attend . . . to the mere incidents of the surface, the reality—the reality, I tell you—fades. The inner truth is hidden—luckily, luckily" (*HD* 93). One needs to shield oneself in work, here defined as part of surface reality, in order to escape from the vague threat of a hidden, second-order reality. Viewed from this angle, the workaday business of "mere incidents" appears to be the domain of timid functionaries, those without the courage to endure the grim secrets of the world.[19]

Although Marlow attributes a higher value to work elsewhere in "Heart of Darkness," he does so only after implicitly redefining it as constituting the inner reality of the *individual*: "I don't like work . . . but I like what is in the work,—the chance to find yourself. Your own reality—for yourself, not for others—what no other man can ever know. They can only see the mere show, and never can tell what it really means" (*HD* 85). Such reversals in Marlow's rhetoric can be disorienting. He sometimes disdains work as merely a necessary distraction from something unbearable; he sometimes describes it as a locus of value.[20] His inside/outside opposition always privileges the former as being more real; but that inner reality can be either the Gothic suggestion of an unknown threat, as in the malevolence seemingly concealed within the jungle, or the private domain of personal values, which, like Prince Roman's "needs" and "aspirations," must remain "secret" and "unexpressed" (*TH* 48). The trope of the privileged yet vulnerable inside will recur in an ironic form in *Nostromo*, where Charles Gould's refusal to divulge his thoughts fails to preserve what he imagines to be the purity of his intentions; he becomes instead a more complex version of the Kurtz-like hollow man.

In "Heart of Darkness" the conflicting interpretations of the hidden inside represent two perspectives on the same problem. Often figured as an eerie stillness or silence, the Gothic menace of the forest suggests to Marlow that reality must be elsewhere—in the concealed inside—and in consequence his own sense of reality must be an illusion, part of the surface truth. But if the blankness of nature overawes consciousness by its utter indifference to human meaning and value, that recognition also triggers what Gillian Beer has described as "a massive compensatory activity within the psyche" that is characteristic of the post-Darwinian mind. Evolutionary theory, Beer argues, fostered a heightened awareness of the "*incongruence* between mind and world" such that the human image-making faculty was forced to struggle to restore man's sense of belonging in the world.[21] The sole source of signification, the inner reality of the individual also becomes the sole locus of value.[22]

Yet the privileged sanctum of Marlow's inner reality is nearly turned inside out by his "remote kinship with this wild and passionate uproar" of the natives on the banks of the river (*HD* 96).

Thus it is not surprising that the undermining of distinctions between Marlow's inner reality and the outer reality of the forest is
literalized in the presence of "restrained" cannibals on board the
steamer. Here, as in "Karain," the collision of cultures triggers an
acute sense of cultural relativity that threatens to deepen into a
full-blown skeptical crisis. If the cannibals on shore seem to Marlow to represent something inhuman in human form, those on
board are humans whose "inhumanity" can be overlooked: "after all, they did not eat each other before my face" (*HD* 94). If pursued, such observations inevitably undermine the very distinctions Marlow would like to preserve, and he soon takes refuge
in his articulation of the necessity of surface truths, which safely
push less tolerable truths out of sight.

The crucial term Marlow uses to define his essential difference
from his environment is "intention," along with other examples
of a strongly teleological vocabulary: "idea," "force," and—the
concrete token and symbolic representative of British efficiency—the "rivet." Veiled threats may secure the rivets required
to repair the steamboat, but intentions require the shelter of consciousness. When consciousness is endangered, Marlow's saving sense of the purposive and pragmatic begins to ebb, and he
derides his dangerous maneuvering up the river to save a human
life as mere "monkey tricks" (*HD* 94). With mindless movement
threatening to supplant ethical action, Marlow's self-description
barely safeguards his intuitive apprehension of the privileged
duality presupposed by man as the symbol-making animal.
"Man's animality is in the realm of sheer matter, sheer motion,"
writes Kenneth Burke. "But his 'symbolicity' adds a dimension
of action not reducible to the non-symbolic—for by its very nature as symbolic it cannot be identical with the non-symbolic."[23]
Inclined by skepticism to subvert his own claims to meaning and
so to collapse the very difference Burke articulates, Marlow is
troubled by the *ease* with which the constructions of consciousness are defeated. He will neither cede his uniquely human difference from blank nature nor admit that all meaning derives
from the symbol-making activity of his mind. Throughout the
story Marlow remains suspended between the suspicion that all
values and meaning are projections and his desire to "see
through" to a moral occult.

Though he is intensely aware of an intention hidden within the "impenetrable forest," Marlow's efforts at interpreting it are completely frustrated until his discovery of actual writing in the wilderness. Finding on a "stack of firewood . . . a flat piece of board with some faded pencil-writing on it" (*HD* 98), Marlow feels as if the forest has suddenly rendered itself legible. Stepping inside an adjacent hut Marlow then comes upon a book, *An Inquiry into some Points of Seamanship*, which exemplifies what he most desires to find—"a singleness of intention"—and instantly feels "a delicious sensation of having come upon something unmistakably real" (*HD* 99). Yet even this avatar of intelligibility is marked by the mystery of the wilderness, for the book is filled with marginalia that to Marlow look like "cipher." Although he realizes that the writing is "plainly referring to the text" and thus is intended as commentary or explanation, the affair remains "an extravagant mystery."[24] The mystery later vanishes with the discovery of the book's Russian owner, but it is this sort of deadlocked dialogue between meaning promised and meaning denied that pushes Marlow into an uneasy rhetoric of the unknowable. An unambiguously human connection would momentarily banish anxieties about what makes such connections possible (or impossible), and the desire for the consolations of reading anticipates Marlow's increasingly intense desire to talk with Kurtz: "I assure you to leave off reading was like tearing myself away from the shelter of an old and solid friendship" (*HD* 99–100).

The deepest fear here is that the mysterious intentions housed in the wilderness will overpower his own, and when Marlow reads nature rather than the abandoned book, the wilderness offers him visions he is not eager to have: "suddenly, as though a veil had been removed from my eyes, I made out, deep in the tangled gloom, naked breasts, arms, legs, glaring eyes,—the bush was swarming with human limbs in movement" (*HD* 110). The "amazing reality of . . . concealed life" here suggests both figurative dismemberment and a troubling confusion of the human and the natural (*HD* 80). Where in Schopenhauer the common ground of the will tends to connect diverse phenomena like a current of electricity ("the powerful, irresistible impulse with which masses of water rush downwards, the persistence and determination with which the magnet always turns back to the

North Pole" [*WWR* I: 117–18]), in Conrad the emphasis falls on a potential loss of the capacity to differentiate between what normally are highly particularized phenomena. The thought that behind every representation lies the same will threatens to level fundamental hierarchies, even to the extent that the human, the animal, and the organic begin to blend into one another. Conrad thus extends the subversive effect of Schopenhauer's implicit claim that "the absolute unity at the root of our essence . . . is the expression or reflection of that homogeneity which results from the lack of a definitive and difference-producing purpose for life."[25] Marlow accordingly finds little comfort in the suggestion by the manager's uncle that he put his trust in the wilderness:

> I saw him extend his short flipper of an arm for a gesture that took in the forest, the creek, the mud, the river,—seemed to beckon with a dishonouring flourish before the sunlit face of the land a treacherous appeal to the lurking death, to the hidden evil, to the profound darkness of its heart. It was so startling that I leaped to my feet and looked back at the edge of the forest, as though I had expected an answer of some sort to that black display of confidence. (*HD* 92)

The man gestures inarticulately with a flipper; Marlow senses the possibility of an articulate response from the forest. By the time Marlow intercepts Kurtz crawling toward his "unspeakable rites," the conflation of the human and the animal has entered the narrative as a direct threat: "A black figure stood up, strode on long black legs, waving long black arms, across the glow. It had horns—antelope horns, I think—on its head" (*HD* 143). If the limbs Marlow sees swarming in the bush do not seem completely human either, their dismemberment becomes literal when Marlow finally reaches the Inner Station and sees the human transformed into the grotesquely ornamental in the form of the heads on pikes around Kurtz's shack. The reader never learns whether Kurtz's "unspeakable rites" involve cannibalism—they remain part of the inaccessible "inside"—yet cannibalism would be an appropriate metaphor for the breakdown of boundaries the story obsessively investigates.[26]

The fantasy of an undifferentiated vision projected in Marlow's descriptive language represents a nightmarish version of his naive response to Kurtz's report on the "Suppression of Savage Customs": "It gave me the notion of an exotic Immensity ruled by an august Benevolence" (*HD* 118). Marlow would like to resolve the confusing multiplicity of the forest into the consoling vision of a benign will—a kindly monarch, apparently—rather than the frightening force of Schopenhauer's will. The quest for a benevolent principle of harmony and hierarchy must be understood in the context of the ironic pilgrimage Marlow finds himself enacting, and following this path will lead us, with Marlow, to Kurtz.

Searching for the God in Man

Literature has registered God's disappearance in a variety of ways.[27] In Dickens, God's presence remains accessible beyond the human labyrinth of the city for those who have eyes to see. George Eliot, in the well-known anecdote of her conversation with F. W. H. Myers, showed greater equanimity in accepting a world whose transcendental sanctions had not receded but vanished. Of God, immortality, and duty she "pronounced, with terrible earnestness, how inconceivable was the *first*, how unbelievable the *second*, and yet how peremptory and absolute the *third*." Beyond equanimity, Lawrence exhibits almost complete indifference when Birkin heralds the new secularism in a dependent clause.[28]

There is a certain belatedness in Conrad's response to the *deus absconditus*, and in this respect he is closer to Dickens than to George Eliot or Lawrence. The shock that reverberates through his work is immediate, emotional, and anguished—like Marlow's when he discovers that Kurtz has escaped:

The fact is I was completely unnerved by a sheer blank fright, pure abstract terror, unconnected with any distinct shape of physical danger. What made this emotion so overpowering was—how shall I define it?— the moral shock I received, as if something altogether monstrous, intolerable to thought and odious to the soul, had been thrust upon me unexpectedly. (*HD* 141)

I take Marlow's anxiety and terror as a synecdoche for Conrad's own response to finding the heavens empty. But well before Marlow's shock over Kurtz's absence, the departure of God in "Heart of Darkness" is closely linked to Marlow's journey toward Kurtz.

When Marlow begins his narration with a rather weak attempt to distinguish between British colonialism and the more brutally rapacious Belgian variety in the Congo Free State, his argument suggests the need for what sounds like a form of primitive religion: "What redeems it is the idea only. An idea at the back of it; not a sentimental pretence but an idea; and an unselfish belief in the idea—something you can set up, and bow down before, and offer a sacrifice to . . . "(HD 51). Kurtz, who comes to be seen as a supernatural being by the natives, practices only a selfish religion, perhaps even a religion *of* the self. Nevertheless, from the amoral hypocrisy of the company manager Marlow turns "mentally to Kurtz for relief—positively for relief" (HD 138). Although Kurtz has plummeted from the culmination of European Liberalism to atavistic savagery, Marlow still prefers the assertion of some form of conviction to a skeptical emptying out of all beliefs.

The extent to which conviction in "Heart of Darkness" is shadowed by a hunger for spiritual value has often been underestimated owing to the distracting ferocity of Conrad's ironic treatment of simpletons like the stave-bearing pilgrims of the Eldorado Exploring Expedition.[29] But irony in Conrad does not always suggest self-righteous indignation. "True irony," says Burke, "is based upon a sense of fundamental kinship with the enemy, as one *needs* him, is *indebted* to him, is not merely outside him as an observer but contains him *within*, being consubstantial with him."[30] Fatuous as they are, the pilgrims are important insofar as Marlow feels *impelled* to cast them away. Kurtz, more obviously one of Marlow's secret sharers, seeks ivory, but Marlow recognizes that the ivory is as much an idol as a commodity: "The word . . . rang in the air, was whispered, was sighed. You would think they were praying to it" (HD 76). The substitution signifies a spiritual void, a hollowness like that of the accountant or the brickmaker, and Kurtz hungers to fill that emptiness as much as his coffers. It is this displaced religious impulse that draws to Conrad admirers such as T. S. Eliot and Graham Greene, a High Anglican and a Roman Catholic.

Before discovering Kurtz's emptiness, Marlow fixates on the desire to hear his voice as a defense, like the shelter afforded by the book of seamanship, against the frightening blankness and silence of the wilderness. Unsettled, at one point Marlow suddenly breaks from his monologue to address his audience more directly, as if challenging them to respond. The rhetorical gesture instantly conjures the social connection whose absence he feared in the wilderness: "how can you imagine what particular region of the first ages a man's untrammelled feet may take him into by the way of solitude—utter solitude without a policeman—by the way of silence—utter silence, where no warning voice of a kind neighbour can be heard whispering of public opinion?" (*HD* 116). The passage assumes that an investment in authority, whether the disciplinary effect of the police or of language, acts as a defense against a kind of "natural" atavism. It also brings out the extent to which Conrad's work is suffused with the fear of loneliness.[31] The narrator of *Under Western Eyes* remarks of Razumov: "Who knows what true loneliness is—not the conventional word, but the naked terror? . . . No human being could bear a steady view of moral solitude without going mad" (*UWE* 39). Such fear is basic to the psychology of skepticism: "As long as God exists, I am not alone. And couldn't the other suffer the fate of God?" This train of thought leads to the hypothesis that "the philosophical problem of the other [is] the trace or scar of the departure of God."[32] Descending from the divine to the human, the problem of the other plays out our anxieties about knowing and being known. For Marlow, Kurtz becomes that other, yet he occupies an unsettling position between the human and something beyond "the threshold of the invisible" (*HD* 151).

Marlow first becomes obsessed with the consolation of Kurtz's voice when his native helmsman is killed by a spear thrown from the riverbank. Whatever his deficiencies, the helmsman had carried out one of the most valuable duties a character in Conrad can perform—like Singleton, he had steered. His death persuades Marlow that Kurtz also must have died in the attack: "I couldn't have felt more of lonely desolation somehow, had I been robbed of a belief or had missed my destiny in life" (*HD* 114). A potential substitution for the helmsman ("And couldn't the other suffer the fate of God?"), Kurtz presents himself to Marlow only as a voice, and the promise of this voice comes to represent the sheltering and sheltered intention he so desires. But before ex-

periencing the deep duplicity of Kurtz's "gift of expression . . .
the pulsating stream of light, or the deceitful flow from the heart
of an impenetrable darkness" (*HD* 113–14), Marlow comes face to
face with a parody of his own desire to believe in Kurtz in the
figure of the Russian harlequin, who babbles with the enthusi-
asm of a disciple of Reverend Moon: "'I tell you,' he cried, 'this
man has enlarged my mind.' He opened his arms wide, staring
at me with his little blue eyes that were perfectly round"
(*HD* 125). Although his own loyalty will run deeper, at this moment Marlow "does not envy him his devotion to Kurtz"
(*HD* 127).

Marlow's preference for the nightmare of Kurtz over that of the
trading company eventually assumes the form of an ambivalent
discipleship. Like a priest presiding over the relics of a saint,
Marlow takes care to alter the text that will perpetuate an idealized version of Kurtz by tearing off the savage postscript to the
"Suppression of Savage Customs." Lying to the Intended, Marlow continues to protect an ideal image of Kurtz, again by paying
tribute only to what Kurtz originally intended. The anxious effort
to suppress publicity about Kurtz's savage customs is of a piece
with Marlow's lame defense of English colonialism in expressing
a longing for the sort of certainty once provided by religion.

Hoping for something human in the wilderness, Marlow finds
the Russian—a blithering zealot—and Kurtz. But Kurtz has
withdrawn into a world of his own creation. From the Russian
Marlow learns that "'you don't talk with that man—you listen to
him'" (*HD* 123). Even before meeting him Marlow remarks, "I
had never imagined him as doing, you know, but as discoursing"
(*HD* 113). Yet when Marlow hears about Kurtz's "monologues,"
he considers that the Russian's devotion may be "about the most
dangerous thing in every way he had come upon so far"
(*HD* 127). In his climactic showdown with Kurtz just beyond the
circle of his worshipers, Marlow understands these monologues
as the expression of a man whose "intelligence," though "perfectly clear," was "concentrated . . . upon himself with horrible
intensity" (*HD* 144). Bracketed within Marlow's first encounters
with the Russian and Kurtz is his horrified discovery that what
seemed "round carved balls" ornamenting fence posts are actually "symbolic" heads on stakes with all of the faces but one

turned in toward Kurtz's house. The heads literalize the potential violence of moral skepticism; the human other has become purely instrumental. Those gazing inward reflect Kurtz's own self-absorption while the one turned outward beckons, like the forest, to Marlow, who ultimately manages to establish the connection he has been seeking all along.

The Russian only listens to Kurtz (and consequently is "filled" and "occupied" by him); Marlow, when faced with the necessity of preventing Kurtz's return to the midnight rites, *talks* him back to the hut. Dialogue emerges here as an antidote to the self-enclosure of monologue. Yet in narrating his story to the audience on the *Nellie*, Marlow reexperiences the danger to which Kurtz has succumbed. To his auditors Marlow had "for a long time" already become, as Kurtz was to Marlow, "no more to us than a voice" (*HD* 83). Marlow himself underlines the problem when, in the passage that begins this chapter, he declares the impossibility of ever communicating "the life-sensation" of his experience in Africa: "We live, as we dream—alone." Providing Marlow with an audience to shape his utterance, Conrad aims to transform a potential prison house of language into what Henry James called "a noble sociability of vision."[33] The breadth of this society, however, is quite limited. "Be civil," someone interrupts: to the extent that dialogue between Englishmen becomes a synecdoche for all civilized discourse, Marlow is.

Although dialogue holds the potential to undo the solipsism of monologue, the fear that language may inevitably fail to communicate whatever is most important runs deep in Conrad. "Your own reality," Marlow claims in his praise of work, is inaccessible to others: "they only see the mere show, and never can tell what it really means" (*HD* 85). For Bakhtin true dialogic structure emerges from what Keats called "negative capability," the capacity to understand all points of view from the inside out and the willingness to accord each an equal say. The monologic is associated with the Romantic cult of the personality and its tendency to objectify whatever cannot be absorbed into its own perspective.[34] Kurtz has long been recognized as the epitome of Romantic individualism,[35] and in "Heart of Darkness" Conrad dramatizes, in the relationships between Kurtz and Marlow and between Marlow and the inscribed audience, the danger of the

collapse of the dialogic into the monologic. Marlow, by with-
drawing his hesitating foot, preserves the capacity to maintain a
dialogue with his audience—though admittedly (if we exclude
the chorus of critical response) a rather one-sided one. In *Nostromo* the collapse into monological authority will be associated
with political and physical violence, the ferocious imposition of
a single will. Although Kurtz's savagery anticipates this theme,
in "Heart of Darkness" Conrad ultimately seems less concerned
with the political critique of colonialism that dominates the first
section of the novella than with the more narrowly social and literary problem that Marlow's narration may become purely self-
reflexive.

By its very nature, however, language cannot become a wholly
private set of dream symbols. If, as Wittgenstein asserted, a
word's meaning is its use, "use" also implies the history of its
use: maverick usage does not necessarily assign a new (and possibly private) meaning to a word.[36] "The fantasy of a private language," according to Cavell, "can be understood as an attempt
to account for, and protect, our separateness, our unknowing-
ness, our unwillingness or incapacity either to know or to be
known."[37] Marlow's rather defensive outbursts against his audience are suggestive of a conflicted attempt to confront his own
sense of isolation. In *Lord Jim*, where Jim reaches "the secret
fount of [Marlow's] egotism," the ambivalent desire to share and
withhold through narration is played out in the disruptions and
dislocations of narrative chronology. Here the emphasis falls less
on the problem of other minds per se than on the capacity of Marlow's narration to rescue "the shade of the original Kurtz," the
one committed to humanitarian ideals, from the encompassing
darkness (*HD* 147).

Watching Kurtz die, Marlow feels "as though a veil had been
rent" (*HD* 149), but the unveiling only leads to an undecidable
question. Kurtz may or may not have been able to reaffirm the
validity of ethical categories in his dying words: he whispers, "at
some image, at some vision"—an image from memory or a vision
of certitudes beyond the human? Deathbed scenes in Victorian
literature, one critic has suggested, may function in part to suppress such uncertainties: "When the heart is so strongly moved,

the skeptical intellect is silenced."[38] The absence of the sentimental response to skepticism in Kurtz's last moments only heightens the indeterminacy of what we are to make of his experience ("the horror, the horror"?) and so intensifies the skeptical confusion inspired in Marlow and the reader. Has Kurtz pierced to the moral occult, or is Marlow again turning to him for relief where none is warranted?

Absent in the moment of Kurtz's death, sentimentality more frequently characterizes Conrad's representation of women. In Marlow's meeting with Kurtz's fiancée, then, we might expect to find a resurgence of the sentimentality resisted earlier.

Marlow's Narration: Toward the Shelter of the Aesthetic

In "the shade of the original Kurtz" Conrad refashions the "tender ghosts of ideals" found in "Karain." The doubleness of what lies beyond the threshold of the visible—the ghost of Kurtz's original intentions or an "initiated wraith from the back of Nowhere" (*HD* 117)—recalls the contrast between the unseen that threatens Karain and what the narrator sees as the "charming shades of loved women." In that story imagination is ambiguously linked to a mode of perception capable of penetrating to a realm of absolute value. In the figure of Kurtz's Intended, Conrad again associates the shadowy realm of the ideal with women, but in so doing he cannot fully accept the imagination as an adequate repository for the ideals of civilization.

In the melodrama of Marlow's interview with the Intended, imagery of the ghostly becomes insistent.[39] Although the encounter is often criticized for its melodrama, it is important to understand why the characteristic excess of the melodramatic imagination comes into play, even when the resulting scene is not as accomplished as many others in Conrad. The extravagant representation—the insistence on the enveloping gloom of the darkness, the cries of the wilderness reverberating through the house—provides a gauge for the intensity of Conrad's desire to make legible signs of the absolute ethical values that Marlow could not read on the face of the African jungle. The representation is, as usual, equivocal: although the darkness absorbs al-

most everything, Marlow preserves what light remains in the Intended's idealized vision of Kurtz by refusing to destroy it with
the one fact she would not have been able to bear. The characteristic optimism of melodrama resists but cannot overcome the
Gothic threat of Conrad's darker vision.

A context for Marlow's lie evolves from his occasional outbursts of misogyny earlier in the narrative. In each he claims that
women live in an ideal realm divorced from reality: their world
is "too beautiful altogether, and if they were to set it up it would
go to pieces before the first sunset. Some confounded fact we
men have been living contentedly with ever since the day of creation would start up and knock the whole thing over" (*HD* 59).
The ideals Kurtz bore into the wilderness ultimately survive only
in the illusions of—a rare bit of wordplay for Conrad—his
Intended.[40] Better there than nowhere, perhaps, but the tone of
the scene wavers uneasily, suggesting at one moment Marlow's
ironic awareness of the Intended's severely limited understanding, at another a breathless idealization of futile feminine nobility. As Howard Felperin has remarked, "when Marlow finally
meets Kurtz's lady, that presiding figure of his romantic quest-
ing, the scene is far from one of unmitigated irony but one of
irony itself ironized to maintain the spell of romance."[41] The logic
of the narrative does not offer woman's capacity to believe as a
symbolic resolution of Marlow's impasse, for the inclination to
idealize the female imagination essentially recovers the vanishing ethical value of the holy only to transform it into the fundamental otherness of woman.[42] By the time he came to write *Under
Western Eyes*, Conrad was able to indulge in parody of his own
tendency to idealize female spirituality in the ridiculously extravagant "feminism" of Peter Ivanovitch, whose sycophantic at-
tentions to the wealthy Madame de S—— are unmasked as symbolic violence in his brutal treatment of Tekla. In "Heart of Darkness" the narrative suspends Marlow between the suspicion that
civilized ideals survive only in the pathetic naiveté of Kurtz's fiancée and the thwarted attempt to pierce to a moral occult. The
novella ends inconclusively by returning us to the narrative
frame and the impossibility of knowing whether any of Marlow's
immediate listeners learned anything from the story, let alone
understood what Conrad called its "secondary notions."[43]

Conrad cannot easily accept the pessimistic implications of Marlow's failure to discover transcendental sanctions for ethical values. Faced with the diabolical specter of Kurtz, Marlow reacts with the anger shown in "The Idiots" by Jean-Pierre, who pounds furiously on the doors of a church that is, predictably, empty. Just as Jean-Pierre rages against futility, Marlow resents "bitterly the absurd danger of our situation, as if to be at the mercy of that atrocious phantom had been a dishonouring necessity" (HD 133). Resentment at feeling dependent may cover a deeper fear. Though dramatized as an active presence, evil is defined as a vacancy, and fear of vacancy haunts the novella.[44] The absence of God in "Heart of Darkness" strips man's honor by leaving him prey to the nightmarish assaults of the numinous as sheer power—ghosts of the Gothic, "atrocious phantoms" lacking the ethical value of the holy.

Conrad's fantasy of the knitting machine, cited in Chapter One, was written a few years before "Heart of Darkness," and it is deeply engaged in the indignity of God's departure:

There is a—let us say—a machine. It evolved itself (I am severely scientific) out of a chaos of scraps of iron and behold!—it knits. I am horrified at the horrible work and stand appalled. I feel it ought to embroider—but it goes on knitting. . . . And the most withering thought is that the infamous thing has made itself; made itself without thought, without conscience, without foresight, without eyes, without heart. It is a tragic accident—and it has happened. You can't interfere with it. The last drop of bitterness is in the suspicion that you can't even smash it. . . .

It knits us in and it knits us out. It has knitted time space, pain, death, corruption, despair and all the illusions—and nothing matters.[45]

Taken one way, the machine can be read as a technological version of Schopenhauer's blind will: it stands beyond the warp and woof of the reality it determines. Or, as I argued in the first chapter, the operation of the machine represents a fiction of skepticism cognate with Descartes's *malin génie*. In the context of the present discussion, the machine represents not a metaphysical postulate but, rather, Conrad's anxious attempt to fill with his imagination the vacancy left by God. (Compare Marlow's impulsive attraction as a child to "the most blank" space on the map—HD 52.) After a glance toward science in the claim that the machine "evolved itself," the passage betrays Conrad's feeling that the "accident" was actually a malicious joke played by God, who absconded after building the machine only as an affront to man's desire for autonomy. "The machine is thinner than air," Conrad continued, a few weeks later, "and as evanescent as a flash of lightning."[46] The resentment Conrad directs at the paradoxically immaterial machine disguises his fear of an absence he cannot face, and the extravagant displacement reinstates God through negation as an absent cause presiding over man's humiliation.

The religious note in Conrad's lamentations sounds quite clearly after the brutal death of Winnie's brother, Stevie, in *The Secret Agent*: "She kept still as the population of half the globe would keep still in astonishment and despair, were the sun suddenly put out in the summer sky by the perfidy of a trusted providence" (*SA* 244). Unlike Winnie, however, Marlow does not believe that the darkness is all. "We live," says Marlow, "in the flicker—may it last as long as the old earth keeps rolling!" (*HD* 49). In "Heart of Darkness" the possibility of "an unselfish belief in the idea" persists in ghosts of the ideal. But Conrad reserves a place for the flicker of belief only in what Marlow presents as the deluded imagination of women.

Although Marlow's lie to the Intended imposes the false closure of popular romance on a radically inconclusive story—"The last word he pronounced," Marlow tells the Intended, "was—your name" (*HD* 161)—the act of narration that constitutes the greatest part of the novella issues as a response to the lie he once told.[47] Retelling his own story within Kurtz's, Marlow rescues what meaning he can from the corruption of Kurtz's idealism. In *Nostromo* Emilia Gould will be forced to conclude that "there was something inherent in the necessities of successful action which carried with it the moral degradation of the idea" (*N* 521). The words, of course, could be cited as a summary of Kurtz's decline. As for Marlow, the possible success of his act of narration may lie in its own failure.[48]

Universal truths, such as those hidden within the shadowy realm of the ideal, can only be compromised by their fall into the particularity of language. A skeptical refusal to commit idealized conceptions to linguistic expression may end, like Charles

Gould, in silence and passivity or, like Jim, who dies with his hand over his mouth, in resignation. Marlow's intensely skeptical expression of the limitations of language in "Heart of Darkness" permits the belief that beyond language may lie a realm of value barely detectable in the spectral signs of its absence. As empiricism shades into mysticism, Marlow, like Conrad, becomes more verbose, straining to make words gesture beyond themselves. Paradoxically, the skeptical probing of Marlow's narration may ultimately shelter the metaphysical significance it simultaneously puts in question by shying away from an absence Marlow cannot face. Although Marlow may not fully understand the significance of his own narration, and although the events he describes are notably bereft of consolation, the compulsion to establish a dialogue with the men on the *Nellie* both mitigates the danger of skeptical self-enclosure and attempts to reinvest, in the words of the Preface, "the commonplace surface of words" with the "magic suggestiveness" of the ideal.

"Heart of Darkness" clears space for a more sustained investigation of the sheltering power of the aesthetic in *Lord Jim*. Moral skepticism, the sense that values may be purely arbitrary inventions, reappears with renewed intensity in Marlow's meditations on "a sovereign power," and skeptical reflections on what "inside," if any, is concealed by the "outside" are also reworked, again with greater urgency, in Conrad's narrative projection of the problem of other minds. Picking up these and related issues from "Heart of Darkness," *Lord Jim* ultimately recasts them within the context of fiction making itself.

Chapter Four

Lord Jim: The Refuge of Art

Inquiry into the skeptical dimension of *Lord Jim* requires that we retrace Huxley's path from empiricism to idealism in order to return to a radical skepticism wholly opposed to the later claims of Kant and Schopenhauer. While Schopenhauer characteristically turns to experience as the ultimate authority for an argument whose validity, we could say, he aims to make us *see*, he does not, clearly enough, follow the empiricist tradition in its rejection of metaphysics. Writing under the twin influences of David Hume and Continental metaphysics, Schopenhauer has been described as Kant seen through the eyes of the British empiricists. Shifting my own angle of vision, in this and the following chapters I will focus on the skeptical side of the divided allegiance shared by Schopenhauer and Conrad, turning first to Hume and then to Berkeley as models for the operation of Conrad's skepticism.

Skepticism in Conrad sometimes approaches what Hume described, only to reject, as "total skepticism"—that is, "a total extinction of belief and evidence" (*THN* 183, 185–86). Hume and Conrad are alike in believing that a vision of total skepticism cannot be sustained. Hume argues that we "naturally" resist the utter nihilism produced by rigorous skeptical inquiry into the fundamental bases of knowledge. We may not "know" the sun will rise tomorrow, but nature prevents the sane from becoming immersed in the doubt that it may not. Of course man's skepticism is also part of nature, and in *Lord Jim* Conrad dramatizes the experience of momentarily penetrating the limits of Hume's naturalism as well as the mind's defensive response to this moment of "seeing through." Conrad thus projects in fictional form a theory of repression—his usual trope is "shelter"—which was implicit in Hume and only recently articulated by Freud.[1]

Lord Jim is dominated by three intensely imagined moments

that receive disproportionate narrative attention. Marlow's first sight of Jim, his consultation with Stein, and his interview with Jewel in Patusan all achieve their peculiar intensity as crises of skeptical thought. To account for these moments of skeptical dissolution I will analyze the modes of consolation, or shelters, which Conrad proposes in response to the potential corrosiveness of total skepticism. As in Hume, consciousness sometimes must be shielded from itself, and Conrad's most encompassing shelter is the power of narration he gives to Marlow. As a first-person narrator and the most dominant of Conrad's voices in the text, Marlow functions as a means of "crisis management" by both expressing and mitigating Conrad's own skepticism.

Bakhtin has argued that the distinctive feature of novelistic discourse is its ability to incorporate multiplicity—"authorial speech, the speeches of narrators, inserted genres, the speech of characters"—into a dialogical network of interrelationships.[2] By refusing to accept any one literary mode or perspective as accurate or true, Conrad's skepticism, generally speaking, brings to the foreground the skepticism inherent in the discourse of the novel; in *Lord Jim* it also determines the novel's shifts among satire, psychological realism, comedy, romance, tragedy, and elegy. Even before the drama of Jim's avoidance of Brown, skepticism motivates and organizes the diverse features of Conrad's text.

Jim and the Limitations of Vision

Conrad once wrote to an aspiring novelist that he should try to write "a novel of *analysis* on the basis of some strong situation,"[3] and Marlow's recollection of his first sight of Jim provides just such a situation. These memories are centered in the static image of Jim, who stands by idly and seemingly unconcerned as his captain enters the shipping office to lie about the fate of the *Patna*.

I liked his appearance; I knew his appearance; he came from the right place; he was one of us. He stood there for all the parentage of his kind, for men and women by no means clever or amusing, but whose very existence is based upon honest faith, and upon the instinct of courage. I don't mean military courage, or civil courage, or any special kind of courage. I mean just that inborn ability to look temptations straight in the face. (*LJ* 43)

Because Jim mirrors not only Marlow's English heritage but also his place in the English maritime tradition, he fears in Jim the possible subversion of some of his most stable assumptions: "I would have trusted the deck to that youngster on the strength of a single glance, and gone to sleep with both eyes—and, by Jove! it wouldn't have been safe. There are depths of horror in that thought" (*LJ* 45). An untrustworthy cynosure, Jim carries with him more than the fear of concealed weakness and lost honor, though for Marlow these are very real concerns. (Indeed, these fears establish the few consolations of continuity available to the reader in the confusing chronology of the early chapters.) More important, Marlow wants to see Jim as an exemplary product of nature and nurture, a young man who comes from the right place and who resists temptations instinctively. But Jim's impulsive self-preservation on the *Patna* suggests that outward signs of inner strength cannot be trusted. To abstract from Marlow's more immediate response, the duplicity of Jim's appearance redeploys a central trope of "Heart of Darkness" by turning a privileged inside into a vulnerable outside: inner resolve becomes as dubiously trustworthy as the cut of one's clothes. Adumbrating Marlow's more comprehensive vision of contingency in Patusan, Conrad focuses in Jim a more limited threat to the essentially English values and standards he seems to embody.

In this early scene Marlow's "depths of horror" sounds a note of excess, for his insistent rhetoric of catastrophic shock recalls the far more momentous story of Kurtz, whose failure to remain loyal to his Intended symbolically implicates all of European civilization. The hidden origin of Marlow's "horror" in the early chapters of *Lord Jim*, I suggest, lies in a constellation of epistemological and aesthetic issues concentrated in the figure of Jim.

Marlow's response to Jim resembles the motive of traditional epistemology: "There is an initial threatening *sense* or fact of something amiss, something which *must* be accounted for; the *going over* of a situation to see where an unnoticed inference or assumption may have been made; the sense that something in this one incident contains a moral about knowledge as a whole."[4] Since Marlow has himself trained "youngsters . . . for the service of the Red Rag" (*LJ* 44), Jim appears as what philosophers call a "best case": if Marlow should be able to "know" anyone, it is Jim; and if he can't know Jim, what can he know? Consonant with the aesthetics of vision in Conrad's Preface, Marlow's inquiry relies as much on his capacity to *see* Jim as on the opportunity to talk with him, and the truths Marlow seeks to glimpse are primarily moral. But Marlow's bafflement brings out a tension latent in the Preface: how well does the aim of paying "the highest kind of justice to the visible universe" square with the intention to give us that "glimpse of truth" for which we forgot to ask? Consider Marlow's role as narrator early on in relation to Conrad's own situation as author.

Marlow locates his frustration in his inability to see Jim's moral deficiency, and limitations of vision in these early chapters are analogous to limitations of language. Marlow first appears in the novel precisely when he makes eye contact with Jim at the inquiry, where the quality of his vision—"an act of intelligent volition" (*LJ* 32–33)—distinguishes his attention from the merely fascinated stare of others. Marlow's desire for a penetrating vision is answered by Jim's desire to bring out "the true horror behind the appalling face of things" through "a meticulous precision of statement" (*LJ* 30). Remarking on the reciprocal desire of the courtroom audience for "some essential disclosure," Marlow goes on to say that "nothing of the kind could be disclosed," for the "official inquiry" into "the well-known fact" was "as instructive as the tapping with a hammer on an iron box, were the object to find out what's inside" (*LJ* 56). Neither the language of the inquiry nor Marlow's gaze can penetrate to what appearances conceal, and Conrad's own textual practice is expressive of an analogous bafflement when faced with the mysterious opacity that first attracts Marlow.[5]

In Marlow's meditations at the Malabar Hotel on Jim's postsentencing opportunities we can detect the formulation and ousting of narrative possibilities. As an insistent yet seemingly insoluble problem, Jim presents Marlow with a crisis of decision, and Marlow's dilemma about what to do with him comes to reflect Conrad's.

Marlow's first effort on Jim's behalf takes the form of a letter to his friend Denver, who provides the first of Jim's many provisional shelters before the retreat into Patusan. In setting Jim up to inherit Denver's considerable wealth and property, Marlow's rescue resembles an authorial decision to relocate Jim in a nineteenth-century novel, where the transfer of property from one generation to the next often determines the dynamics of plot. In *Lord Jim*, however, filial relations exist only to be ruptured, along with many of the correlative assumptions of nineteenth-century fiction,[6] and Jim's flight from Denver will initiate the compulsive pattern of retreat that lands him in Patusan. But other options arise before Marlow settles on Denver, and the formation of friendship represented by his letter of introduction must first withstand the temptation located in Chester and Holy Terror Robinson.

Before the sentencing, Chester had solicited Marlow's support for a scheme to place Jim on a barren island in order to supervise a band of coolies in the grand labor of amassing large quantities of guano. At the time Marlow angrily rejected their plan, but while trying to "take refuge" in letter writing, he is possessed of a vision: "All at once, on the blank page, under the very point of the pen, the two figures of Chester and his antique partner, very distinct and complete, would dodge into view with stride and gestures, as if reproduced in the field of some optical toy. I would watch them for a while. No! They were too phantasmal and extravagant to enter into any one's fate" (*LJ* 174). However fleeting the appeal, the scheme clearly holds an ambivalent fascination for Marlow or it would never have leapt to mind. Marlow's response is again indicative of Conrad's. The "optical toy" suggests the intensely visual nature of Conrad's characteristic representations, and ultimately it is Conrad who has just introduced the possibility of a relationship between Jim and these "phantasmal and extravagant" figures. For Conrad, through Marlow, to "reproduce" Chester and Robinson in the field of his representation at this juncture is to acknowledge the appeal of death as closure. Like Brierly at the inquiry, Marlow momentarily grasps at a final solution: "for a second I wished heartily that the only course left open for me were to pay for his funeral" (*LJ* 174). (Brierly too would have been happy to underwrite the expense, but only if the grave were designed to his specifications: "let him creep twenty feet underground and stay there!" [*LJ* 66].) These moments pass, however, and when Conrad finally puts a stop to the expansive narrative of Jim's life, the funeral arrangements are left to Doramin.

The intrusion of Chester and Robinson into the narrative also allows Conrad to give vent to biting commentary on the imperious demands of Jim's narcissism: "I could guarantee the island wouldn't sink under him," Chester sneers, "and I believe he is a bit particular on that point" (*LJ* 168). Moral skepticism, here the disposition to view another purely as an instrument, issues through Chester as satire. Yet satire typically depends on a stable moral pespective from which to level judgment, and in *Lord Jim*, after the anonymous narrator's irony in the first four chapters, Conrad uses Marlow to put in question precisely such moral certainties. Given that the dissolution of the moral often pushes the satiric toward the comic, it is not surprising that a touch of cruel Dantesque comedy also slips into Marlow's imaginative response to Chester's offer: "I had a rapid vision of Jim perched on a shadowless rock, up to his knees in guano, with the screams of seabirds in his ears, the incandescent ball of the sun above his head; the empty sky and the empty ocean all a-quiver, simmering together in the heat as far as the eye could reach" (*LJ* 167). Yet these comic and satiric perspectives, however compelling, are not sustained.

Readers have often noted that the psychological realism of the first half of the novel, in which Jim tells Marlow the story of the *Patna*, is superseded by romance in the second half. In this pivotal moment before Patusan, Marlow's rejection of Chester and Robinson can be read as Conrad's dismissal of comic and satiric modes in favor of the romantic treatment he later provides. Similarly, Jim's refusal to remain ensconced in the bourgeois security provided by Denver marks the narrative's distance from novels of inheritance and home. (Earlier on, after an odd digression on the unhappy marriage of "poor Selvin," Conrad has Marlow remind himself that "we are concerned with Jim—who was unmarried" [*LJ* 156].) None of these narrative modes, finally, can be sanctioned as an adequate response to Jim.

The shelter of the aesthetic is thus a problematic one. Conrad's narration of Marlow's attempt to tell Jim's story aims, at the very least, to sustain the possibility of understanding as a bulwark against skepticism. But aesthetic solutions can come to seem no solution at all if art ultimately fails to articulate the ethical or veridical insights which Marlow explicitly seeks within the fiction and which Conrad cites as his own aim in his pronouncements about fiction. Skepticism produces the need for "consoling forms," but those forms may turn out to be expressive only of "that pure love of the external beauty of things" that Conrad praises in Hudson.[7] Marlow's narration of Jim's story, that is, may never achieve a penetrating vision but, rather, to return to Marlow's own trope, remain futilely absorbed in playing over the surfaces of a box whose secrets it will never unlock.

Marlow's desire for a "truer" vision mirrors Conrad's attempt to find a mode of representation adequate to the moral complexity of Marlow's response to Jim, and when Marlow experiences ·Jim as a threat to English virtue and honor, the extremity of his horror drawns on Conrad's investment in the ethical status of his own intensely visual fictions. Can contemplation of the "sublime spectacle," in the words of *A Personal Record*, really be "a moral end in itself" if Marlow's expert observation of Jim is so profoundly mistaken?

Adequate or not, the formation of defenses is required by radical skepticism, and in *Lord Jim* the discourse of skepticism results in a progressive construction and discarding of various literary modes of consolation. In order to analyze the pattern of dissolution and recuperation played out within the encompassing shelter of Conrad's novel, I will turn first to issues of authorial skepticism as they are reflected in the narrative strategies leading up to Marlow's skeptical crisis in Patusan.

Skepticism and Analogical Form: From Dickens to Conrad

The Chester and Robinson episode is only one of a series of perspectives Conrad brings to bear on Jim's case, and the technique of an encompassing network of analogies suggests a connection between Conrad's narrative method and that of Dickens.[8] Marlow's narration of Jim's story before Patusan proceeds thematically rather than temporally, and his conversations with the *Patna*'s chief engineer and the French lieutenant, as well as the inset stories of Brierly and little Bob Stanton, are all suspended in the narrative discourse as analogues to the central situation of Jim's experience on the *Patna*. The primary difference between the analogical procedures of Conrad and Dickens is that Dickens employs multiple plots, whereas Conrad naturalizes the analogies in *Lord Jim* as the flow of Marlow's memory in his struggle toward a moral understanding of Jim. In each, nonetheless, it is analogy that structures the text.[9]

Recent critical theory has challenged the use of analogy as a means of thematic totalization in critical commentary by challenging the concept of the unified text itself. Peter Garrett, for instance, has argued persuasively that many critics have used analogy as a strategy "to limit the play of meanings by imposing a center" rather than leaving the text open to "the multiplicity and instability of decentered structure."[10] Garrett's dialogical approach has the virtue, for my purposes, of highlighting affinities between the narrative strategies of Dickens and Conrad, even though in so doing Garrett sometimes exaggerates the ironic leveling effect of Dickens's analogical method. Thus in *Bleak House*, Garrett argues, the drawing together of seemingly heterogeneous elements through analogy produces a subversive juxtaposition between Harold Skimpole's self-serving vision of social harmony and Esther Summerson's affirmation of the providential design underlying her encounter with Lady Dedlock: "For all their obvious moral differences, both versions of providence emerge as individual creations and imply the fictiveness of all objectified moral orders."[11]

Yet Dickens places these ethical differences more in the foreground than Garrett's commentary would suggest, and the uncertainty of the cosmic order glanced at in *Bleak House* does not produce the equivocal judgments characteristic of Marlow. Having punctuated his account of Jim on the *Patna* with the stories of Brierly and the chief engineer, Marlow explicitly acknowledges the ethical relativity Garrett attributes to Dickens: "I was made to look at the convention that lurks in all truth and on the essential sincerity of falsehood" (*LJ* 93). Dickens probably would not recognize the thought as his own, for (as Garrett admits) most of his novels posit a transcendental realm that sanctions a moral order identified more with Esther than with Skimpole. Miller has made the point well, though here too the thought becomes more appropriate to Conrad as it unfolds: "As in all Dickens' work, there is at the centre of *Bleak House* a tension between belief in some extra-human source of value, a stable center outside the shadows of the human game, and on the other hand the shade of a suspicion that there may be no such centre, that all systems of interpretation may be fictions."[12]

Miller's last clause applies better to Conrad than to Dickens, who keeps his eye more steadily on the human game. In Conrad, Dickens's "shade of suspicion" becomes anguished investigation into and retreat from the idea of a "stable center." Belief in a center that holds presumes that truth is univocal and could be unveiled in a moment of comprehensive vision. Marlow does not quite lament the *absence* of such a truth; rather, he laments the impossibility of ever laying to rest "the most obstinate ghost of man's creation . . . the *doubt* of the sovereign power enthroned in a fixed standard of conduct" (*LJ* 50, emphasis mine). Through Marlow, Conrad resists the notion that the social and moral orders exist only as arbitrary human constructs utterly divorced from transcendental confirmation, and the collapse of Kurtz in "Heart of Darkness" and Brierly in *Lord Jim* registers the fear that man's internal moral sense may itself provide inadequate compensation.[13] More radically than in Dickens, Conradian networks of analogy run counter to the ideal of a definitive unveiling and posit truth instead as something closer to what Nietzsche called "a movable host of metaphors, metonymies, and anthropomorphisms."[14] In *Lord Jim* this epistemological tension takes on psychological motivation in Marlow's desire for a definitive vision of Jim, but the effort can result only in a series of analogies that postpones the revelation of the "whole" truth Marlow desires.

Yet the narrative strategies of *Lord Jim* also reflect a deep nostalgia for recovering the whole truth. Although Marlow believes that the official inquiry will never "get inside" Jim, elsewhere *Lord Jim* does present moments of definitive revelations and complete decodings. When Marlow visits the chief engineer of the *Patna* in the hospital, the reader, unlike the doctor, surely can discover the "thread of logic" in the engineer's delirium that allows one to read "pilgrims" for "pink toads." On a larger scale, the narrative strategy of the first section of the book depends on the reader's interest in discovering the withheld fact, hidden like an object in a box, that the *Patna* did not sink. Even the first direct encounter between Jim and Marlow—the yellow dog incident— is predicated on a miscommunication that the two men eventually can decipher. Marlow's discourse on Jim implicitly promises to be another such revelation of the essential, for Marlow is able to identify the shortcoming of the official inquiry: "Its object was not the fundamental why, but the superficial how, of this affair" (*LJ* 56). Attending to the "why" promises that Marlow will see beyond the limitations of the court officials, but his inquiry never quite arrives at the desired moment of vision.

Marlow's initial remarks about his conversations with Jim at the Malabar Hotel combine our two models of truth in a visualization of frustration: "The views he let me have of himself were like those glimpses through the shifting rents in a thick fog—bits of vivid and vanishing detail, giving no connected idea of the general aspect of a country" (*LJ* 76). The promise of a definitive vision dwindles into a perception of parts that do not adequately define a whole. As discontinuous as "bits of vivid and vanishing detail," the analogies Marlow brings to bear on Jim's case compensate for his inability to see through the fog to the whole truth he assumes must lie behind it.

The elusive irony of Conrad's method complicates the very first of these analogies: Brierly during and after the inquiry. Listening to Jim's testimony, Brierly apparently takes the Conradian virtue of sympathetic identification to a fatal extreme. Simply imagining Jim's dishonor and weakness is enough to seduce Brierly into the suicide Jim himself had considered while floating in the lifeboat. If we contrast Jim's ability to stand up under the inquiry, he comes out favorably, for unlike Brierly he refuses to abandon the conviction that the next time he would not fail. Yet Conrad undoes the redemptive force of the analogy a few pages later when Marlow remarks of the late captain: "Who can tell what flattering view he had induced himself to take of his own suicide" (*LJ* 64). If Brierly remained a narcissist to the end, perhaps Jim's perseverance also amounts to little more than a narcissistic inability to understand the significance of his own experience. Indeed, Marlow will refer on the last page of the novel, just before Jim's death, to his "exalted egoism." Conrad further complicates Marlow's presentation by including, as a subordinate narrator, Brierly's first mate, Jones, whose bad luck, surliness, and resentment contrast with yet also resemble qualities associated with Jim and Brierly. All of Marlow's analogical connections (or disconnections) partake of this ironic counterpoise. Although each teases us with the promise of fuller understanding, none will allow the mind to repose in any one answer.[15]

After the story of Brierly, the most extended analogical commentary on Jim emerges from Marlow's conversations with the French lieutenant. Owing to the complexity of Conrad's presentation here, I want to devote considerable attention to two issues associated with this figure: the ethical indeterminacy generated by the skepticism inherent in Marlow's vagrant discourse, and the implication of the French lieutenant in Conrad's internal debate on the moral significance of his fiction.

The first man to board the *Patna* after its abandonment, the French lieutenant remained on its decks for thirty hours as it was towed to port, with every expectation that it might sink, with an axe to cut the hawsers lest it pull down the tow, and a precarious escape for himself. Complaining only of a lack of wine with his meals, the lieutenant would appear at first to offer a damning contrast to Jim's terrified paralysis. Preparing to respond to Marlow's account of Jim's trial and their subsequent conversations, the lieutenant is described as if he holds the key to the "inside" that remains inaccessible to the clumsy probing of the official inquiry: "in his occult way [he] managed to make his immobility appear profoundly responsive, and as full of valuable thoughts as an egg is of meat." The lieutenant so impresses Marlow that he feels as if he were "taking professional opinion on the case" (*LJ* 145).

Yet in a typically Conradian retreat, Marlow is not permitted to feast on "valuable thoughts" from the lieutenant, and the essential "inside" remains hidden. The lieutenant, Marlow is pleased to discover, instantly perceives that it was Jim's moral isolation amid the rest of the crew which induced the "poor young man [to run] away along with the others," and he openly admits that no one can choose not to be afraid. "Given a certain combination of circumstances," the lieutenant notes, "fear is sure to come" (*LJ* 146). Yet Marlow's intense anticipation has prepared us for more compelling insight, and we are soon forced to reassess our reading of the French lieutenant's authority. For what from one angle appears to be an "immobility [that is] profoundly responsive" may from another become a sign of limitation and restriction.

Here Conrad's peculiar ability to bring small, seemingly random details to our attention comes into play. Guided by Marlow's habits of observation, the reader must linger over the lieutenant's scars, a "starred" gunshot wound on the back of his hand, and "also the seam of an old wound, beginning a little below the temple and going out of sight under the short grey hair at the side of his head—the graze of a spear or the cut of a sabre" (*LJ* 140). Together with similar passages, these observations foster a quality of attention sensitized to any signs that might allow us to articulate the meaning they seem to promise yet withhold, and when bodily details next appear we are prepared to receive them not only as positive signs of the lieutenant's past heroism in battle but also as indications of a debility that may transcend the merely physical: "The three last fingers of his wounded hand," Marlow notes, "were stiff and could not move independently of each other, so that he took up his tumbler with an ungainly clutch" (*LJ* 146). The Frenchman's rigidity emerges more distinctly as a quality of mind in his response to Marlow's mistaken notion that he inclines toward leniency: "He drew up his heavy eyelids. . . . I was confronted by two narrow grey circlets, like two tiny steel rings around the profound blackness of the pupils. The sharp glance, coming from that massive body, gave a notion of extreme efficiency, like a razor-edge on a battle-axe" (*LJ* 148). Transformed into an unthinking tool of his trade, the French lieutenant and the excessive rigidity of his code of honor are presented here in vivid visual terms: "when the honour is gone . . . I can offer no opinion—because—monsieur—I know nothing of it." Although Marlow and the lieutenant are momentarily equated in their comic immobility ("we faced each other mutely, like two china dogs on a mantelpiece"), it is the latter whose "pronouncement was uttered in the passionless and definite phraseology a machine would use" (*LJ* 159).[16] Marlow apparently respects the French lieutenant's commitment to honor, yet he also bridles at its categorical nature, which admits no mitigations. The implication that honor can become a calcifying of the necessary "stiffness before the inner and outer terrors," and so a threat to one's humanity, typifies Conrad's habit of indulging a sudden and ironic shift of perspective on a concept elsewhere construed as a value.[17]

Though capable of performing his duty, as Jim was not, the French lieutenant lacks the powers of self-reflection that, however much a curse as well as a blessing, constitute complete humanity in Conrad's world. This lack assimilates the lieutenant to the unthinking impassiveness of the *Patna*'s helmsman, whose limited understanding during the inquiry produces a parody of the solace of tradition in an incantatory recitation of the names of past ships. While the lieutenant's range of consciousness clearly exceeds the helmsman's, their shared limitation reminds us that participation in a tradition without the capacity to reflect intelligently on it may become a form of superstition—in the helmsman's case, a string of proper names whose fetishistic power obviates the need to think. When Marlow tries to praise such figures, as he does in "Heart of Darkness" while lamenting the loss of his (again) native helmsman, he typically returns to an objectification identical in its rhetorical form to his description of the French lieutenant: "I missed my late helmsman awfully. . . . [H]e had steered; for months I had him at my back—a help— an instrument" (*HD* 119). Although racial condescension may overlap nationalistic superiority in a novel that must continually posit a "them" in order to define "one of us," what I wish to emphasize here is the ethical indeterminacy produced in the juxtaposition of Jim with a figure as intrinsically equivocal as the French lieutenant.

Readers have often misinterpreted the French lieutenant as a figure of unquestioned moral authority, in part because his initial appeal for Marlow evidently extends beyond mere trustworthiness and in part because the attention lavished on him suggests the possibility of an ambivalent authorial identification.[18] To make visible the particular lines of force that converge in the French lieutenant, we need to step back from the immediacy of the dramatic situation and view the narrative space surrounding him as a zone of contact between competing ideas about art. For by examining the qualities parceled out between the lieutenant and

Jim, we can detect within the folds of Conrad's complicated presentation an inquiry into the visual and moral dimensions of his
fiction.

Describing Jim's physical and moral paralysis on the *Patna*,
Marlow likens his frightened fantasies of death to those of a "finished artist." Less explicitly, Marlow's ruminations about the
French lieutenant also involve the twin association of ethics and
art. For Marlow even the lieutenant's commonplace remark—
"how the time passes"—produces a "moment of vision":

> It's extraordinary how we go through life with eyes half shut, with dull
> ears, with dormant thoughts. Perhaps it's just as well; and it may be that
> it is this very dulness that makes life to the incalculable majority so sup-
> portable and so welcome. Nevertheless, there can be but few of us who
> have never known one of these rare moments of awakening when we
> see, hear, understand ever so much—everything—in a flash—before we
> fall back again into our agreeable somnolence. (*LJ* 143)

The passage distinctly recalls the well-known "roar which lies on
the other side of silence" in *Middlemarch*—the onset of a more intense mode of perception—and the "flash" of understanding intensifies the promise of the kind of authoritative testimony that
can be provided only by an expert witness.[19] Like those in the
"unvisited tombs" in the last paragraph of *Middlemarch*, the
French lieutenant, "one of those steady, reliable men who are the
raw material of great reputations, one of those uncounted lives
that are buried without drums and trumpets under the founda-
tions of monumental successes" (*LJ* 143–44), has been left behind
by a receding heroic age. The lieutenant's moral pedigree, vali-
dated by echoes of Eliot, also comes with impeccable aesthetic
credentials: "his torpid demeanor concealed nothing: it had that
mysterious, almost miraculous, power of producing striking effects by means impossible of detection which is the last word of
the highest art" (*LJ* 141–42). The description recalls Conrad's
praise of James's artistry in *The Spoils of Poynton*: "The delicacy
and tenuity of the thing are amazing. It is like a great sheet of
plate glass—you don't know it's there till you run against it."[20]
Although Marlow's immediate desire in this scene is to hear
grounds for exculpating Jim from a man with direct experience
in the affair, the language of his account often exceeds the de-

mands of the narrative and, in so doing, characterizes the lieutenant as both an emblem of "the highest art" and "the mouthpiece of abstract wisdom" (*LJ* 147). I argued earlier that Conrad's
critical writing posits the ideal of "good service" as a third term
mediating between ethical commitment and an aestheticism
lacking moral value. An icon of good service, the French lieutenant is presented as the ideal spokesman for a pronouncement capable of fusing the aesthetic and the moral in the manner later
theorized in "A Familiar Preface" and *A Personal Record*.

There is a sense, moreover, in which the lieutenant's consciousness is not only more discerning than Jim's but more lucid
than Marlow's too, for the lieutenant is one of the few characters
(Stein is another) who does not invoke demonic powers behind
the circumstances of Jim's crisis. Finding it "extraordinary how
he could cast upon you the spirit of his illusion," Marlow is easily
drawn into Jim's grim fantasy that he "had suffered himself to be
handled by the infernal powers who had selected him for the victim of their practical joke" (*LJ* 108–9). Because Jim missed his first
opportunity for heroism while standing paralyzed in "the brutal
tumult of earth and sky, that seemed directed at him, and made
him hold his breath in awe" (*LJ* 7), we might want to see Jim himself as the origin of such paranoia. But Marlow's own Gothic
imaginings—he speaks of the submerged derelict as "a kind of
maritime ghoul on the prowl to kill ships in the dark . . . a special arrangement of a malevolent providence" (*LJ* 159)—suggest
that fear of nature's sublime energies cannot be limited to Jim's
psychology. We need not puzzle long over the uncanny power of
Jim's persuasiveness, for Conrad himself preferred the thought
of a demonic order to the nightmare of no order whatsoever.
Thus even the rhetorical flourishes of the anonymous narrator
are suffused with a sense of divine malice, as when the *Patna*
smolders in "a luminous immensity, as if scorched by a flame
flicked at her from a heaven without pity" (*LJ* 16).[21]

This pattern suggests a desire to evade moral responsibility by
displacing intentionality from the self and relocating it in a per-
sonified set of circumstances.[22] In Jim's case the text associates
this evasion with the visual nature of his imagination. Jim becomes paralyzed on the *Patna*, according to Marlow, because his
imaginative vision completely usurps his ability to think:

. . . he could *depict* to himself without hindrance the sudden swing up-wards of the dark sky-line, the sudden tilt up of the vast plain of the sea, the swift still rise, the brutal fling, the grasp of the abyss, the struggle without hope, the starlight closing over his head for ever like the vault of a tomb—the revolt of his young life—the black end. . . . *And you must remember he was a finished artist in that peculiar way, he was a gifted poor devil with the faculty of swift and forestalling vision.* The sights it showed him had turned him into cold stone from the soles of his feet to the nape of his neck. (*LJ* 96–97, emphasis added)

Jim's self-absorbed immobility at the Malabar may be even more intense than the paralysis here on the *Patna*, for his visual imagination during the conversations with Marlow comes to seem virtually pathological: "'See and hear. . . . See and hear,' he repeated twice, at long intervals, filled by vacant staring" (*LJ* 106). Conrad's letters suggest that he too was troubled by the gift of "a swift and forestalling vision": "it is a fool's business to write fiction for a living," he once wrote. "One's will becomes the slave of hallucinations, responds only to shadowy impulses, waits on imagination alone."[23] Jim, the slave of his own hallucinations, disrupts the vision on the *Patna* only to jump, an act whose motivation first drops out of his syntax—"I had jumped . . . It seems"—and then more explicitly: "It was their doing as plainly as if they had reached up with a boat-hook and pulled me over" (*LJ* 111, 123). Jim's failure to act is attributed to an involuntary conjuring of vivid images; the responsibility for the one action he does take he displaces onto the other officers. If Jim is a "finished artist," he is a version of the artist as disabled aesthete that Conrad would like to exorcise.

The analogy can be taken further. Just as Jim cannot bring himself even to describe certain key actions, such as his jump, Conrad, at this point in his career, also had trouble finding words for actions. "'You will discover, if you read my books,'" Conrad remarked to R. L. Mégroz, "'how I am writing towards some fixed event or scene I can see, but I do not know how I shall ever get there.'"[24] The displacement of moral significance from narrative event to visual tableau and discursive commentary anticipates what would become a more pervasive insistence in modernist narrative on a gap between event and meaning. Here Conrad's particular conjoining of paralysis and the visual imagination suggests that Jim's projection of moral responsibility onto external circumstances may be read as a dark analogue to Conrad's own problems with confronting action in his fiction.

In contrast to Conrad, Jim, and Marlow, the French lieutenant remains free of the fantasy of a demonic subversion of the will and thus seems a perfect man of action. Yet the lieutenant's severe moral rectitude is also associated with a lack of imagination; he would be "finished" as an artist before he could begin. Troped as the demonic, the "special arrangement of a malevolent providence" is simply the aesthetic order created (malevolently or not) through metaphor and plot. Although the impulse to order that Conrad channels through Marlow and Jim is implicitly criticized as paranoia by the lucidity of the French lieutenant, that hardheaded lucidity also implies a moralistic dismissal of the irresponsibility of art. (The submerged links among paranoia, the demonic, and authorship become more explicit in *Nostromo* and *Under Western Eyes*.) Thus we arrive again at a typically Conradian deadlock: if the artistry of Jim's vision evades moral responsibility, the vision of the French lieutenant is deprived of artistry through an overinvestment in moral imperatives.

Conrad's internal debate on the ethics of authorship is played out more explicitly (and with more anguish) in *A Personal Record*, where he muses over his ambivalent identification with Don Quixote, a figure who, though gifted with "the irresistible grace of imagination," is "not a good citizen" (*PR* 36–37). In the account of the *Patna* disaster, the oscillations of the skeptical regard are turned toward Jim, producing the network of analogies that surround the central fact of Jim's jump.

Marlow would like to find some repose in his restlessly imaginative inquiry, but adding more links to the analogical chain does not help. Directly after Marlow's account of the French lieutenant, the story of Bob Stanton (a first mate who, unlike Jim, went down with his ship) becomes a link in Marlow's chain of associations through Stanton's one-time occupation as an insurance canvasser—the only job, according to Marlow, as spiritually debilitating as Jim's post-*Patna* job as a water clerk. The analogy quickly gives way to another when Marlow recounts a description of Stanton's fatal effort to save a woman from a sinking ship: "One of the hands told me, hiding a smile at the recollection, 'It was for all the world, sir, like a naughty youngster fighting with his mother'" (*LJ* 150). Stanton's death can be considered another version of unglamorous heroism: the contrast between the splendid Brierly and the French lieutenant here moves to another figure more grotesque than the lieutenant but still, for all his ludicrousness, honorable. Yet however we construe the analogy, the play of similarities and differences does not bring Jim into sharp focus. It is as if one were to superimpose, for purposes of comparison, one image on another, like the negatives for two photographs, only to find that the distinctive features of each had become blurred and indistinguishable.

A good deal of this blurring effect derives from the nature of analogy itself, for analogy asserts a general likeness or mutual relevance with a reticent vagueness that is both peculiar to itself and particularly well suited to the irresolutions of skepticism. I argued earlier that Conrad's unwillingness to abandon his belief in the absolute results in a spectral imagery of the possible in his early fiction. Analogical organization also corresponds to the possible rather than to the absolute, for analogy posits resemblances without necessarily organizing them into a stable hierarchy.[25] Although metaphor and simile can be considered two ways of proffering analogy, analogy more closely resembles simile than metaphor given that simile "*proposes*" a transfer of meaning from one thing to another rather than assuming, like metaphor, that "the transference is possible or has already taken place."[26] It is therefore fitting that Conrad's style reflects a marked preference for simile over metaphor.

Yet the nature of the trope alone cannot account for the radically interrogative nature of Conrad's text. Implicit questions are raised in the juxtaposition of Jim with Brierly, the French lieutenant, and Bob Stanton, but Marlow also raises explicit questions of knowledge and belief which find no answer, and those that do are often contradicted by his later pronouncements. Since no perspective on Jim establishes a better purchase than another, the reader may come to share Marlow's sense that Jim may not exist apart from our efforts to make sense of him. The reader, that is, may participate in Marlow's sensation of seeing Jim vanish before his "dazzled eyes as utterly as though . . . blown to atoms" (*LJ* 178). To the extent that Marlow retains an imaginative hold on him, Jim remains an intelligible character, and the activity of interpretation becomes a defense against the total dissolution of meaning latent in authorial skepticism. Conrad's strategy of involving us in the process of Marlow's moral understanding is designed to establish a community of belief in the *possibility* of such an understanding, even though that possibility may never be translated into a definitive statement of the value and meaning of Jim's life.

Marlow's narration nevertheless reveals its limitations by tending toward an analogical flow that runs on without making significant progress toward the moral understanding that is its goal. Marlow's decision to consult Stein, "an eminently suitable person to receive my confidences about Jim's difficulties as well as my own" (*LJ* 203), initiates a movement from the limited consolations of Marlow's essentially rational perspective to a species of shelter more closely associated with Jim's own romantic vision.

Stein and the Romance of the Past

The Stein episode occupies a crucial place in the structure of the novel.[27] The decision to send Jim to Patusan results in a shift in the mode of representation from psychological realism to a world constructed of romance conventions. The shift is far less drastic than those between the later episodes in Joyce's *Ulysses*, but *Lord Jim*, without itself becoming a fully self-conscious fiction, anticipates such experimentation. The romantic begins to emerge here in the figure of Stein as a way to call a halt to Jim's flight from job to job and, at a higher level, to the skeptical play of analogies that structures the narrative to this point. Here even more than with the French lieutenant, Marlow rouses our expectations of revelation, but the sheltering conception proposed during his conversation with Stein will itself be threatened by skepticism in a new way.

Stein's own romanticism occupies a privileged position in *Lord Jim*.[28] Only Stein has lived a life capable of satisfying the claims of the spirit and the body, the ideal and the real. "This man possessed an intrepidity of spirit and a physical courage that could have been called reckless had it not been like a natural function of the body—say good digestion, for instance—completely unconscious of itself" (*LJ* 203). Although we could easily mistake this for the equivocal limitations of the French lieutenant, Stein's early career in Celebes unfolds in a place seemingly innocent of self-consciousness. It is, in the logic of the novel, a virtually unfallen world. Despite the political intrigue and armed battles, in Stein's retelling Celebes is a place where the rift between thought and action did not exist. The nature of Stein's utopia becomes clear in his story of having survived an ambush sprung by political enemies.

Stein's self-representation recalls Hal's mocking characterization of Hotspur in *Henry IV*, Part I: "he that kills me some six or seven dozen of Scots at a breakfast, washes his hands, and says to his wife, 'Fie upon this quiet life! I want work'" (II.iv.103–6). For Stein, taken utterly unawares, nevertheless managed to outwit and kill most of his attackers; at the same time, he also captured an "extraordinary perfect specimen" of a rare species of butterfly. To evoke his exhilaration Stein quotes from Goethe's *Torquato Tasso*: "I hold it, then, at length within my hands, / And in a certain sense can call it mine" (*LJ* 211).[29] Goethe's Duke Alfonso is talking at once about a volume of poetry that Tasso wrote for him and about the happiness the gift has brought him. Stein is thinking of a butterfly, one that symbolizes, as Tony Tanner has observed, the high aspirations and unattainable ideals that haunt Jim.[30] We need not rely on the symbolic connection between butterflies and elusive ideals, however, to see that Stein clutches an abstraction as tenuous as Alfonso's. After the quotation, Stein describes his perfect joy in that distant time of wish-fulfilling romance: he was young, strong, and triumphant; he had the love of a woman and child; and "even what I had once dreamed in my sleep had come into my hand, too!" Jim's daydreams remain in the realm of the imagination, in "the sea-life of light literature" (*LJ* 6). Stein, however, has experienced a world in which complete success can literally be grasped; he has *lived* the dreams of glory that the collision of the *Patna* shatters for Jim.

Yet Conrad has pushed the world of Stein's achievement into an inaccessible past. Stein now lives a sedentary life, and his butterflies are dead. The scene suggests, however, that Stein may find compensation for this loss through art. Stein's actions no longer can incarnate the ideal, but his butterfly collection at least permits him to contemplate its image: "He looked at a butterfly, as though on the bronze sheen of these frail wings, in the white tracings, in the gorgeous markings, he could see other things, an image of something as perishable and defying destruction as these delicate and lifeless tissues displaying a splendour unmarred by death" (*LJ* 207). Each butterfly represents for Stein an ideal synthesis of art and nature, a "masterpiece of Nature—the great artist" (*LJ* 208). Tanner's otherwise fine discussion of butterflies and beetles fails to distinguish between living butterflies and a collector's specimen, and it is the former which fully incarnates Stein's dream. Even though the little corpses display "a splendour unmarred by death," we are reminded also that nothing can restore their full vitality: "The frail and beautiful wings quivered faintly, as if his breath had for an instant called back to life that gorgeous object of his dreams" (*LJ* 211). These beautiful objects, which offer an imperfect mimesis of life, represent a version of ideal art, for "*les valeurs idéales*" are preserved here in the delicate tracings and beautiful markings on the wings of a butterfly.[31] Art substitutes for the wholeness of being Stein enjoyed in his youth.

Although only Stein is permitted to live in a time when ideal value could be found in the real world, the first description of Marlow as a narrator has already suggested that art may have the power to recover a lost unity: "Marlow's body, extended at rest in the seat, would become very still, as though his spirit had winged its way back into the lapse of time and were speaking through his lips from the past" (*LJ* 33). Here two dualities—spirit/body and past/present—are momentarily overcome in the act of narration. But Conrad's more fundamental aim, I have argued, is to invest Marlow's narration with the power to overcome what Conrad considered an equally fundamental duality. By articulating moral values within a primarily visual mode of representation, Conrad aims "to make us see" the ideal values associated with the dream that comes into Stein's hand. The trope of incarnation underwrites these passages and anticipates the logic of incorporation operating in Patusan. Incarnation posits a synthesis that in practice Marlow's discourse cannot sustain, and quite often Marlow's discursive treatment of abstract issues completely disengages itself from the sharp immediacy of any embodied scene.[32] In Marlow's consultation with Stein, however, Conrad confronts more directly than anywhere else the relationships among action, vision, and voice.[33]

As Marlow sits alone in a pool of light from which he watches Stein's prowling shadow, Stein closes the lid of a display box,

and taking up the case in both hands he bore it religiously away to its place, passing out of the bright circle of the lamp into the ring of fainter light—into shapeless dusk at last. It had an odd effect—as if these few steps had carried him out of this concrete and perplexed world. His tall form, as though robbed of its substance, hovered noiselessly over invisible things with stooping and indefinite movements; his voice, heard in that remoteness where he could be glimpsed mysteriously busy with immaterial cares, was no longer incisive, seemed to roll voluminous and grave—mellowed by distance. (*LJ* 213)

The image summoned is one of a priest who bears to the altar a reliquary containing sacred offerings.[34] Stein's words, though "mellowed by distance," begin to come more quickly as he becomes absorbed in the problem, and his preoccupation sweeps him into the exclamations of his native language: "*Wie? Was? Gott in Himmel!*" The religious portent of the scene conspires with the rhythms of ritual in Stein's words to make us feel that Stein is conscious of a truth that will end Jim's seemingly endless flight from job to job. But Stein's abstraction is excessive. "*Robbed* of substance," he can "no longer [be] incisive." His words, too, lose their substance: although the darkness allows Stein to formulate the enigmatic "truths" on which he insists so dramatically, "as though away there in the dusk he had been inspired by some whisper of knowledge" (*LJ* 214), his certitude withers in the light. His hand falling lamely to his side, Stein can only repeat the now empty injunction, "in the destructive element immerse." Marlow's response to Stein's reminder that Jim is romantic ("perhaps he is . . . but I am sure you are") reflects his skeptical sense that the elder man remains enclosed in his own experience.[35]

Stein's words nevertheless evoke from Marlow a series of revelatory moments, and these revelations yield insight into Marlow's final evaluation of Stein's remarks and into Conrad's strategies of representation. Marlow first contemplates an inner landscape inspired by Stein's romantic pronouncements, "a vast and uncertain expanse, as of a crepuscular horizon on a plain at dawn—or was it, perchance, at the coming of the night?" (*LJ* 215). The picture resists Marlow's desire for a clear choice, yet it captures in visual terms both the indeterminacy and potential danger of Stein's advice: "it was a charming and deceptive light, throwing the impalpable poesy of its dimness over pitfalls—over graves." Marlow and Stein then acknowledge their failure to find "a practical remedy"; their conversation has been entirely theoretical, and its very abstractness threatens to blot out Jim's living reality: "We avoided pronouncing Jim's name as though we had tried to keep flesh and blood out of our discussion, or he were nothing but an erring spirit, a suffering and nameless shade." "In the morning," says Stein, "we shall do something practical" (*LJ* 215).

But as Marlow heads for bed he describes, in perhaps the most beautiful passage in the novel, the interior of Stein's house in such a way that we sense already the restoration of Jim's full humanity that was lost in their previous conversation.

[Stein] lit a two-branched candlestick and led the way. We passed through empty dark rooms, escorted by gleams from the lights Stein carried. They glided along the waxed floors, sweeping here and there over the polished surface of the table, leaped upon a fragmentary curve of a piece of furniture, or flashed perpendicularly in and out of distant mirrors, while the forms of two men and the flicker of two flames could be seen for a moment stealing silently across the depths of a crystalline void. (*LJ* 215–16)

It is impossible to read this passage without sensing the full engagement of Conrad's sensibility. The passage replaces Stein's insistence on the practical with an intensely vivid and lyrical representation of the men bent on taking action on Jim's behalf. Marlow has for some time been peering through "shifting rents in a thick fog" to see Jim; now he sees a reflected image of himself accompanied by a reflection of Stein. Marlow sees himself instead of Jim because, in considering Jim's future, he must view him, as Stein has, in light of his own experience; the fragmentary quality of the image preserves the sense of mystery and isolation that prevents truly reciprocal communication between solitary individuals. More troubling, however, is the sense in which their reflected images also signify a danger inherent in their desire to help Jim.

Mirrors and self-consciousness figure frequently in Conrad, as when Razumov catches "sight of his own face in the looking-glass" and, his "mental stagnation" disturbed, he begins to ponder the meaning of his disrupted life (*UWE* 69). But here, after gazing in the mirror, Marlow senses a consciousness of self that verges on solipsism. When Stein asks, in his Germanic syntax, "What is it that by inward pain makes him know himself? What is it that for you and me makes him—exist?", Marlow hesitates: "At that moment it was difficult to believe in Jim's existence—starting from a country parsonage, blurred by crowds of men as by clouds of dust" (*LJ* 216). Relieved of his personal history and idealized as a textbook example of "the romantic," Jim vanishes along with his individuality. Up to this moment Marlow has struggled to see through the face Jim presents to the world, but now even Jim's "erring spirit" has disappeared. Marlow's experience here recalls one of Conrad's most sweepingly skeptical statements: "Life knows us not and we do not know life—we don't know even our own thoughts. Half the words we use have no meaning whatever and of the other half each man understands each word after the fashion of his own folly and conceit."[36] Asserting a radical detachment not only from others but from himself, Conrad pushes the thought to its skeptical extreme, perhaps using as a model, as Cedric Watts has suggested, *Marius the Epicurean*, which Garnett had mailed to him that spring. Given Conrad's echoes of Pater elsewhere, he may well have been influenced by Marius's reflections on "this closely shut cell of one's own personality."[37] But even apart from the question of influence, Marlow's sense of Jim's sudden effacement and of Stein's self-regarding nostalgia brings him to the threshold of a solipsistic vision that follows inevitably from the assumption that only our own impressions are real: another's pain becomes our bundle of sensory experience.

But Marlow recoils from the eerie spectacle of "a crystalline void." We escape the solipsism of total skepticism with respect to others by acknowledging the reality of another's pain, for with acknowledgment comes the capacity to relate to others as a moral agent.[38] The question of acknowledgment engages Conrad throughout *Lord Jim* and will return in a different guise in *Nostromo*. Here it may well be an awareness of Jim's "inward pain" that suddenly forces its way into Marlow's mind.

> [Jim's] imperishable reality came to me with a convincing, with an irresistible force! I saw it vividly, as though in our progress through the lofty silent rooms amongst fleeting gleams of light and the sudden revelations of human figures stealing with flickering flames within unfathomable and pellucid depths, we had approached near to absolute Truth, which, like Beauty itself, floats elusive, obscure, half submerged, in the silent still waters of mystery. (*LJ* 216)

The passage accomplishes many things at once. It is, first of all, an explicit vision of the inevitable elusiveness of Jim's essential being and of all truth. But the possibility of achieving moral insight is not wholly abandoned. By repeating and interpreting Marlow's earlier perceptions of the room, the passage turns back on itself to interrogate the possibility of abstracting knowledge from visual impressions. Although the "absolute Truth" Marlow desires remains unattainable, Conrad's depiction of Marlow's visual imagination captures the process of moral understanding, whose goal is always beyond reach. Moral consciousness is understood as a triumph over skeptical self-enclosure, and by granting to Jim a measure of autonomy he has not always acknowledged, Marlow establishes the preconditions for a moral relationship.

Up to this point Marlow's narration of Jim's experience has frequently hinted at the danger of solipsism. Although Marlow no doubt honestly desires to help Jim, his attentiveness during their conversations at the Malabar sometimes takes on a certain morbidity, as if Jim were one of Stein's butterflies, pinned against the wall. (Indeed, one of the chief burdens of the Author's Note is precisely Conrad's attempt to counter the charge of morbidity brought by an unnamed female reader.) Marlow's narration of these conversations often assumes the quality of an internalized dialogue between the halves of a divided self, particularly when his language dissolves the boundaries between Jim's consciousness and his own. Part of this blurring results from ambiguities inherent in Marlow's frequent use of free indirect discourse, for what might be called the "third voice" produced in this mode hovers between the minds of narrator and character, drawing on the language of each.[39] But Marlow often takes over the narration in a more direct fashion by effecting a transition into his own projection of what Jim's experience must have been like through phrases such as "I can easily picture him to myself . . ." or "I can see him glaring at the iron . . ." This is narration by conjecture (a method later perfected by Faulkner), and we can only accept Marlow at his word when he assures us that "I would have been little fitted for the reception of his confidences had I not been able at times to understand the pauses between the words," or when he notes that Jim "related facts which I have not forgotten, but at this distance of time I couldn't recall his very words" (*LJ* 105). At one level Conrad merely means to explain why Marlow does not quote Jim more copiously. But it is equally important that the cognitive aim of understanding Jim is also motivated by Marlow's emotional *need* for those experiences, as if by living through Jim's crisis vicariously he might find within himself the strength Brierly evidently lacked. The relationship between Marlow and Jim at these moments is thus analogous to that between Marlow and Kurtz; in both instances Marlow is able to cross over into the experience of another, yet still withdraw his "hesitating foot."

In these early chapters Marlow's vicarious participation in Jim's experience approaches a selfish appropriation that never becomes an issue in "Heart of Darkness." Entering into their friendship, it would undermine, at the very least, the possibility of a truly reciprocal relationship. Pushed to an extreme, it might reveal, in the manner of *The Nigger of the "Narcissus,"* Marlow's sympathy as a form of egoism. (Marlow at one point admits that Jim "had reached the secret sensibility of my egoism"—*LJ* 152.) Entering into Marlow's *narration* of that friendship, such an appropriation puts into question, from the standpoint of his audience, the autonomy of Jim's existence. The possibility thus arises that Marlow's presentation of Jim could become a projection of Marlow's own fears rather than the portrait of an individual whose life remains independent of Marlow's story. Marlow himself betrays some awareness of his potential usurpation of Jim's consciousness in his occasional efforts to disentangle Jim's language from his own ("That's his simile," Marlow interjects, "not mine"—*LJ* 112) and in the sudden distance he achieves through passing characterizations of the imagined scene on board the *Patna* as a particular form of spectacle (farce, low comedy, etc.). To what extent is the Jim Marlow describes faithful to the man he knew? How much of Marlow's narration, that is, is informed by memory and how much by imagination?

Marlow's epiphany at Stein's offers an implicit response to these otherwise unanswerable questions. Dispelling the potential for solipsism in Marlow's narration, it replaces Marlow's reflection in the mirror with the "imperishable reality" of someone whose otherness is now acknowledged. Crediting Marlow's inquiry with the possibility of sustaining its ethical integrity, Conrad also affirms the ethical value of his own fiction.

One can imagine the novel closing rather rapidly here with a Jamesian open-endedness: Marlow strides into the night having made a resolution regarding Jim which is never fully revealed to the reader. But the novel does not end here, and the decision to send Jim to Patusan puts back into play the tendency toward self-enclosure that Marlow's vision had countered. Conrad's generosity in allowing Stein and Marlow to provide Jim with a second chance is doubled by the sense that sending Jim to Patusan may represent another version of Brierly's desire to bury Jim out of sight, or even Chester's plan to set Jim up as lord of the coolies on his own guano island. Jim, of course, *wants* a dangerous adventure, and Stein and Marlow are more than up to the challenge of providing one: "Neither Stein nor I had a clear conception of what might be on the other side when we, metaphorically speaking, took him up and hove him over the wall with scant ceremony. . . . He wanted a refuge, and a refuge at the cost of danger should be offered him" (*LJ* 229–30).

Patusan: Incarnating the Dream

Stein and Marlow heave Jim over the wall into a world that brings into the narrative present the romantic realm previously constituted as Stein's mythic past. Projecting in narrative form the shelter of romance articulated in the Stein discussion, the second half of the novel continues the exploration of possible literary responses to Jim that began with satire and psychological realism.[40] Romance requires the suppression of skepticism, and in Patusan it provides a sustained shelter against skeptic incursions until, with the resurgence of skepticism, romance modulates into tragedy.

The world of Patusan has a peculiar and precarious status. It seems at once to be a "real" place in relation to the *Patna* half of the narrative and also a wholly internalized locus of the imagination. Conrad's contemporary readers would have recognized Jim's life in Patusan as a version of the historical adventures of Sir James Brooke, who established himself as rajah of Sarawak, Borneo, in 1841.[41] Yet Conrad appropriates this history as metaphor, much as he refashioned the history of the Congo Free State in "Heart of Darkness" in order to investigate "secondary notions" beyond the initial critique of colonialism. Through Jim's experience in Patusan, Conrad continues to investigate the nature and power of his own art, for these adventures read simultaneously as an extension of the mimetic project of the first half of the novel and as an allegorical investigation of the power of aesthetic ordering to replace the fixed standard of conduct.

Although Patusan clearly offers Jim the opportunity to bring order to a community, Marlow describes his success there not as a political ordering but as an artistic one: "He left his earthly failings behind him and that sort of reputation he had, and there was a totally new set of conditions for his imaginative faculty to work upon" (*LJ* 218). Where "absolute Truth" was once "like Beauty," now it *is* beauty. From the first chapters of the novel the narrative focuses on the nature of Jim's imagination, which has been conditioned in a Bovaryesque fashion by the "light holiday literature" he reads before discovering "his vocation for the sea." Once on the training ship, when unable to enjoy the sense of removed superiority afforded by his elevated station in the foretop, Jim "would forget himself, and beforehand live in his mind the sea-life of light literature":

He saw himself saving people from sinking ships, cutting away masts in a hurricane, swimming through a surf with a line; or as a lonely castaway, barefooted and half naked, walking on uncovered reefs in search of shellfish to stave off starvation. He confronted savages on tropical shores, quelled mutinies on the high seas, and in a small boat upon the ocean kept up the hearts of despairing men—always an example of devotion to duty, and as unflinching as a hero in a book. (*LJ* 6)

It is precisely this tendency to lose himself in his imagination that causes Jim's failure to act when faced with an emergency on the training ship. Jim rationalizes this failure as an opportunity unworthy of his attention and takes solace in considering himself an epic hero *in potentia*: "he exulted with fresh certitude in his avidity for adventure, and in a sense of many-sided courage" (*LJ* 9).[42] But Jim's early experiences disappoint him: "After two years of training he went to sea, and entering the regions so well known to his imagination, found them strangely barren of adventure" (*LJ* 10). Entering Patusan, Jim finds a world that perfectly matches the imaginary regions inspired by his boyhood reading. Of Doramin and his family Jim exclaims to Marlow: "They are like people in a book, aren't they?" (*LJ* 260). The reader shares with Jim the sense of stepping into a world fashioned by Jim's own imagination.[43]

In Patusan Jim's "word was the one truth of every passing day," and to his success, remarks Marlow, "there were no externals" (*LJ* 272, 226). Marlow is referring not to the psychological interiority of Patusan but to its physical remoteness within thirty miles of surrounding forest, and this tension between realistic and allegorical readings of Patusan recurs in a number of forms, including Marlow's tribute to Patusan's romance setting: ". . . do you notice how, three hundred miles beyond the end of telegraph cables and mail-boat lines, the haggard utilitarian lies of our civilisation wither and die, to be replaced by pure exercises of imagination, that have the futility, often the charm, and sometimes the deep hidden truthfulness, of works of art?" (*LJ* 282). Technology would seem to mark the boundary between Patusan and outside reality. Yet in Patusan modernity does not dissolve into the unspoiled nature of Axel Heyst's island hermitage; "utilitarian lies" are replaced by art, a pure exercise of the imagination that effaces the otherwise inescapable network of cables and lines crisscrossing the modern world. The palpable geography of here and there, as well as the historical span of premodern and modern, is reconstrued by a nostalgic aesthetic as the inner realm of the pure imagination as against the decay of external reality. From the moment Jim flees from the rajah's request to fix a watch to Marlow's sense that in leaving the interior he was "going back to the world where events move, men change, light flickers, life flows" (*LJ* 330), Jim's leap into Patusan is figured as a leap out of time and into a timelessness that is at once an outpost just beyond the reach of progress and an unlocalized interior landscape.[44] Like Stein's butterflies, Patusan represents an idealized image of art, and what is at stake is whether that art is characterized by "futility" or a "deep hidden truthfulness."

Beyond its mimetic solidity, then, Patusan can also be considered a fragile narrative hypothesis. Its order derives not from a code of conduct but—as if his language had the power of authorial fiat—from Jim's word, "the one truth of every passing day." The communal bond effected by the "sovereign power enthroned in a fixed standard of conduct" thus becomes "a new sovereign," the power of an authorial imagination now purged of the "infernal alloy" that formerly contaminated it (*LJ* 45). In "Heart of Darkness" the infernal alloy of skepticism remains very much with Marlow, who fears that "We live, as we dream—alone." In *Lord Jim* Marlow feels at Stein's that he has escaped the self-enclosure of radical skepticism, and the world of Patusan seems (if we generalize from Marlow's sense of its unreality) at once an internalized romance and a narrative space purged of skepticism.

Yet the threat of solipsism often returns, as at the beginning of Chapter Thirty-Four, where the anonymous narrator describes Marlow looking at his audience "with the eyes of a man returning from the *excessive* remoteness of a dream" (*LJ* 320, emphasis added). His aim, Marlow informs them a few moments later, is "to tell you the story, to try to hand over to you, as it were, its very existence, its reality—the truth disclosed in a moment of illusion" (*LJ* 323). Marlow conjures this dream of an unmediated vision in response to having recalled the skeptical crisis of his interview with Jewel, to which I now turn.[45]

The Collapse of Shelter: Jewel and the End of Romance

As if intensified through its suppression, skepticism resurfaces in Marlow's encounter with Jewel to initiate the unravelling of romance that culminates in Jim's tragic encounter with Brown. Jewel fears that Marlow has come to take Jim away, and the story of her mother's death, offered as a version of the fate she wishes to escape, elicits a seemingly excessive response. In the obscurity of its immediate motivation and the intensity of Marlow's reaction, the passage recalls the overdetermination of his first sight of Jim.

[Jewel's story] had the power to drive me out of my conception of existence, out of that shelter each of us makes for himself to creep under in moments of danger, as a tortoise withdraws within its shell. For a moment I had a view of a world that seemed to wear a vast and dismal aspect of disorder, while, in truth, thanks to our unwearied efforts, it is as sunny an arrangement of small conveniences as the mind of man can conceive. But still—it was only a moment: I went back into my shell directly. One *must*—don't you know?—though I seemed to have lost all my words in the chaos of dark thoughts I had contemplated for a second or two beyond the pale. These came back, too, very soon, for words also belong to the sheltering conception of light and order which is our refuge. (*LJ* 313)

At this moment the sense of crisis that charges the entire novel achieves its clearest articulation. The apparent catalyst for Marlow's sudden vision is the disrupted relations within Jewel's family: weeping, her mother dies as Jewel struggles to hold the door against her stepfather, Cornelius; her true father had abandoned them long before. Marlow is moved, clearly enough, by Jewel's earlier lack of any tolerable life, her torment and precarious escape through Jim. The *depth* of his emotional upheaval suggests that he views the family as the one dependable refuge in this world—"the hearthstone," he says elsewhere, is where "the humblest of us has the right to sit" (*LJ* 221)—but with Jewel's words he senses "the still rise of a flood in the night, obliterating the familiar landmarks of emotions" (*LJ* 312). (The context here restores to "familiar" its etymological connection with "family.") Jewel's fear of abandonment seems well grounded: she has lost both her parents, and her stepfather, having already turned against her mother, now plots the betrayal of her lover. How can Marlow assuage Jewel's anxiety about the trustworthiness of her relationship with Jim if the weight of her experience argues for the inevitability of separation and loss? "She should have made for herself," Marlow laments, "a shelter of inexpugnable peace out of [Jim's] honest affection" (*LJ* 313). In his own relationship with Jim, Marlow has aimed to construct just such a shelter, but in Jewel's story he now comes to recognize the fragility of all forms of human connectedness, for she has raised the problem of evil in a way that permits no anodynes or shallow consolation.

As if by contagion, Marlow's faith in all "sheltering conceptions" becomes threatened by Cornelius's violation of the family as shelter, and his emotional crisis begins to open into a more broadly epistemological one. Although the "passive, irremediable horror" of Jewel's family history has distinct Oedipal resonance, a psychoanalytic reading obscures Marlow's deeper fear of losing his words to the undifferentiated darkness.[46] Standing at some distance from Marlow's experience, one might say that the semiotic crisis is more fundamental than the Oedipal one; from within the fiction, that Marlow, faced with the loss of immediate relationships, would at least like to remain committed to the promise of community afforded by language. To be overwhelmed, however, by the sense that we live as we dream—alone—is to reexperience with nightmarish intensity a child's fear of being trapped forever alone in the dark.[47] Jukes, the first mate of *Typhoon*, suffers from this very fear, and only Captain MacWhirr's voice has the power to restore his confidence and combat the destructive furor of the storm.[48] Here, as even the shelter of articulation vanishes, Marlow's skeptic vision crosses over from the limited skepticism that empties perceptions of meaning into a Pyrrhonism that threatens consciousness itself: Jewel and her claims have disappeared; Jim has disappeared; Marlow remains alone in a "chaos of dark thoughts" that are literally unspeakable. At a moment when he most needs his ability to communicate intimately, all knowledge—and language itself—comes to seem, in Marlow's defensively ironic phrase, a false order, a "sunny . . . arrangement of small conveniences."

For Conrad such a breakdown would interrupt the novel by making writing impossible. Radical skepticism undermines one's belief in the existence of a "usable" audience—like Jim, a writer thrives on the confidence inspired by an imagined audience—and a novelist who permanently loses all faith in language has a short career.[49] Here even the descriptions of the dissolution of visible forms in the surrounding scene suggest the extinguishing of Conrad's visual imagination and the possible end of his narrative.[50] Located in Marlow, the crisis is contained; the vision is intolerable, and the perspective afforded by Marlow's retro-spective narration permits him to describe the sensation of being forced back into the shell of conventional understanding. Mar-low's last shelter, we could say, appears as the quotation marks Conrad places around his words.

The most telling analogue to Marlow's vision occurs not in fic-tion but in Hume's meditations on the relationship between the phenomenology of "common life" and the conclusions of rigor-ous skeptical inquiry in Book I, Part IV, of *A Treatise of Human Nature.*[51] Hume's discussion has a rhythm of insight and retreat that closely resembles Marlow's withdrawal from the nihilistic vi-sion occasioned by Jewel. Hume argues that whereas reason un-leashed on itself has the power to subvert itself and to annihilate the evidence of the senses, "nature" prevents us from remaining in the void reason opens up (*THN* 180–85). He good-naturedly acknowledges that no matter how powerful the conclusions pro-duced by his skepticism, "an hour hence" his readers will take for granted the independent existence of the external world and any other concepts vitiated by total skepticism. "Nature, by an absolute and uncontroulable necessity has determin'd us to judge as well as to breathe and feel" (*THN* 218, 183).

But in his extraordinary conclusion to Book I, Hume returns to the issue by reflecting on whether the disjunction between his rational inquiry and ordinary life deprives his philosophical en-terprise of value—not simply for his audience but for himself. In a startling moment of convergence Hume's use of a well-known topos for vocation momentarily issues as a Conradian adventure yarn: "Methinks I am like a man, who having struck on many shoals, and having narrowly escap'd ship-wreck in passing a small frith, has yet the temerity to put out to sea in the same leaky weather-beaten vessel, and even carries his ambition so far as to think of compassing the globe under these disadvantageous cir-cumstances" (*THN* 263–64). More than fears of thwarted ambi-tion connect the two writers. Having marshaled his reason to open fissures in his own rational enterprise, Hume describes his predicament as skeptic in terms that increasingly come to resem-ble those of Jim, Marlow, and Conrad: "I am first affrighted and confounded with that forelorn solitude, in which I am plac'd in my philosophy, and fancy myself some strange uncouth mon-

ster, who not being able to mingle and unite in society, has been
expell'd all human commerce, and left utterly abandon'd and dis-
consolate. Fain wou'd I run into the crowd for shelter and
warmth" (*THN* 264). The fear of isolation recalls Marlow's struggles with language and Jim's lonely eminence on Patusan; and,
like Hume, each has sought consolation in the sheltering conceptions of society.[52] Yet Hume cannot simply reject the solitary
investigation that produces the dilemma of either accepting what
experience insists is absurd or denying the value of his philosophical system.

In the following paragraphs we see him approaching the intolerable vision that neither he nor Marlow ever names as madness:[53]

The *intense* view of these manifold contradictions and imperfections in
human reason has so wrought upon me, and heated my brain, that I am
ready to reject all belief and reasoning, and can look upon no opinion
even as more probable or likely than another. Where am I, or what?
From what causes do I derive my existence, and to what condition shall
I return? Whose favour shall I court, and whose anger must I dread?
What beings surround me? and on whom have I any influence, or who
have any influence on me? I am confounded with all these questions,
and begin to fancy myself in the most deplorable condition imaginable,
inviron'd with the deepest darkness, and utterly depriv'd of the use of
every member and faculty.

But the tortoise must withdraw within its shell:

Most fortunately it happens, that since reason is incapable of dispelling these clouds, nature herself suffices to that purpose, and cures me
of this philosophical melancholy and delirium, either by relaxing this
bent of mind, or by some avocation, and lively impressions of my
senses, which obliterate all these chimeras. I dine, I play a game of backgammon, I converse, and am merry with my friends; and when after
three or four hour's amusement, I wou'd return to these speculations,
they appear so cold, and strain'd, and ridiculous, that I cannot find in
my heart to enter into them any farther. (*THN* 268–69)

Rather than become a restaurateur or professional gambler,
Hume chooses to continue in his leaky vessel, allowing his mind
to widen the fissures only when he is "naturally" so inclined.
Then, reflecting on where his writing has taken him, Hume re-

cuperates the incompatibility of total skepticism and common life as new knowledge of human nature, "the only science of man," but "hitherto the most neglected" (*THN* 273). The decision to turn toward society for solace amounts to a necessary repression of the intolerable, one that allows him to write Books II and III, "Of the Passions" and "Of Morals." Marlow might have turned away from Jim, as Brierly tries to, after first experiencing the deep uncertainty Jim inspired. Instead he continually crosses Jim's path to see if he needs bailing out. Even after retreating from the shock of his conversation with Jewel, Marlow later chooses to write out the final events of Jim's life and send it to the privileged man. Both writers, then, find ways to "manage" the crises brought on by radically skeptical thought.

Marlow's first sight of Jim, his interview with Jewel, and Hume's reflections on skepticism all partake of what Cavell has described as the "three phenomenologically striking features of the conclusion which characterizes skepticism: the sense of *discovery* expressed in the conclusion of the investigation; the sense of the *conflict* of this discovery with our ordinary 'beliefs'; the *instability* of the discovery, the theoretical conviction it inspires vanishing under the pressure (or distraction) of our ordinary commerce with the world."[54] In each case the pressure of convention exacts a price. Hume feels that though his "follies shall at least be natural and agreeable," he nevertheless "must be a fool" (*THN* 270). Marlow's retreat within his shell associates him with the complacency of Jim's father, whom Marlow later envisions "grey-haired and serene in the inviolable shelter of his book-lined, faded, and comfortable study," "equably trusting Providence and the established order of the universe" (*LJ* 341). Yet just as one imagines that Hume was never your typical backgammon player, Marlow's sheltering conceptions can be distinguished from those of Jim's father, for Marlow's self-consciousness about the difference between inside and outside has been earned by his momentary penetration beyond conventions.[55] Such a penetration may take the form of a journey into the Congo or an awareness of the imminence of death, or it may lie in "the capacity to look consciously," as Marlow does in the Jewel interview, "under the surface of familiar emotions" (*LJ* 169).

Despite the losses entailed by curtailing skepticism, both Hume and Conrad respond by reaffirming their vocations. Hume affirms himself as a philosopher by continuing the *Treatise* out of "an ambition" to contribute to "the instruction of mankind" (*THN* 271). Conrad asserts the ethical value of his authorship by having Marlow stand up "like an evoked ghost"—the barely visible sign of Conrad's absent presence—"to answer for [Jim's] eternal constancy" (*LJ* 416).

Marlow's readiness to bear witness notwithstanding, if one of *Blackwood's* installments had ended with the last lines of Chapter Thirty-Five, few readers would have expected more:

He was white from head to foot, and remained persistently visible with the stronghold of the night at his back, the sea at his feet, the opportunity by his side—still veiled. . . . For me that white figure in the stillness of coast and sea seemed to stand at the heart of a vast enigma. The twilight was ebbing fast from the sky above his head, the strip of sand had sunk already under his feet, he himself appeared no bigger than a child—then only a speck, a tiny white speck, that seemed to catch all the light left in a darkened world. . . . And, suddenly, I lost him. . . . (*LJ* 336)

The tableau bodies Jim forth as the hero he would like to remain. A perfectly realized symbolic scene, the passage recalls the anonymous narrator's description of Marlow settling into his story at the end of Chapter Four, where his "spirit" speaks "through his lips from the past." There the idea of incarnation anticipates the ideal narration Marlow later describes in which words would embody meaning in such a way that Jim's reality could be handed over to the audience. In Patusan Marlow borrows the trope to characterize Jim's supremacy as "the visible, tangible incarnation of unfailing truth and of unfailing victory" (*LJ* 361). In the false ending Conrad substitutes the trope of reflection as Jim—Don Quixote in a tragic key—becomes the last mirror of a lost age of heroism, catching "all the light left in a darkened world."

Yet once more the novel does not end here. Each shelter that emerges as a possible response to skepticism fails to provide closure. The anonymous narrator's satire gives way to Marlow's rationalism, which in turn modulates into Stein's romanticism and the world of Patusan. But the refuge of romantic art, as we will see, cannot cope with the problem of evil or the finality of loss. The narrative heads inexorably toward the moment when skepticism no longer will be forestalled but tragically embraced.

Brown and the Tragedy of Skepticism

Explicit language of incarnation runs throughout Conrad, and the ending of *Lord Jim* derives much of its meaning and power from a return to imagery of disembodied spirits.[56] Both Jim's death and the representation of Jewel are drawn into the logic of incarnation versus self-division. More so than Kurtz's Intended, Jewel throughout much of the novel symbolizes Jim's new opportunity and all he has acquired by seizing it—success, trust, and love; and in naming her himself, Jim underlines Jewel's role as a "vehicle of imaginary value."[57] Yet Jewel is not always as abstract a character as Aeneas's Lavinia, who functions only as a symbolic counter, the idealized mother of the future heroes of the Roman empire. Jewel's appearance outside the charmed world of Patusan at Stein's, where she mourns Jim's death, startles us into believing in her flesh and blood, as if her ability to cross over from the world of romance into the novelistic space of Stein's reception room were a guarantee of independent existence. In Patusan Jewel can be at once the "opportunity" Marlow imagines sitting "veiled by [Jim's] side like an Eastern bride" and the actual woman Jim embraces after slaying his would-be assassin. Like Jim, she appears to be a "visible, tangible incarnation."

But after Brown's arrival, the narrative relentlessly moves toward the moment when Jim will have to choose between alternatives that no longer can be realized in one figure. In his last moment, Marlow imagines, Jim may have "beheld the face" of that "Eastern bride." But once unveiled, the bride is not Jewel. In the aftermath of Brown's slaughter of Dain Waris and his men, the world of irreconcilable claims returns to enforce a distinction between Jim's ideal object of desire and Jewel: dying from Doramin's single shot in the chest, Jim "goes away from a living woman to celebrate his pitiless wedding with a shadowy ideal of conduct" (*LJ* 416). Although by leaving behind the living woman Jim seems finally to marry perfection in death, even there unity becomes duality as he too suffers a self-division that is expressed as the exile of his ideal self from its mortal body:

> Now he is no more, there are days when the reality of his existence comes to me with an immense, with an overwhelming force; and yet upon my honour there are moments, too, when he passes from my eyes like a disembodied spirit astray amongst the passions of this earth, ready to surrender himself faithfully to the claim of his own world of shades. (*LJ* 416)

Jim's dream of perfect heroism can be achieved only in the books of his youth. His spirit seems to depart for the idealized realm of shades projected in "Karain."

Alive in Patusan, however, and incarnated as the truth of his own imagination, Jim has a power that approximates Stephen Dedalus's ideal of the artist as God, though unlike Stephen's indifferent deity, Jim is all too visible.[58] Conrad himself was not committed to the self-glorifying concept of the artist as God: agonizing over God's absence, he was not prepared to take up the role himself. Yet Conrad allows Jim to realize such an aspiration, for in Patusan nature the great artist has her surrogate in Jim, whose martial and political arts—the focus of readings attuned exclusively to the mimetic—seem also to regulate things "as much beyond his control as the motions of the moon and the stars" (*LJ* 221).

Having failed to live up to the code of conduct on the *Patna*, Jim establishes in Patusan a principle of order that (until the deadly reassertion of Doramin's power) originates solely in himself. Because Marlow repeatedly describes this order as an act of aesthetic realization, we can read the collapse of Jim's communal order on Patusan as the revenge of the real on Jim's idealized art, the triumph of the anarchy Marlow glimpsed beyond the pale over the reordering power of the romantic. Gentleman Brown appears in Patusan in the doubled role of the villain required by romance conventions and as the reality those conventions have previously excluded from the narrative. Romance certainly can be more, but in Patusan it finally appears as a facile embodiment of ideal values, a story in which the closing of the gap between intention and action represents a falsification of reality.[59] Romance in Patusan thus takes on the quality of Marlow's lie to the

Intended, which undermines the validity of romantic closure by setting it against the "horror" of Kurtz. In *Lord Jim*, unable to credit the idea of art as an autonomous realm, Conrad gives up the fantasy of a sovereign artist-god spinning an inviolable sanctuary of romance and turns back to the more mundane figure of Marlow.

Jim's romance depends on a suppression of the divisive skepticism that charges the first half of the novel. While Jim leads a charmed life, Marlow's skeptical crisis in the Jewel interview anticipates the appearance of Brown, whose violation of Jim's sheltered retreat undoes its constitutive repression. Consistent with the precarious doubleness of Patusan itself, Brown arrives both as the emissary from the outside world feared by Jewel and as the resurgence of Jim's repressed guilt.[60] As a figure from the world that has expelled Jim, Brown brings with him the richly particularized personal history we expect from a novel; as the embodiment of the worst of Jim's past, his significance lies in the "sickening suggestion of common guilt" he inspires (*LJ* 387). Before Brown's arrival, his counterpart within Patusan, Cornelius, has been held in check by Jim's sovereign power. United, however, they bring Jim's house down on his head by reopening the gap between the old man and the new. When Jim's repression breaks down, his romance breaks down, and Marlow's letter to the privileged man, which takes Brown as its starting point, records the collapse of romance into tragedy.

Conrad's epistemological and moral skepticism, dramatized in Marlow's response to Jim's deceptive appearance and brought to a crisis in the Jewel interview, forecloses on Patusan's romance in the tragic form of the novel's ending. Ian Watt has claimed that "to postulate self-knowledge as a criterion of tragedy . . . may be yet another of the modern secularized versions of the consolations which religion offers in the face of suffering, waste, and evil."[61] Perhaps so, but Conrad seeks just such consolation, and a tragic hero need not *achieve* self-knowledge in order for the criterion to have relevance. Jim's tragedy begins at the moment he refuses to acknowledge his affinities with Brown, and his refusal ever to awaken to his own denial only adds to its tragic force.

Here I follow Cavell's suggestion that "tragedy is the story and study of a failure of acknowledgement . . . the form of tragedy is the public form of the life of skepticism with respect to other minds."[62] Doubting, from time to time, the reality of another, we evade a deeper doubt about our own autonomy, our powerlessness to know another, and our powerlessness to be known. Although accepting the existence of another may establish, as it does in the Stein discussion, the preconditions for a moral relationship, acknowledgment also reminds us of the reality of our own existence as partial and dependent.

Jim cannot accept Brown as both a version of himself and as wholly other. While Jim himself has committed a crime despite having the best of intentions, Brown, driven by a "complex intention," contains "an undisguised ruthlessness of purpose, a strange vengeful attitude towards his own past, a blind belief in the righteousness of his will against all mankind" (*LJ* 370). Brown's ruthlessness may be undisguised to Marlow, but it is not to Jim, who tells Jewel: "Men act badly sometimes without being much worse than others" (*LJ* 394). Jim's homespun philosophy may be true enough in his own case, but it does not see into Brown. We may be tempted to share in Jim's blindness to himself by seizing on Brown's final savagery as an all-determining distinction in kind, but Brown's desire for sovereignty over Patusan mirrors even as it inverts Jim's benevolent dictatorship.

Although "Jim did not know the almost inconceivable egotism of the man which made him, when resisted and foiled in his will, mad with the indignant and revengeful wrath of a thwarted autocrat" (*LJ* 394), Brown's thirst for destruction should not distract us from the mad egotism of Jim's belief that the "fierce purpose in the gale" on the training ship was directed at himself. Nor should we dismiss the cool ferocity of Jim's response to the oncoming assassin as wholly different in kind from the violence of Brown:

[He experienced] a feeling of unutterable relief, of vengeful elation. He held his shot, he says, deliberately. He held it for the tenth part of a second, for three strides of the man—an unconscionable time. He held it for the pleasure of saying to himself, That's a dead man! (*LJ* 301)

Jim could not know Brown's mind because he would not. His refusal to acknowledge Brown's otherness does not constitute a denial of Brown's humanity—Jim won't leave him to die "like a rat

in a trap" (*LJ* 381). Rather, it is a denial of their common humanity, a refusal to acknowledge that human nature includes Brown,
and that Jim himself contains "the opposite poles of that conception of life which includes all mankind" (*LJ* 381). To think of
Brown as a part of himself is to destroy the fantasy of having
turned his idealized self-image into a sovereign power free of all
infernal alloys.

With Brown's challenge Jim again must make his actions live
up to his dream. Marlow's symbolic tableaux, which typically
rescue from time a moment of significant repose, sometimes
crystallize an instant of perfectly lucid apprehension set apart
from the demands of action. Consider the scene when Marlow
joins Jim at the site of his defeat of Sherif Ali:

> And there I was with him, high in the sunshine on the top of that historic
> hill of his. He dominated the forest, the secular gloom, the old mankind.
> He was like a figure set up on a pedestal, to represent in his persistent
> youth the power, and perhaps the virtues, of races that never grow old,
> that have emerged from the gloom. I don't know why he should always
> have appeared to me symbolic. (*LJ* 265)

Here we see the picture of virtuous success earned by the melodrama Jim has fought and won. Yet such moments of static apprehension cannot last, and when action resumes, the idealized
figure must descend from the pedestal and confront the recalci-
trant stuff of the real. (The reality neither Marlow nor Jim wishes
to confront includes more virulent expressions of the divisive-
ness latent in Marlow's tentative assessment of Jim's racial virtues.) The Patusan episode essentially offers Jim a prolonged in-
terlude of sovereign imagining, a time when actions achieve the
clarity of abstract intention. But the romance of Patusan can only
defer Jim's collision with something beyond himself that is initiated by Brown and finished by Doramin.

Only the trope of incarnation temporarily reconciles the claims
of ideal values and the world of action. Conrad once described
his difficulties writing as "the despair of thought without expression, or the wandering soul without a body."[63] After Jim's death,
we are left with Marlow's disembodied voice speaking hesitantly
to us of a wholeness that has departed the world. The last lines
of the novel, in which Stein "waves his hand sadly at his butter-

flies," constitute an elegiac lament for the time when, in Stein's words, "what I had once dreamed in my sleep could come into my hand" (*LJ* 211). The "malevolent Providence" that arranged the "practical joke" of the *Patna* collision and the "demon" that whispered advice in Brown's ear return to the narrative foreground in the figure of Doramin, and the scene of Jim's death in Doramin's court reads like a ritual encounter in which the dream of incarnation is finally dispelled by an angry father. If, as Cornelius insists, Jim is a "mere child," what Jim finally discovers outside himself at the end is a father less forgiving than Stein or Marlow. Conrad's generosity, manifested first in providing Marlow to shelter Jim from the satiric perspective of the anonymous narrator, induces him to hold off Doramin's inevitable last shot before saying, like Jim contemplating the assassin, "That's a dead man." Conrad ultimately sacrifices the emerging artist-god on the altar of his skepticism, which will not permit an idealized spirit to remain safely "within the envelope of . . . common desires," or a symbolic figure to rest secure on its pedestal.

Chapter Five

Nostromo and *The Secret Agent*: The Ethics of Form

One of the most significant developments in Conrad's fiction after "Heart of Darkness" and *Lord Jim* is the disappearance of Marlow, who reappears only in "Youth" (1902), a slight allegory of innocence and experience, and *Chance* (1913), where his presence as narrator is, at the very least, only occasionally a virtue.[1] The power and interest of *Lord Jim* lie in the unleashing and countering of Conrad's skepticism, which is both expressed and mitigated through Marlow. Contrasting "An Outpost of Progress" and "Heart of Darkness" in Chapter One, I argued that without Marlow's mediation, Conrad is drawn toward a more monological mode. My aim in this chapter is to devote more sustained attention to the ways in which skepticism enters into Conrad's texts in the absence of a recognizable substitute for Marlow, such as the teacher of languages in *Under Western Eyes*, and in the absence of the problematics of vision associated with Schopenhauer. The two issues I will bring into focus are epistemological skepticism as it turns inward toward the self, and moral skepticism as it exerts a reciprocal influence on narrative form and the status of character.

Skepticism, Character, and Agency

Skepticism leads naturally to an anxiety about agency, and the problem of agency establishes a useful link between epistemological and moral skepticism in Conrad. As I noted earlier, the deepest motive for skepticism is "the attempt to convert the human condition . . . into an intellectual difficulty, a riddle." Our "powerlessness" to give another a true sense of our separateness "presents itself as ignorance—a metaphysical finitude as an intellectual lack."[2] If skepticism calls forth the desire to posit another in order to substantiate one's own sense of self, it also tries to manage a corresponding fear of dependency. Pushed to an extreme, fear of dependence becomes the nightmare of determinism.

The tradition of epistemology since Descartes produces striking evidence of this connection. Descartes thought to conquer skepticism by establishing beyond doubt the reality of the *cogito*, from which he then claimed to derive a range of objective truths, including, in the "Third Meditation," the reality of God. But the positing of a power beyond can take a dangerous turn. Before "proving" the existence of God, Descartes gives free rein to skepticism in the "First Meditation," where he entertains the idea that "not a supremely good God, the source of truth, but rather an evil genius, as clever and deceitful as he is powerful . . . has directed his entire effort to misleading me."[3] Descartes attempts to exorcise the *malin génie* with what amounts to an elaborate tautology: our idea of God is one of perfection, and perfection precludes "fraud and deception"; given that ideas must resemble their cause, an undeceiving, perfect God must exist. But this and other arguments advanced in the wake of Descartes clearly cannot lock out the demon, who may have inspired the idea of God's perfection in the first place. Berkeley later tried to refute skepticism by grounding reality in God's perception of the world, but no logic can prevent God's metaphysical sanction from becoming the deceptions of Descartes's evil genius.[4] Contemporary philosophical debate has returned to the fear that consciousness might be determined by a malign external power in the grotesque (and rather comic) hypothesis that we may be brains in vats tended by an evil scientist.[5]

Turning away from the other and inward toward the self only recapitulates the problem. The anxiety that Descartes allays through recourse to God ("when I turn my powers of discernment toward myself, I . . . understand that I am something incomplete and dependent upon another"[6]) recurs with renewed urgency in Hume. If the self, as Hume describes it, is "nothing but a bundle or collection of different perceptions . . . in a perpetual flux and movement" (*THN* 252), is there any validity in ascribing the power of agency to it? This thought emerges quite distinctly in the middle of the extended passage (quoted at greater length in Chapter Four) in which Hume faces "the *intense* view" of the "manifold contradictions" of skepticism: "Where am I, or what? From what causes do I derive my existence, and to what condition shall I return? Whose favour shall I court, and whose anger must I dread? What beings surround me? and on whom have I any influence, or who have any influence on me? I am confounded with all these questions" (*THN* 269). These issues represent the legacy of the skepticism inherent in the empirical tradition, and they find expression in *Nostromo* and *The Secret Agent*, where crises of identity are closely linked to struggles for personal autonomy.

These struggles are played out as the revolt of characters against how others within the fiction attempt to define or control them and, on another level, as the resistance of characters to the narrative design itself. Although tracing these tensions beyond the frame of the fictions into the realm of the metafictional entails an increasingly speculative argument, both *Nostromo* and *The Secret Agent* contain ample textual grounds for the discussion. Skepticism dominates the relationship between character and author in *The Secret Agent*, where the withdrawal of a moral attitude dehumanizes characters, and the resulting black comedy pushes to an extreme the comic potential of the reduction of the human to the mechanically repetitive. In *Nostromo* the tension between skepticism and Conrad's refusal to accede to it completely produces something more recognizable as a traditional novel. To approach the question of the interrelations among the discourses of character, narrator, and author, I will again turn to the narrative poetics of Bakhtin, whose investigation of types of double-voiced discourse helps to illuminate the peculiar status of character in *Nostromo* and *The Secret Agent*.

Decoud and the Discourse of Skepticism

Nostromo marks a shift away from stories drawn from Conrad's years at sea, and it is the first of three novels which claim to look closely at the nature of political behavior. Yet the resemblances to the earlier fiction are strong: despite the new historical breadth and range of *Nostromo*, it also recasts the study of idealization and skepticism that lies at the heart of *Lord Jim*. In the absence of Marlow, the locus of skepticism shifts from participant-narrator to character (though one who also takes up the role of narrator at a key moment in the narrative) in the figure of Martin Decoud, whose struggle with commitment explicitly dramatizes the tension between skepticism and belief formerly rendered more subjectively in Marlow's first-person discourse. Decoud's fate, when he is isolated on a small island, is to find that the self, to adapt Winnie Verloc's well-known phrase, doesn't bear much looking into. Given the peculiarities of his death by what has been described as an authorial exorcism, Decoud may be one of the few characters in fiction ever to die of skepticism.[7] Yet Decoud's expulsion does not altogether purge the text of the skeptical malady, which persists in various forms on several levels of the fiction.

In *Mimesis* Erich Auerbach complains that Virginia Woolf's skepticism seems to deny her access to the minds of her own characters.[8] The relationship between Marlow and other characters, many of whom tend to become absorbed into Marlow's subjectivity, both reflects and resists this new sense of the limitations of what an author or narrator can know about his or her own characters. Contingent on Marlow's perceptions of them, characters in *Lord Jim* and "Heart of Darkness" often seem tenuous or fragile, as when Jim vanishes before Marlow's "dazzled eyes as though . . . blown to atoms." Although characters are less likely to dissolve before our eyes in *Nostromo*, the instability of character recurs in the crises of identity through which Nostromo, Decoud, and others suffer. The inwardness of Marlow's "chaos of dark thoughts" in Patusan is described from a greater remove in *Nostromo* as "the intimate impressions of universal dissolution" (*N* 417). Nostromo's crisis both recalls Marlow's and anticipates Decoud's.

Before turning to *Nostromo*, Conrad wrote *Typhoon*, a funny story whose comedy—an "antidote"[9] to the skepticism of *Lord Jim*—has obscured its affinities with the skeptical crises of *Nostromo*. In Captain MacWhirr Conrad supplies the first mate, Jukes, with the dependable figure of authority whose absence on the *Patna* permits Jim's panic to go unchecked. When MacWhirr chooses to steer directly into a massive typhoon, the strength of his stolid and unimaginative character helps the crew weather the storm. The possibility of dialogue between Jukes and MacWhirr contrasts sharply with the isolation and self-enclosure of Jim's imagination on board the *Patna*, and it allows Jukes to find in his captain a saving example of self-possession. Jukes's state of mind depends completely on his proximity to MacWhirr, and the narration of the storm pays close attention to the rhythm of their momentary separations and reunions. Alone, Jukes is incapacitated by "a momentary hallucination of swift visions," whereas contact with MacWhirr produces "an access of confidence, a sensation that came from outside like a warm breath" (*T* 52, 89). (Note that the relationship between MacWhirr and Jukes also restages the contrast between Jim's visual imagination and the unimaginative stolidness of the French lieutenant.) Although MacWhirr's often hilarious literal-mindedness ("D'ye mean to say, Mr. Jukes, you ever had your head tied up in a blanket?"—*T* 25) anticipates the comic obtuseness of Captain Mitchell in *Nostromo*, MacWhirr survives a much greater test than does Mitchell, whose stubborn confrontation with Sotillo achieves only the return of his watch. Yet *Typhoon* finally draws back from its tentative assertion of MacWhirr's value by closing with Jukes's unflatteringly ironic letter at the captain's expense: "He got out of it very well for such a stupid man" (*T* 102). While the irony denies MacWhirr the unequivocal status of hero, the narrative clearly imbues him with the power to counter Jukes's potential loss of self, and the comedy restrains the more introspective meditations on identity found in *Lord Jim*.

The fear of a dissolution of self runs deeper in *Nostromo*. Of Charles Gould, the administrator of the San Tomé mine, the engineer-in-chief remarks: "'He must be extremely sure of himself.'" To which Dr. Monygham replies, "'If that's all he is sure of, then he is sure of nothing'" (*N* 310). Having broken down under torture years before, Monygham has good reason to doubt the strength of the individual will. Yet the exchange also presupposes what are, in effect, two competing versions of the self: Monygham's remark challenges the engineer-in-chief's implicit understanding of the self as a fulcrum on which actions turn with the suggestion that the self may be "nothing." When Nostromo later feels betrayed by those in power, he considers himself "undone, destroyed," and hopes to have "restored to him his personality—the only thing lost in that desperate affair" (*N* 436, 434). The narrator's characterization of Monygham in the same scene locates a dynamic common to many figures in the novel: "Having had to encounter single-handed during his period of eclipse many physical dangers, he was well aware of the most dangerous element common to them all: of the crushing, para-lyzing sense of human littleness, which is what really defeats a man struggling with natural forces, alone, far from the eyes of his fellows" (*N* 433). Isolation within nature—a negative sublime in which the boundlessness of the world overwhelms the mind's capacity to comprehend it—substitutes in *Nostromo* for the sub-limities of a penetrating vision in the earlier fiction. Arnold Ben-nett, uncharacteristically indulging in hyperbole, felt that Higue-rota, the snow-capped peak that dominates the mountain range outside Sulaco, was "the principal personage in the story," which contains many scenes of human beings dwarfed by the immensi-ty and indifference of nature.[10] Society and consciousness alike, to borrow from the abstract language of *The Secret Agent*, are en-dangered by "the majesty of inorganic nature" (*SA* 14).

Charles Gould confronts nature head-on through his obses-sion with redeeming both the moral and economic value of the silver mine; Nostromo tends to his reputation in order to create a fiction of indomitable self-sufficiency. Both struggle to impose their selves on the world (social and natural) in order to become grounded in something more substantial than subjective self-awareness. In Decoud's case, it is apparently the inability to ground himself outside of illusion that undermines his will to live.[11] A coroner's report, admittedly, would not brook such ab-straction, nor would many novels; but if we locate Decoud in the larger patterns of the text, his cause of death, if not quite plausible within the canon of probability established by the nineteenth-century novel, at least makes sense. Although the complexity of the novel prevents a comprehensive summary, some of the intricacies of the narrative development are impor-tant to my argument, and a brief sketch will be useful here.

Nostromo traces the violent history of Sulaco, a coastal city in the South American province of Costaguana, and the lives of the people who are involved in Costaguana's revolutionary politics. Most important in the novel's huge cast of characters are Charles

Gould, an Englishman with a European education who was born in Sulaco; Decoud, another Costaguanan returned after life abroad; and Nostromo, the Italian *capataz* of the longshoremen. The political and economic significance of Sulaco lies in the San Tomé silver mine, which Gould inherits from his father. One of a series of Costaguanan governments ("the fourth in six years") forced the elder Gould to take up the mine as a perpetual concession and to pay heavy duties on it. Ruined by what amounted to officially sanctioned extortion, he advised his son never to take up the Gould concession. But after his father's death, Charles becomes stubbornly idealistic in his belief that the wealth of the mine will necessarily improve Sulaco's standard of living in both economic and moral terms: "Only let the material interests once get a firm footing, and they are bound to impose the conditions on which alone they can continue to exist. . . . A better justice will come afterwards" (*N* 84). Gould's ultimately maniacal commitment to the mine resembles Nostromo's obsession with his reputation; each is eventually mastered by his own idealization.

While more remains to be said of Nostromo and Gould, Decoud's place in this pattern is more complex. Decoud undergoes the classic Conradian shift from spectator to actor when revolutionaries, who have seized control of the capital and the eastern part of the country, aim once again to capture the mine. As part of their forces approach by land, another part by sea, Gould chooses to load the semiannual shipment of silver on a lighter in order to save it for the financing of a separatist counterrevolution to be underwritten by his American backer, Holroyd. Decoud and Nostromo set out into the Golfo Placido, but their lighter collides with the transport of the incoming revolutionaries; the two men escape to one of the nearby Isabel islands, where they hide the silver. Since Decoud's newspaper editorials excoriating Montero, the invading revolutionary general, have made him a marked man, Nostromo returns to shore alone, leaving Decoud with provisions to await a more propitious time for return. After ten days in solitude, Decoud commits suicide.

The presentation of Decoud uneasily combines Conrad's conservative distrust of political ambition per se with a narrative celebrating the emergence of a commitment that is understood as more authentic. *A Tale of a Tub* and *Casablanca*, to pair two unlikely

works, suggest themselves as analogues: Swift satirically identifies frustrated sexual desire as the origin of military adventur-
ism, while in *Casablanca* an idealistic woman helps a cynical,
world-weary man break out of his skeptical pose and enter the
battle for the good. In the former, private motivation discredits
public actions; in the latter, it lays the foundation for them. In
Decoud both stories struggle to get told at once. "Blinded . . . to
the genuine impulses of his own nature," Decoud cannot acknowledge that his article on Costaguanan politics commis-
sioned by the *Parisian Review* bespeaks a patriotic commitment
that belies the "spirit of levity" in which it was conceived. Later,
even his sister is surprised at Decoud's "earnestness" in carrying
out a mission to buy new rifles for Sulaco (*N* 154). Yet the letter
from the small-arms committee arrives in the handwriting of Antonia Avellanos, and Decoud's decision to return to Sulaco with
the shipment is motivated, his sister surmises, by a desire to see
Antonia again. Once he has returned, all of Decoud's impas-
sioned speeches about Costaguana are uttered, as if elicited by
her disdain for his skepticism, in Antonia's presence, and his
love for her emerges most readily in the context of love for his
country.[12] Thus Decoud's claim to be subject to "no patriotic illusions" but "only the supreme illusion of a lover" is merely a
partial self-deception (*N* 189). He uses each commitment to
shield himself from the other, preferring to dismiss either, in bra-
vura displays of unconcern, as mere illusion.

Albert Guerard has lucidly described the problem that arises
from Decoud's presentation generally and his suicide in particular. Setting out to help Nostromo save the silver, Decoud remains an interesting figure of unresolved commitments. Yet the
narrator's harsh condemnation of Decoud before his death reduces the complexity of the character that has emerged as if in
defiance of the narrator's earlier disdain for him as an "idle bou-
levardier" whose assumed "cosmopolitanism" is "in reality a
mere barren indifferentism posing as intellectual superiority"
(*N* 152). "Conrad," Guerard suggests, "may be condemning Decoud for a withdrawal and skepticism more radical than Decoud
ever shows; which are, in fact, Conrad's own." Demonstrating
that there is "a marked discrepancy between what Decoud does
and says and is, and what the narrator or omniscient author says

about him," Guerard concludes that Conrad condemns by proxy his own tendency toward skeptical immobilization.[13] (I will return to Guerard's important hesitation between "narrator" and "omniscient author.") There is no doubt that Decoud is made a scapegoat for a radical skepticism that the narrator never relinquishes; but the manner of Decoud's expulsion demands closer attention.

Were it not for the brilliantly vivid rendering of the scene, with "the great waters spread out strangely smooth, as if their restlessness had been crushed by the weight of that dense night," the time Nostromo and Decoud spend on the gulf would read as a crude allegory of skepticism and faith (*N* 261).[14] Nostromo, whose family name is Fidanza, throws himself into the adventure with melodramatic intensity; he is utterly resolved to make it "the most famous and desperate affair of [his] life" (*N* 265). For Decoud, however, the sudden loss of familiar surroundings, or any discernible surroundings whatsoever, undermines, in a classic crisis of skepticism, his sense of the real: "All his active sensations and feelings from as far back as he could remember seemed to him the maddest of dreams. Even his passionate devotion to Antonia into which he had worked himself up out of the depths of his scepticism had lost all appearance of reality. For a moment he was the prey of an extremely languid but not unpleasant indifference" (*N* 267). The empty darkness recalls Jim's descent into the lifeboat from the decks of the *Patna*, and both scenes resemble the hypothetical realm of Dostoevsky's Grand Inquisitor, "a black cavern" of moral isolation where everything is permitted.[15] Nostromo's ardent belief in the importance of his own actions enables him to carry on; Decoud requires Nostromo's example and, more fundamentally, the immediacy of ordinary reality. Earlier, as he sits alone in Viola's café, Decoud is described as a "man with no faith in anything except the truth of his own sensations" (*N* 229). Yet skepticism does not prevent him from writing to his sister: "In the most sceptical heart there lurks at such moments, when the chances of existence are involved, a desire to leave a correct impression of the feelings, like a light by which the action may be seen when personality is gone, gone where no light of investigation can ever reach the truth which every death takes out of the world" (*N* 230). One thinks of Hume alone in his writing chamber, doubting even his sensations, and recognizing the need to turn to the anodyne of society. Faced with his own mortality, Decoud too experiences the limits of skepticism, not only by reaching out to his sister but also by affirming, in the absence of anything else, the "truth" of his own impressions. It is through Decoud, clearly, that skepticism first enters Conrad's fiction as an explicit theme, and in so doing, threatens to dominate the story through the philosophical and sometimes allegorical language that attends it.

For with Decoud's marooning on the Great Isabel, the narrative shifts into a more abstract discourse that examines Decoud as if he were a laboratory specimen. We might ask, in the manner of Joyce's "Ithaca" episode, of what did Decoud die? The narrator supplies several answers. "The truth was that he died from solitude" (*N* 496). Despite his mildly contemptuous attitude, Decoud admires, even envies, the power Nostromo commands, and Nostromo's absence in Decoud's prolonged period of crisis (Decoud knows he will be tortured and killed if captured by Montero) no doubt would unnerve him. But enough to cause suicide? The account presses us to believe that Decoud "was not fit to grapple with himself single-handed." Deprived of the reassurance found in "the sight of some human face, Decoud caught himself entertaining a doubt of his own individuality."[16] Consciousness seems to extinguish itself, and we are told that Decoud's individuality "merged into the world of cloud and water, of natural forces and forms of nature" (*N* 497). The case study, proceeding virtually day by day, then identifies Decoud's feeling of impotence—cosmic despair also registering faintly as sexual anxiety—as a contributing factor in his demise:

In our activity alone do we find the sustaining illusion of an independent existence as against the whole scheme of things of which we form a helpless part. Decoud lost all belief in the reality of his action past and to come. On the fifth day an immense melancholy descended upon him palpably. He resolved not to give himself up to these people in Sulaco, who had beset him, unreal and terrible, like jibbering and obscene spectres. He saw himself struggling feebly in their midst, and Antonia, gigantic and lovely like an allegorical statue, looking on with scornful eyes at his weakness. (*N* 497–98)

All the vivid particulars of the scene in the Golfo Placido have disappeared, leaving the allegorical scheme with only minimal embodiment in Antonia's statue: isolated from Faith, Skepticism dies and is scorned by Love. The abstraction here recalls Marlow's most philosophical moments in *Lord Jim*, but Marlow's sense of philosophical urgency—the *need* to know—has been replaced by the pressure of unmitigated and *knowing* irony. It is as if, to remain with the analogy, the kind of sympathy Marlow interposes between Jim and the anonymous narrator has broken down. Yet even the anonymous narrator in *Lord Jim* tempers his irony by showing glimpses of the world through Jim's eyes. Decoud's skeptic vision—the seemingly unmediated sensory impressions *evoked* as subjective experience for the reader in the earlier fiction—is now objectified from a removed perspective: "He beheld the universe as a succession of incomprehensible images" (*N* 498).

With the emergence of skepticism as both a dominant character trait and an explicit term in the narrative discourse, the treatment of Decoud modulates into the "observational and theoretical vocabulary" typical of "the natural and social sciences," a quality of attention P. F. Strawson cites as a consequence of moral skepticism.[17] As the abstract language lifts away from the imagined life of the character, the representation of Decoud's death no longer provides the kind of characterization and setting that nineteenth-century fiction teaches us to expect. Iris Murdoch's classic critique of the modern novel speaks to this issue: "Modern literature presents us with . . . the triumph of myth as a solipsistic form. . . . [W]e feel the ruthless subjection of the characters to the will of their author."[18] Murdoch probably does not pause, like Guerard, over the relation between author and narrator because her argument is concerned to chart broad developments in philosophy and the novel, not to analyze particular texts. Yet both sense the coercive presence of the author *in the text* as a problem. Guerard offers a speculative interpretation of the language describing Decoud's suicide as an authorial falsification or deformation of Decoud's presentation elsewhere. Murdoch argues that authorial intention intrudes itself in a coercive form as the imprisoning quality of the myth or moral fable that often underlies modern novels. Here one thinks of the first chapter of *Nostromo*, which recounts the legend of two *gringos* who die on Azuera, the rocky peninsula at the northern lip of the gulf, while searching for lost treasure. The ensuing narrative, for all its complications and characters, essentially fleshes out the scheme delineated by the introductory legend. The problem of the author's location in the text takes on a particular urgency in Decoud's suicide and, more generally, in the relationship between narrator and characters in both *Nostromo* and *The Secret Agent*.

The only author we can discuss with complete certainty in this context is what Bakhtin has called the "secondary author," "the image of the author" created within the text by the "primary" or historical author.[19] In opposition to formalist or structuralist approaches to narrative, Bakhtin's theory constitutes a poetics of utterance in which statements on all levels of fictional discourse are understood as refractions of authorial intention.[20] In the ideal of the polyphonic novel, each character embodies an autonomous perspective that carries the same authority as the discourse of the author; yet each character is at the same time determined by the all-encompassing intention of the author as realized in the design of the fiction. (The relationship between these individual centers of intentionality and the more pervasive authorial intention can be considered analogous to the subordination of individual wills to the metaphysical will in Schopenhauer.) If we attend to the competing voices within the fiction, authorial intention can only be divided against itself in a network of dialogic tensions. Yet these independent perspectives are combined (not merged) on a higher level as a unified multiplicity—polyphony—organized by the author.[21]

In this context we can understand Guerard's criticism of *Nostromo* and Murdoch's critique of the modern novel as responding to deviations from Bakhtin's ideal of the autonomy of perspectives in the polyphonic novel. The obtrusive sense of authorial coercion noted by Guerard and others represents the loss of Decoud's otherness in relation to the author, and he is consequently absorbed into the abstraction of a philosophical monologue that can be understood as an expression of the author's unified and dominant consciousness.[22] The merging of Decoud's individuality "into the world of cloud and water, of natural forces and forms of nature" can thus be read as a thematization of his reduction to the wholly objectified status of the austere natural scenery that

opens the novel. Murdoch's "solipsistic form" is the extreme
expression of Bakhtin's "monologic form."

In *Lord Jim* Conrad dramatizes a struggle to overcome solipsism: Marlow's effort "to know" Jim reveals what Murdoch (and
Bakhtin) considers "incomparably the most important thing" a
novel can reveal, namely, "that other people exist"—exist, that
is, independently of the author.[23] In Decoud's death, however,
the hardening of Conrad's moral skepticism into a form of imprisonment from which Decoud, unlike Jim, cannot escape suggests that without the mediation of a fully dramatized narrator,
Conrad tends toward heavy irony, as in "An Outpost of Progress," or philosophical monologue. Murdoch or Bakhtin very
likely would prefer *Lord Jim* to *Nostromo*, but an appreciation of
Nostromo does not require that one relinquish the values of freedom and autonomy they understandably embrace. For despite
the apparent fatalism of the narrative, *Nostromo*, like *Lord Jim*,
contains signs of resistance to authorial coercion. As in all of Conrad's best work, the slide into more radical forms of skepticism
elicits a response.

Resistance to skepticism in earlier Conrad can be found in the
visionary mode associated with Schopenhauerian contemplation. In these later novels the tension between skeptical and antiskeptical impulses is best approached from the standpoint of
character and ironic form. Some recent theories of fiction have
virtually dispensed with character altogether by bringing structure or textuality to the foreground. But this theoretical reorien-
tation does not answer to Murdoch's critique, since she does not
welcome the confluence of poetry and fiction that takes place in
the modern novel and would likely consider the dismantling of
character in critical theory symptomatic of the problem. The interest of *Nostromo* in this context derives from the way in which
it shows that one need not choose between the illusion of characters acting independently of their author, "the deconstruction
of character," or the reduction of character to "actant."[24] For, to
return to Decoud, once the author has, so to speak, condemned
and executed the marooned skeptic, the concrete language describing the moment of his death permits us to recuperate the
sense of authorial willfulness as the expression of a problem of
characterization that recurs throughout the novel.

Decoud, Hirsch, and Resisting the Machine

The language describing Decoud's fatal tenth day links him with Hirsch, the hide merchant from Esmeralda stranded in Sulaco by the revolution. To Decoud, in his last hours, "the solitude appeared like a great void, and the silence of the gulf like a tense, thin cord to which he hung suspended by both hands" (*N* 498). The cord clearly recalls Hirsch, who is tortured by strappado before being shot by Sotillo, the revolutionary commander whose troop transport struck the lighter.[25] Typically regarded only as an example of anti-Semitic stereotyping, Hirsch has a more complex role to play. During the rioting in town Hirsch hides himself in the lighter that Nostromo and Decoud take out into the Golfo Placido, and when it collides with the troop transport, he is swept off the lighter into Sotillo's vessel. Sotillo, unable to face the possibility that he has sunk the silver, refuses to believe Hirsch's garbled version of the plan to save the shipment and eventually shoots him in a fit of enraged frustration. But Hirsch is more than merely a victim of Sotillo's ferocious greed, and the significance of his connection with Decoud emerges from the bracketing of the account of his torture and death by a conversation between Monygham and Nostromo about victimization and responsibility.

Without Hirsch, as Gould later unwittingly acknowledges, the story could not advance as it does: "And but for him we might not have known anything of what has happened" (*N* 381). The development of the narrative, that is, *requires* the dissemination of Hirsch's misinformation. Nostromo comes upon Hirsch's still suspended body in the Custom House after awakening ashore to what seems to him the intolerable necessity of remaining incognito. Happening upon Nostromo, Monygham is shocked to find him alive because Hirsch's story of the collision has led him to believe, with Sotillo, that Nostromo and Decoud perished along with the silver. After discovering Hirsch's body, Monygham and Nostromo begin to discuss the fate of Sulaco while the corpse, described in lurid detail, dangles before them. When Nostromo, no longer trusting the Gould circle, allows Monygham to continue believing that both Decoud and the silver are lost, the narrative flashes back to the scenes culminating in Hirsch's death and then returns to their conversation.

We know from earlier scenes that Monygham has exploited Hirsch's unfortunate choice of hiding places by encouraging Sotillo's belief that the silver was never actually sent out into the gulf; the longer Sotillo searches for the silver, Monygham reasons, the more time there will be to seek help from the loyal forces of Barrios, whose troops remain many miles to the south in Cayta.[26] Nostromo, fiercely indignant that Monygham cares little for his recent heroics, is quick to point out Monygham's complicity in Hirsch's death: "if you had not confirmed Sotillo in his madness, he would have been in no haste to give the estrapade to that miserable Hirsch" (*N* 438). Confessing that he gave no thought to Hirsch's welfare, Monygham nevertheless tries to mitigate his responsibility with the claim that Hirsch was "doomed from the moment he caught hold of the anchor. . . . Just as I myself am doomed—most probably" (*N* 439). Monygham's characteristic equivocation opens out into the issue of freedom and determinism, and the entire conversation with Nostromo returns obsessively to the question of the individual's autonomy within networks of relationships lying beyond his control. To Monygham's bitter (and at this moment ruthless) mind, "the fate of Hirsch presented itself as part of the general atrocity of things," and the meaning of Hirsch's death must be understood in this larger context.

Surveying "the general atrocity of things" in the novel, or, to return to the language describing Decoud's death, "the whole scheme" of which some characters may "form a helpless part," we may be surprised to realize how many people suffer torture at the hands of a powerful oppressor: in the novel's "prehistory" Don José Avellanos, Monygham, and Sotillo's family are all tortured or persecuted by the dictator, Guzman Bento, and Gould's uncle is publicly executed by Bento; within the fictional present Gould is nearly executed by Montero, Monygham is nearly hanged by Sotillo, Hirsch is tortured and shot by Sotillo, and Decoud, hanging by his hands on a cord of silence, is tortured by . . . the author? As my own involved summaries may suggest, the narrative of *Nostromo* sometimes resembles, as it so often does in Dickens, a complicated machine. Hirsch, we could say, is both a crucial cog in the novel's narrative machinery and a victim of it. Could the same be said of Decoud? If so, we might expect to find thematizations of such an author-character relationship elsewhere, and we do, I suggest, in the struggles for autonomy enacted by Nostromo, Gould, and other characters. The example of Nostromo requires further attention.

When Monygham discovers Nostromo alive in the Custom House, he imagines that "Nostromo's return was providential. He did not think of him humanely, as of a fellow-creature just escaped from the jaws of death. The Capataz for him was the only possible messenger to Cayta" (N 431–32). Yet Nostromo, acutely conscious of himself as a mere instrument, is not so pleased with "providence." His sense of self has always depended on the audience for his theatrical self-displays, and the silver fiasco has both proved an unnecessarily risky bit of theater and deprived him of the public recognition he craves. (Conrad brilliantly evokes the sense in which Nostromo is both master of and mastered by his reputation at the end of Part One, where, encircled by a throng of eager admirers, Nostromo cuts the silver buttons off his coat to appease his lover's demand for a gift.) Sullen and resentful, Nostromo claims that the *blancos*—the aristocrats associated with Gould—have transformed him into "nothing." Though slow to accept responsibility for his own actions, Monygham does not hesitate to rebuke the capataz: "It was your place to think like a man" (N 456). Two issues underlie the entire dialogue: a tension between evasion and the assumption of responsibility (reminiscent of Jim after the *Patna* debacle) and a tension between Nostromo's angry feeling of personal inconsequence—"I am nothing"—and Monygham's response: "Not at all. You are everything" (N 457). The counterpoint here between "everything" and "nothing" recapitulates the implicit debate about the nature of the self articulated earlier by the chief engineer and Monygham. Although it may seem ironic for Monygham to take up the position he formerly challenged, the flipflop is merely apparent: for Monygham, Nostromo's self is simply a vessel to be filled or an object to be manipulated.

The mission to Cayta will provide Nostromo a means to recover his "personality," "the only thing lost in that desperate affair"; but before Monygham asks him to undertake this new risk, their conversation is interrupted by the story of Hirsch. A man caught up in forces greater than himself, Hirsch dies because he finally dares to assert himself by spitting in Sotillo's face, and the narrative lingers over the particulars of his torture for nearly a third of the chapter. Having witnessed Hirsch's death, we are then returned to Monygham and Nostromo, who have no idea why Hirsch was shot. Given the choice between "accepting the mission to Barrios, with all its dangers and difficulties, and leaving Sulaco by stealth, ingloriously, in poverty" (*N* 455), Nostromo chooses not to spit in Monygham's face. But neither does he immediately accept the commission. Instead, he vows to avenge Hirsch, a man for whom he has shown nothing but disdain, threatens to strangle Monygham, and runs impulsively out of the Custom House into the street. Understandably confused, Monygham chases after Nostromo; yet Monygham's pursuit (he is "beside himself with the fear of the man doing away with his usefulness") points toward the reason for Nostromo's erratic behavior. Though we cannot be sure that Nostromo recognizes Hirsch as an extreme version of his own helplessness, he clearly fears and despises Monygham as a man with seemingly demonic influence over the course of his life: "the king of the devils himself has sent you out of this town of cowards and talkers to meet me to-night of all the nights of my life." "The devil," Monygham responds, "has nothing to do with this," though Charles Gould, he implies, does (*N* 462).

In fact, no one has anything to do with the affair but Monygham, who has concealed his plan to stall Sotillo from all but Emilia Gould for fear that Charles would not permit Monygham to put his own life at risk. When a dangerous deed has needed doing, Nostromo has always been the preferred agent of Gould's will; but only Monygham knows that Nostromo survived the sinking of the lighter. Though Nostromo wants to meet with Gould, Monygham recoils from the idea of letting him head for the senior administrator's house, mainly because he fears for Nostromo's safety but also because his instinct is to keep Nostromo sealed off from the man who has controlled his fate from behind the scenes. At this moment Monygham is essentially taking over Gould's role as the man who "runs" Nostromo, and the charged intensity of the dialogue indicates that the relations between them embody a crucial narrative dynamic.

The gap between Gould and Nostromo can be understood, of course, as the "social space" that inevitably separates the aristocrat from the hired hero. If Monygham is to draw Nostromo into his clandestine plot to occupy Sotillo while Barrios is summoned, it is in his interest to preserve that separation. But on another level, Gould, the man who has directed Nostromo's adventures, can be considered Nostromo's "author," and it is therefore fitting that they not meet.[27] Before Monygham ventures out and happens upon Nostromo in the Custom House, "it was on the tip of Charles's tongue to say that only the late Capataz de Cargadores could have been employed with some chance of success" (N 409). Since Monygham's plan is designed to abet Gould in his monomaniacal commitment to the security of the mine, we can say that Monygham functions to mediate Gould's "authorial intentions."

Here Edward Said's argument that "the real action" underlying the "richly documented surface" of *Nostromo* "concerns man's overambitious intention to author his own world because the world as he finds it is somehow intolerable" converges with Bakhtin's understanding of the secondary author as the historical author's projection of his or her own image into the text.[28] Gould's efforts to bring order to Sulaco (which resemble Jim's labors in Patusan) provide the chief example of such authoring, and Nostromo is the heroic figure Gould needs to carry out the project he envisions. In *Lord Jim* we can see an authorial dilemma in Marlow's anxiety that his narration may not be true to Jim's experience: what if Jim comes to seem a puppet of Marlow's invention?[29] In Marlow's absence we begin to get at the problem from the other side: a character seems to rebel against an author who, like Monygham, orders his life without attending to him as a "fellow-creature." I do not mean to suggest that Nostromo is aware of himself as a character in a novel, though we can easily imagine him anticipating Razumov's defiant declaration to the narrator of *Under Western Eyes*: "I am not a young man in a novel" (*UWE* 185–86). (Like Nostromo, Razumov deeply resents that control of his life has passed out of his own hands.) Rather, when Monygham sees providence in Nostromo's return and Nostromo sees the devil, their responses can be read as expressions of the novel's problematic relationship between character and author.

On one level *Nostromo* dramatizes the individual's struggle for autonomy: Nostromo wishes to free himself from the increasingly restrictive demands of reputation; Gould seeks freedom from the graft and extortion of Costaguanan politics; virtually everyone else wants to escape from the cycle of revolutions. The pattern of concealed figures of power underwriting the apparently free actions of other characters or institutions extends throughout the novel: Holroyd, the American financier, stands behind Gould just as America stands behind the Sulacan republic and Gould stands behind Monygham and Nostromo. The irony of Nostromo's name, a corruption of the Italian for "our man," lies in the question of whose man he is, just as the title of the novel asks that question of all the characters within it.[30] Sometimes the analogy of author-character relationships is virtually forced on us through Conrad's narrative method, as when he hands the narration over to Captain Mitchell in Part Three, Chapter Ten. There the reader is drawn into the text through the figure of a visitor to Sulaco who is subjected to Mitchell's long-winded summing-up of events left hanging at the end of the previous chapter. To imagine Nostromo (or Decoud's ghost) overhearing the harangue, which transforms complex events into a newspaper's daily soap opera summary, is to get a sense of what motivates the rebellion of characters against categories of understanding imposed by others. When we associate these designs with the narrative design of the fiction itself, the tension between freedom and determinism can be understood as extending to the relationship between characters and figures who, like narrators and subordinate narrators, seem to refract the intentions of the author responsible for the fiction as a whole.

I have been referring so far to the "narrator" of *Nostromo*, but the term does not do justice to the complexities of the narrative voice. Just as the reader remains intermittently aware of Marlow as the instrument of Conrad's art, we sense different levels *within* the discourse of the narrator of *Nostromo*. The narrating voice has a literary or written style, and it is characterized by an omniscience that resists revealing itself as such. Sometimes characters pitch in to get the story told in the form of spoken summaries or a conveniently informative letter like Decoud's; more often we are told about people and events as if we already knew all about them or had already read the book. When the language of the narration bristles, as it often does, with Spanish phrases and allusions to local proverbs, it becomes a form of "stylization," a discourse oriented toward the native languages whose inflections and verbal texture it aims to imitate. At other moments the narrative voice sounds more like direct authorial discourse, a language oriented toward purely referential and communicative functions.[31] These modulations create the illusion of sometimes attending to the mediated voice of a narrator, sometimes to the voice of the author. Our sense of the author's presence, then, need not be located wholly in a particular authorial mouthpiece, whether a character or narrator, for it can register as a quality of the discourse of either.

In the midst of the rioting, for instance, as forces converge from various directions, we begin to detect the author presiding over the narrative machinery as if to reacquaint himself with the operations of his own invention.

The riot which [Fuentes] feared and expected broke out in less than an hour after Father Corbelàn had left him. Indeed, Father Corbelàn, who had appointed a meeting with Nostromo in the Dominican Convent, where he had his residence in one of the cells, never managed to reach the place. From the Intendencia he had gone straight on to the Avellanos's house to tell his brother-in-law, and though he stayed there no more than half an hour he had found himself cut off from his ascetic abode. Nostromo, after waiting there for some time, watching uneasily the increasing uproar in the street, had made his way to the offices of the *Porvenir*, and stayed there till daylight, as Decoud had mentioned in the letter to his sister. Thus the Capataz, instead of riding towards the Los Hatos woods as bearer of Hernandez's nomination, had remained in town to save the life of the President Dictator, to assist in repressing the outbreak of the mob, and at last to sail out with the silver of the mine.

But Father Corbelàn, escaping to Hernandez, had the document in his pocket, a piece of official writing turning a bandit into a general in a memorable last official act of the Ribierist party, whose watchwords were honesty, peace, and progress. Probably neither the priest nor the bandit saw the irony in it. (*N* 352–53)

The complexity of the narrative line is such that the paths of characters often require a good deal of supervision. Here a discursive strain is obliquely acknowledged in the allusion to Decoud's highly improbable letter, which to a large extent functions to tie up Conrad's loose ends. Had Conrad foreseen the principle of omission later established by Joyce, he would have worked out the minutiae of comings and goings only to suppress them; as it is, he seems intent on displaying the meticulous connections that Joyce only refers to coyly: "See?" Leopold Bloom remarks. "It all works out."[32] Conrad's summaries in the second part of the novel contrast with the confusing series of chronological dislocations and rapid juxtapositions of the first part; montage coalesces into the fullness of a panoramic perspective. Yet these methods are complementary: the reader is struck in the first part by the absence of conventional ordering and in the next two by frequent efforts to recover moments of coherence. In the first part the author, like the absolute for which Conrad's stories always yearn, is conspicuous through his absence. In the extended passage quoted earlier, we sense the author hovering over the scene like the God whose eye cannot penetrate the "blind darkness" of the first chapter.

In the telling of Decoud's death, when the character is "sentenced" and the reader harangued, the officiousness of the speaker, always a little too quick to point a moral or underline an irony, modulates into a coercive authorial presence. Identical verbal formulas lock Decoud and Nostromo into the moral scheme prefigured by the first chapter:

> A victim of the disillusioned weariness which is the retribution meted out to intellectual audacity, the brilliant Don Martin Decoud, weighted by the bars of San Tomé silver, disappeared without a trace, swallowed up in the immense indifference of things.
> . . . .
> The magnificent Capataz de Cargadores, victim of the disenchanted vanity which is the reward of audacious action, sat in the weary pose of a hunted outcast through a night of sleeplessness as tormenting as any known to Decoud, his companion in the most desperate affair of his life. (*N* 501–2)

Decoud and Nostromo are indeed victims, but not of weariness or vanity as much as of the rigidity of the author's moral fable. This is not a case of catching Conrad out. For the verbal and structural connections I have been tracing between Decoud's suicide and Hirsch's murder suggest the author's *awareness* of the extent to which the narrative machinery of *Nostromo* may exist in order to torture its characters. Conrad's vision of life will not permit him to create a fictional world in which characters can triumph over external forces of determination, whether history, economics, or the brutality of a dictator.[33] But Decoud's suicide brings to the foreground the sense in which *any* character in fiction is simultaneously free and utterly determined. Making the text turn back on itself, Conrad criticizes his own complicity in the many instances of torture his text recounts, and this reflexive commentary saves the story from becoming reductively fatalistic or even sadistic.

It is not enough, then, to say that Conrad performs an exorcism of authorial skepticism. True to Conrad's larger vision, the individual's attempt to create his own reality in *Nostromo* is always defeated by a narrative that will not accommodate itself to that individual's needs. But by making us see such determinism as *an extension of authorial intention*, Decoud's "execution" reveals what amounts to a confession of the author's responsibility for the fate of his characters. "A writer of imaginative prose," in the words of *A Personal Record*, "stands confessed in his work. His conscience, his deeper sense of things, lawful and unlawful, gives him his attitude before the world" (*PR* 95).

Edward Said cites Conrad's letter to Graham about the self-evolved knitting machine as evidence that Conrad saw himself as another figure in the chain of would-be authors who are themselves authored. If all authority for Conrad lies outside the self, then Conrad too, according to Said, must in some sense disclaim responsibility for the "knitting" of his own texts. Said thus gives Conrad's letter something like the status of Milton's invocations to *Paradise Lost*. If the muse, unbidden, nightly visits the poet in order to dictate his "unpremeditated" verse, so "Conrad, life's harried agent himself authored by life," allows life to author *Nostromo* through him.[34]

A writer for whom writing was "the conversion of nervous force into phrases," Conrad clearly was aware of the involuntary dimension of his own fiction.[35] And, like many thinkers, he no doubt was inclined to objectify his own unconscious compulsions as a vision of metaphysical necessity. But if my understanding of the Hirsch connection has any validity, Decoud's suicide suggests that the author of *Nostromo* is more willing to assume full authority for his fiction than the author of the letter Said cites. (Though I would not argue for a revolution in Conrad's world-view, a period of seven years or more separates *Nostromo* and *A Personal Record* from the letter to Graham.) Hirsch's final defiance of Sotillo and Nostromo's hostility toward Monygham, in this reading, represent acts of rebellion against the coercion of at-tempts to transform them into instruments of another's will, and the resistance to being caught up in "the general atrocity of things" can be taken as a figure for resistance to the intentions governing the construction of the fiction as a whole.[36] "Authorial intention" in this sense is divided against itself in a dialogic struc-ture dominated by the tension between a desire for autonomy and a determinism produced by deep moral skepticism. This point may become clearer if *Nostromo* is compared with *The Secret Agent*.

Skeptic Comedy and the Coercion of Character

Much more so than in *Nostromo*, characters in *The Secret Agent* often seem ruthlessly subjected to the author's will, and the coer-civeness of that will must be separated into the events of the nar-rative and the manner of their narration. Setting aside for the mo-ment the discourse of the narrator, I will turn first to the narrative logic of Winnie's suicide, which has been cited as an analogue of the gratuitous dispatching of Decoud.[37] The severe irony govern-ing narrative development in *The Secret Agent*, like the ironic per-spective of the narrator, derives from a moral skepticism that transforms black comedy into what can be called the comedy of skepticism.

As in "Heart of Darkness," the narrative of *The Secret Agent* constitutes a gradual revelation of the intolerable within the be-nign. Here cannibalism, often suspected as Kurtz's "unspeakable rites," becomes a more explicit metaphor for the horror concealed behind perceptions conditioned by convention. Karl Yundt, one of the anarchists in Adolf Verloc's circle, condemns capitalism within earshot of Stevie, Winnie Verloc's retarded younger brother: "Do you know how I would call the nature of the present economic conditions? I would call it cannibalistic. That's what it is! They are nourishing their greed on the quivering flesh and the warm blood of the people—nothing else" (SA 51). Late that night, when Verloc comes upon Stevie "gesticulating and murmuring in the kitchen," he heads upstairs to alert his wife, and for the first time he thinks about Stevie and his wife's mother, who also lives in the house, as two more bodies "to provide for" (SA 55). Verloc has just returned from his interview with Mr. Vladimir, whose insistent demand for a series of outrages must be met if Verloc is to keep his job as an agent provocateur. It is in part this economic pressure that induces Verloc to send Stevie on his ill-fated mission to blow up Greenwich Observatory, where the Professor's bomb reduces him to "what might have been an accumulation of raw material for a cannibal feast" (SA 86). A few pages later, as Inspector Heat examines Stevie's remains, Conrad pushes the grotesquerie further: "the Chief Inspector went on peering at the table with a calm face and the slightly anxious attention of an indigent customer bending over what may be called the by-products of a butcher's shop with a view to an inexpensive Sunday dinner."

In my summary the story takes on the aspect of a belabored and macabre joke. But in Conrad's handling cannibalism takes on the status of what Frank Kermode has called a narrative secret, a hidden story or pattern whose significance emerges only when the story is retold in order to draw together and reorder details whose connection might otherwise pass unnoticed.[38] Winnie's gradual recognition that it was Stevie who died in the explosion mirrors the reader's, for Conrad's manipulation of narrative chronology withholds the full meaning of "the thing" first mentioned in Chapter Four until Chapter Nine, where Winnie, "carving knife and fork in hand," is told by her husband, "you know you can trust me" (SA 192–93). We learn at the end of Chapter Two that Winnie almost married a young butcher, but, as we discover still later, there was not enough "room" in his "boat" for Stevie. For the security of her mother and brother she eventually married Verloc, whose "barque seemed a roomy craft" (SA 243). In a grim suggestion of malignant fatality, Verloc, who happened to be rooming in their boarding house, turns out to be more like her first suitor than she ever could have imagined. As the word "butcher" slides from a benign designation of livelihood to a gruesomely sardonic perspective on Stevie's death, the "clearly providential" nature of Verloc's availability recalls and amplifies the irony latent in Monygham's perception of providence in Nostromo's unexpected appearance in the Custom House.

Winnie's discovery of Verloc's failed plot is a shock that shatters her complacent assumption that her husband would at least be a good provider, and it confirms her suspicion that "things do not stand much looking into" (*SA* 177). The closer one looks "into" things in *The Secret Agent* (just as Heat looks closely into Stevie's remains), the more one finds that "inside" the shell of social, political, and familial conventions lurks one horror after another. Though in "Heart of Darkness" the "hidden" remains more mysterious—the "unspeakable" remains just that, available to the reader only in the ambiguity of Kurtz's last words—the narrative logic in both texts depends on the opposition of inside and outside, surface and depth. But in *The Secret Agent* the narrative does not build toward moments of Schopenhauerian vision. No longer charged with the mysterious promise of total knowledge, the inside is less a sanctum than an emptiness guarded by repression, a kind of fold or pocket in the social fabric.

In this logic we see Conrad at his most Swiftian. One thinks of the more distinctly satiric use of cannibalism in "A Modest Proposal," but *A Tale of a Tub* once again suggests a clearer parallel. "Happiness," writes the Grub Street Hack, "is a perpetual possession of being well deceived."[39] The world is peopled by fools, those who remain secure in their delusions, and knaves, those who insist on "unmasking" the underlying horror. The hack writer seems at first to prefer the fool's existence: "so far preferable is that wisdom, which converses about the surface, to that pretended philosophy which enters into the depth of things, and then comes gravely back with informations and discoveries, that in the inside they are good for nothing." Insight requires violence: if surfaces do not satisfy, "then comes reason officiously with tools for cutting, and opening, and mangling, and piercing, offering to demonstrate, that they are not of the same consistence quite through." The ambivalence is apparent already; neither choice will suffice. But Swift gives the argument a few more turns. Lest the reader rest easy with what came to be the Romantic commonplace that "we murder to dissect," the hack condemns analysis of the inside as "the last degree of perverting nature," only to assert in a sudden rhetorical pirouette that "reason is certainly in the right, and that in most corporeal beings, which have fallen under my cognizance, the outside hath been infinitely preferable to the in." The movement of the sentence forces one to experience the impossibility of choosing.[40] We expect that if reason is right, the inside should be preferred, but in the famous anatomizing of the "carcass of a beau" (an ancestor of Stevie?), reason is again literalized as a form of murderous dissection. The categories of fool and knave are irreconcilable, irreducible, and inclusive.

Winnie Verloc, whose "philosophy consisted in not taking notice of the inside of facts" (SA 154), is, as Swift would have it, in "the serene peaceful state of being a fool among knaves" until Stevie's death unmasks her husband. The logic of Conrad's narrative offers no other place for her: "She did not see any alternative between screaming and silence, and instinctively she chose the silence" (SA 246). Once Ossipon's betrayal harshly renews the lesson of the world's knavishness, she can escape from the governing categories of fool and knave only through suicide. Formerly a fool, Ossipon the knave is, at book's end, left paralyzed by passage from one state to the other.

What drops out of this summary is the overbearing presence of the narrator, whose harsh ironies at the characters' expense generally exceed those in *Nostromo*. The ironic treatment of character in *The Secret Agent* has drawn considerable critical attention.[41] Conrad wrote to Marguerite Poradowska that he was fond of *The Secret Agent* "because I think that in it I managed to treat what is after all a melodramatic subject by the method of irony."[42] This irony is usually well controlled, as in the description of Verloc's walk to the embassy that begins Chapter Two: "It was unusually early for him; his whole person exhaled the charm of almost dewy freshness; he wore his blue cloth overcoat unbuttoned; his boots were shiny; his cheeks, freshly shaven, had a sort of gloss, and even his heavy-lidded eyes, refreshed by a night of peaceful slumber, sent out glances of comparative alertness" (SA 11). The light humor of the sentence is of a piece with the rest of the long passage from which it is excerpted. But in other places, as in the description of Karl Yundt, irony verges on vituperation and revulsion: "His worn-out passion, resembling in its impotent fierceness the excitement of a senile sensualist, was badly served by a dried throat and toothless gums which seemed to catch the tip of his tongue" (*SA* 43). Irving Howe was the first to argue that in the absence of anyone to admire in the sordid world of *The Secret Agent*, the novel lacks "a moral positive to serve literary ends."[43] Clearly the sustained ironic treatment implies a range of unstated moral criteria that are necessary to make sense of the ironies, but Howe and others would like to see this moral awareness located in the characters. The technical virtuosity of Conrad's ironic method parts company with the moral imagination as embodied in character.[44]

I confess that I am one of those readers ready to find redeeming value in the technical brilliance and intellectual rigor of *The Secret Agent*, even as I am inclined to recoil from the tensely controlled fury and indignation that informs it at every point. The text holds, one could say, the "fascination of the abomination" (*HD* 50). The comic control of *Typhoon* becomes in *The Secret Agent* a rage for order that finds explicit thematic expression when Vladimir bullies Verloc into the Greenwich Observatory bombing in order to induce a police crackdown on anarchist activity. The order remains a comic one, but it is far blacker than in *Typhoon*.

Characters in *The Secret Agent* resist the imposition of an oppressive order only in the resentment and indignation that dominate their emotional lives. Verloc's delayed response to Vladimir when speaking with Winnie brings out the violence latent in these tensions: "If I hadn't thought of you I would have taken the bullying brute by the throat and rammed his head into the fireplace" (*SA* 239). Vladimir himself descends "from generations victimized by the instruments of an arbitrary power" (*SA* 224). But the Assistant Commissioner, whose consciousness is more comprehensive than any other in the novel, brings out most distinctly the nature of the dynamic I have located in Hirsch: " 'Here I am stuck in a litter of paper,' he reflected, with unreasonable resentment, 'supposed to hold all the threads in my hands, and yet I can but hold what is put in my hand, and nothing else. And they can fasten the other ends of the threads where they please' " (*SA* 115). Not quite a puppet, the Assistant Commissioner nevertheless resents not having the power to be the puppeteer. The "unreasonableness" of the resentment locates the moment as a node in the text's crosscurrents of rebellious energy: no character in *The Secret Agent* is ever allowed to hold all the strings. Inspector Heat, though initially more in the know than the Assistant Commissioner and consequently less frustrated, shares "the dislike of being compelled by events." An encounter with the Professor, whom Heat knows is wired as a human bomb, irritates him because it did not leave him with that "satisfactory sense of superiority the members of the police force get from the unofficial but intimate side of their intercourse with the criminal classes, by which the vanity of power is soothed, and the vulgar love of domination over our fellow-creatures is flattered as worthily as it deserves" (*SA* 122). Whereas characters in *Nostromo* struggle to preserve their autonomy by resisting the tendency to become dominated by a monological order, the author of *The Secret Agent* remains unconcerned with his apparent implication in "the vulgar love of domination."

In consequence, his discourse approaches—from the point of view of the characters, primarily, but from our own as well—what Bakhtin has called authoritative discourse, a language that "demands that we acknowledge it, that we make our own; it binds us, quite independent of any power it might have to persuade us internally." Bakhtin's love of terminology induces him to oppose the "internally persuasive" to the authoritative, yet we can recognize the familiar distinction between the monologic and the fundamentally dialogic, in which every word is "half-ours and half-someone else's." Translated into the relationship between author and character, an orientation toward internally persuasive discourse requires that "the author's discourse about a character [be] organized about *someone actually present*, someone who hears him (the author) and is *capable of answering him*." Characters in Conrad frequently lack the capacity to respond directly to one another, let alone to the author. Nostromo, like Jim, is very often, as Bakhtin would have it, "the mute, voiceless object" of another's words, but in both novels a dialogic tension remains, whether in Marlow's acknowledgment of Jim's essential otherness or in the confessional and rebellious dimensions I have mapped out in *Nostromo*.[45] Characters talk past one another more dramatically in *The Secret Agent* (consider Winnie's last scene with

Verloc, or her ensuing conversation with Ossipon), and the sense of inevitably crossed purposes is compounded in the implied domination of character by author.

For the skeptic voice of *The Secret Agent* establishes an authoritative perspective on characters as wind-up toys capable of expressing only the thoughts programmed into them by the author. Although the London they inhabit is one of dissolving boundaries and disturbing metamorphoses,[46] the exchanges between narrator and character form, as it were, a one-way street. Near the middle of the text an appropriation of the characters' language by the narrator underlines the sense in which the author may listen, but characters are denied the capacity to respond. After Sir Ethelred mentions to the Assistant Commissioner his "Bill for the Nationalization of Fisheries," the Assistant Commissioner is described as "a queer foreign fish" and the city streets as "a slimy aquarium from which the water had been run off" (*SA* 145, 147). The foreignness of the Assistant Commissioner's appearance receives more attention a few pages later when he enters an Italian restaurant and surveys the bland homogeneity of its patrons:

These people were as denationalized as the dishes set before them with every circumstance of unstamped respectability. Neither was their personality stamped in any way, professionally, socially, or racially. They seemed created for the Italian restaurant, unless the Italian restaurant had been perchance created for them. But that last hypothesis was unthinkable, since one could not place them anywhere outside those special establishments. (*SA* 149)

England and its representative Sir Ethelred seem to conspire "to nationalize" or assimilate fish, food, and people alike into a tightly controlled and lifeless order.[47] Even the cooking is "fraudulent." The Assistant Commissioner's foreign difference momentarily sets him apart from the others in the restaurant, yet the fish imagery, which recurs in later pages, tends to reassert control over him and pull him into the "unconscious stream of people on the pavements" (*SA* 63). The fact that the Assistant Commissioner experiences a sense of "evil freedom" (*SA* 148) after leaving his desk work to pursue Verloc only heightens the discrepancy between the characters' lack of self-awareness and the more comprehensive, authoritative perspective established by the narrative voice.[48] As verbal patterning draws our attention to the whir of narrative machinery operating beyond the characters' awareness, our understanding of the characters may become analogous to the Assistant Commissioner's attitude toward those in the restaurant: we see them as created for the story, unless the story has been created perchance for the characters, though one could not place them anywhere outside those special establishments.

Only Stevie actively resists the complacency of the established order in *The Secret Agent*. When Winnie and Stevie take their mother to a retirement home as if in "the Cab of Death itself," Winnie's cynical account of the police as oppressors of the poor upsets Stevie because "he had formed for himself an ideal conception of the metropolitan police as a sort of benevolent institution for the suppression of evil" (*SA* 172). He refuses at first to ride in the cab out of compassion for the emaciated horse, and after the cabman has forced on him a sense of the "close association" of "human and equine misery," Stevie utters the sad truth that it is a "bad world for poor people" (*SA* 171). But Conrad deals harshly with Stevie's compassion. Although the narrative provides lines of crossed purposes to account for the destruction of Stevie, the verbal patterning of the text also suggests that his dismemberment literalizes the "magnanimous indignation [that] swelled his chest to bursting" (*SA* 169). Stevie's death also literalizes the moral disintegration found in Verloc's disregard for Stevie's safety and in his subsequent response to the accident: "Stevie had stumbled within five minutes of being left to himself. And Mr. Verloc was shaken morally to pieces" (*SA* 230). What may be called a violence of thematization—the sense that the author violently processes characters into expressions of theme—recurs in Verloc's death when, after Winnie stabs him, his dripping blood, ticking "fast and furious like the pulse of an insane clock," is cruelly transmuted into an expression of the text's recurrent concern with time (*SA* 265).[49] Winnie's grotesque vision of Stevie's death, moreover, reads both as a confused recollection of his misadventures in a staircase with some catherine wheels and as a transformation of Stevie into an emblem of his characteristic response to "tales of injustice and oppression" (*SA* 9): she sees "smashed branches, torn leaves, gravel, bits of brotherly flesh and bone, all spouting up together in the manner of a firework. . . . where after a rainlike fall of mangled limbs the decapitated head of Stevie lingered suspended alone . . . like the last star of a pyrotechnic display" (*SA* 260). Since Stevie suffers the most gruesome of the three deaths in the novel, we may surmise that it was unwise of him to rebel against the morally suspect institutions the author constructed around him.[50]

Challenging the autonomy of character, the attack on the body in *The Secret Agent* may also represent a perverse expression of Conrad's longing for a form of rationality that does not (as Decoud's does) consume its own order in skeptical dissolution. Skeptic discourse requires the myth of the body as separating in order to account for the fact of our separation, even though it is not the body that shields one mind from another but consciousness itself.[51] Thus an impatience with the process of inference from empirical evidence produces Sterne's fantasy in *Tristram Shandy* of the body with a window to its inner workings. The desire for a *purely* rational world, one in which buildings do not seem to wander from their proper addresses or words (like Marlow's "wretched cur") do not stick to the wrong object, must inevitably do greater damage to the body. (Compare the inscription of the law directly onto the body in *The Penal Colony* or the suffering human figures within the rigorously mapped Aristotelian structure of Dante's hell.) Violence against the body in *The Secret Agent* may be related to the proliferation of seemingly inexplicable geometric details associated with Verloc, whose code name appears in the text as a triangle, and Stevie, who obsessively scrawls "circles, circles, circles; innumerable circles, concentric, eccentric; a coruscating whirl of circles" (*SA* 45). Such details often surface in descriptions of the London scene too: Winnie's cry that Verloc "was a devil" seems "lost as if in a triangular well of asphalt and bricks, of blind houses and unfeeling stones" (*SA* 276). Given Conrad's fascination with anarchy, it is perhaps inevitable that geometric precision is also persistently shadowed by the impossibility of rational order, just as the "repeated curves, uniformity of form, and confusion of intersecting lines" mapped by Stevie's circles suggest "a rendering of cosmic chaos." The play between geometry and chaos recalls Nietzsche's remark that "among philosophers as well as artists, one finds a passionate and exaggerated worship of 'pure forms': let no one doubt that he who *needs* the cult of surfaces to that extent has at some time or other made a calamitous attempt to get *beneath* them."[52] Stevie and Verloc look beneath the familiar only near the end of their lives, but Winnie's widely shared inclination not to look too deeply into things must be read against Conrad's insistent suggestion that he himself has.

As it does violence to the body, Conrad's desire for order in *The Secret Agent* also transforms the status of character. Although the narrator often dips into a character's mind to discuss his or her motivation, verbal patterning, along with the abstract commentary of the narrator, comes to supplant the kind of characterization found in the traditional novel. If we pursue character analysis, the apparent arbitrariness of Winnie's collapse into fear after murdering Verloc may be understood as a version of the monomania rampant in Conrad's fiction. Winnie's fixed idea is the sheltering of Stevie, and when the deaths of Stevie and Verloc free her for the first time in her life, rather than becoming an independent agent, she fills her inner void with fears of retribution. When Ossipon comes on the scene, she simply clings to him as her new object of devotion and begins to consider the possibility of escape. One might argue further that such behavior makes sense as the typical response of an unexpectedly widowed or divorced woman who has never been independent.

But the text does not really solicit a naturalistic motivation for Winnie's behavior. She has been presented from the start as a somnambulist, and the most important act of her life, the murder of her husband, is described in utterly nonnaturalistic terms: "Mr. Verloc heard the creaky plank in the floor, and was content. He waited. Mrs. Verloc was coming. As if the homeless soul of Stevie had flown for shelter straight to the breast of his sister, guardian, and protector, the resemblance of her face with that of her brother grew at every step, even to the droop of the lower lip, even to the slight divergence of the eyes" (*SA* 262). The passage inscribes Winnie into the pattern of explosive overreaction exemplified in Stevie, for whom "the anguish of immoderate compassion was succeeded by the pain of an innocent but pitiless rage" (*SA* 169); Stevie's response has become Winnie's. If metempsychosis is difficult to accept as a motive, we could read this as a parody of a certain kind of sentimental writing.[53] Or, given that Ossipon later (*after* discovering Winnie has murdered Verloc) meditates on "the fact of that resemblance" (*SA* 298), perhaps we should simply read the passage as the expression of emotional affinities between brother and sister that later heighten Ossipon's sensitivity to overlooked physical similarities. But rather than trying to preserve the authority of an earlier fictional paradigm, we should focus on the interesting way in which the passage hovers between naturalistic illusion and the purely textual. Responding to Winnie's elliptical allusion to her murder of Verloc, Ossipon figures the response of the reader: "There were suggestions of triumph, relief, gratitude in the indefinable tone of these words. It engrossed the whole attention of Ossipon to the detriment of mere literal sense" (*SA* 277).

Winnie's mind has always been dominated by a single concern—whether Stevie, Ossipon, or, when she looks into "the very bottom of this thing," "the gallows" (*SA* 267)—and so the entry of Stevie's soul into her body suggests, like Monygham's manipulation of Nostromo, the filling of an empty vessel. Resonating with the language of disembodied souls elsewhere in *The Secret Agent*, the trope of possession establishes a network of narrative secrets that points, I suggest, toward the absent presence of the author who supervises the kind of Conradian transmigrations that also figure prominently in *Nostromo*. First, more examples from *The Secret Agent*.

The only true author in *The Secret Agent* (aside from Ossipon, who is only a pamphleteer) is Michaelis, who spends night and day writing his "Autobiography of a Prisoner." Michaelis pours himself into the project because it allows him "the liberation of his inner life, the letting out of his soul into the wide world" (*SA* 120). The trope describing Michaelis's self-expression picks up the language of disembodied souls and can be read as reflexive commentary on the idea of authorship implicit in the text.[54] Indeed, his self-engrossment resembles the narrator's monologic indifference to the fate of the characters: "Michaelis pursued his idea. . . . He talked to himself, indifferent to the sympathy or hostility of his hearers, indifferent indeed to their presence" (*SA* 44). In the Author's Note to *The Secret Agent* Conrad defends the book by claiming that "there was no perverse intention, no secret scorn for the natural sensibilities of mankind at the bottom of my impulses" (*SA* viii). A reader of the resulting text may well quarrel with Conrad's reconstruction of his intentions; their realization, in any case, is quite often perverse in the sense of being deeply misanthropic. Judging from the recurrent concerns of the Note, Conrad too, when rereading *The Secret Agent* after thirteen years, may have had misgivings: "I confess that it makes a grisly skeleton. But still I will submit that . . . I have not intended to commit a gratuitous outrage on the feelings of mankind" (*SA* xv). When Winnie wishes to set right an ill-considered outburst against Verloc, the narrator attributes her threat to "the demon of perverse inspiration" (*SA* 196). Although "perverse" here primarily means "contrary," the expression also picks up the language of the Author's Note and anticipates the translation of Stevie's soul into Winnie when the inspiration to murder Verloc fully possesses her.

Conrad often described his own creation of a fictional world in language that closely resembles the account of Michaelis's authorship. As implied in "Karain" and *Lord Jim*, the trope of incarnation is basic to Conrad's understanding of artistic realization: "I write very little, but inspiration comes to me in looking at the paper. Then there are soaring flights; my thought goes wandering through vast spaces filled with shadowy forms. All is yet chaos, but, slowly, the apparitions change into living flesh, the shimmering mists take shape, and—who knows?—something may be born of the clash of nebulous ideas."[55] From vapor to living flesh, the idea clothes itself as a living character, and a fictional world is set in motion. Although it is impossible to offer conclusive substantiation for issues extending beyond the fictional frame,[56] I believe that Conrad's writing as a whole legitimates my claim that the imagery of disembodied souls in *The Secret Agent* and *Nostromo* traces the circulation of authorial intentions. In this argument, Conrad's presence in the text—Bakhtin's secondary author—is not limited to incarnated figures for the writer.

In *The Secret Agent* wandering souls are hard-pressed to find a human body to enter, and from the mechanical quality of the characters Conrad derives a good deal of Bergsonian comedy.

When Winnie, in shock from the revelation of Stevie's gruesome death, suddenly stands up "as if raised by a spring," her husband remarks uneasily, "you're looking more like yourself" (*SA* 251). The arbitrary and mechanical in Winnie's behavior is more explicit in Verloc when, just after his return from the botched bombing, Winnie asks him to answer the door: "Mr. Verloc obeyed woodenly, stony-eyed, and like an automaton whose face had been painted red. And this resemblance to a mechanical figure went so far that he had an automaton's absurd air of being aware of the machinery inside of him" (*SA* 197). Most of the characters in *The Secret Agent* are more or less self-conscious robots, ghosts in machines, and the cruel edge of the comedy sometimes draws a smile that may as quickly become a grimace. During the prolonged conversation preceding Verloc's stabbing, the narrator resolutely ignores the emotional charge of the scene as Verloc tries ineptly to console his wife. Rendered from a perspective unflinchingly removed from human emotions, the couple's nervous movements around the room become comic spectacle: "It all had the appearance of a struggle for the possession of a chair, because Mr. Verloc instantly took his wife's place in it" (*SA* 234–35). The sentence resonates nicely with the implication in the first chapter that Verloc, who "took over" Winnie's mother "with the furniture," is the type of man who, in the absence of a chair, might absentmindedly sit on his mother-in-law.

Reducing the human to the mechanical, the comedy of moral skepticism can be understood in its place both as a classic issue of skepticism and as an expression of Conrad's cultural moment. One form that the philosophical discussion of other minds often takes is the problem of articulating how one could distinguish a self-conscious automaton from a human being.[57] As early as the mid-eighteenth century La Mettrie, inspired by Descartes's hypothesis of the animal as machine, championed the idea of the man-machine. Though it was inevitable that "what Descartes said of animals would one day be said of man,"[58] during the early nineteenth century the idea's heretical appeal to Enlightenment rationalism was eclipsed by the ascendancy of philosophical idealism and the Romantic valorization of introspection and the organic. The problem of other minds, which now may seem a purely academic discussion (of the "who cares?" variety), began to take on urgency later in the nineteenth century in the wake of the redefinitions of consciousness sparked by physiological psychology, Darwinian biology, and renewed interest in philosophical materialism.[59] By 1894 T. H. Huxley could write of three proto-Darwinian essays he first published thirty-two years earlier: "most of the conclusions . . . are now to be met with among other well-established and, indeed, elementary truths, in the text-books."[60] And in 1874 Huxley voiced a thought to which *The Secret Agent* may now seem a monument: "We are conscious automata."[61] As the twentieth century draws to a close we can expect to see Huxley's slogan recirculated in debates about computer simulations of human consciousness or "artificial intelligence."

With the boundaries between men, machines, and animals eroding, the concept of the soul becomes increasingly important to those invested in preserving man's privileged position in the world.[62] In this context Conrad's language of disembodied souls registers as a response to the prominence of the mechanical in the second machine age and as a shadow of resistance to the effacement of the newly dubious category of "the human."[63] (Even the description of the writing process Conrad sent to H. G. Wells, "the conversion of nervous force into phrases," presents the human under the aspect of mechanical physics.) Ironically, what may be called the soul of authorial intentions in *The Secret Agent* has the effect of dehumanizing the human by turning the ghost in the machine into the specter of the mechanical.[64]

In *Nostromo*, as in *The Secret Agent*, tropes of embodiment and disembodiment come to the foreground in moments of crucial decision. In *Nostromo*, however, characters are less inclined to acquiesce easily to the manipulations of the author whose intentions "take possession" of them.

Supernatural Naturalism

The legend of two "tenacious *gringo* ghosts" who "cannot tear themselves away from their bodies" in *Nostromo* anticipates Joyce's ironic use of the *Odyssey* in *Ulysses*. Yet there is an important difference between the status of these subtexts. Even though we may know that Leopold Bloom must return home in order to sustain the Homeric parallel, we do not normally think of him as *compelled* to do so. In *Nostromo*, however, the underlying legend is present to the minds of the characters, especially to Nostromo, who thinks of it as having the power of a curse he must resist: "There is something in a treasure that fastens upon a man's mind," he tells Monygham. "Doctor, did you ever hear of the miserable gringos on Azuera, that cannot die? Ha! ha! Sailors like myself" (*N* 460). Although the language of curses, possession, and the supernatural appears throughout the story, very little critical commentary acknowledges it.[65] Some instances, such as the fear that Monygham has "the evil eye" or the description of Emilia Gould as a "good fairy," seem at first relatively inconsequential. Yet the patterns established by Gould and Nostromo encourage an antithetical reading of what otherwise would remain of no consequence.

If life for Decoud is not "a moral romance derived from the tradition of a pretty fairy tale" (*N* 218), *Nostromo* may be read as just such a confluence.[66] Charles Gould's father describes the Gould Concession as a "curse" and implores his son never to return to Costaguana. Charles nevertheless falls under "the spell" of the mine, though his is "another form of enchantment," an idealistic fervor which demands that the "absurd moral disaster" of his father be transformed into "a serious and moral success" (*N* 59, 66). Charles's excessive devotion to the mine ultimately transforms him into a "stony fiend of a man" (*N* 403). Nostromo's curse descends not from his father but from his adopted mother, Teresa Viola, whose dying request for a priest he refuses in order to save the silver with Decoud. (Characters in Conrad should tread softly when confronted with demands sanctioned by the Church.) Teresa's ironic imperative becomes unconscious prophecy: "Get riches at least for once, you indispensable, admired Gian' Battista, to whom the peace of a dying woman is less than the praise of people who have given you a silly name—and nothing besides—in exchange for your soul and body. . . . They have been paying you with words. Your folly shall betray you into poverty, misery, starvation" (*N* 256–57). Teresa's "curse," the legend of the spectral gringos, and Nostromo's resentment over being exploited by Gould all converge in the Custom House when Nos-

tromo talks with Monygham. This convergence helps account for
the force of Nostromo's angry exclamation that Monygham's new
commission has found him *"to-night* of all the nights of my life."
It is at this moment, as he senses control over his own life passing
out of his hands, that Nostromo accuses Monygham, the agent
of Charles Gould's "authoring," of having an "evil eye." The evil
influence of a powerful observer together with the fear of being
controlled by someone else's language suggests again that these
scenes allegorize the dialogic tension between character and author that emerges most distinctly in the verbal link between Decoud and Hirsch. When Sotillo's torture of Hirsch results in a
"comical" expression on Hirsch's screaming face, readers may
want to absolve the author of cruelty by ascribing the perspective
to the "evil eye" of Sotillo—but Sotillo and his soldiers have just
left the room, leaving Hirsch "all alone" (N 447). Only the author
gazes at Hirsch, and it is the author's eye that remains fixed on
Decoud as he hangs suspended from a thin cord in the solitude
of the gulf.

In Nostromo's later decision to steal the silver, the connection
between his fears of a malign external influence and the presence
of a demonic author becomes more insistent. As in Winnie's murder of Verloc, one set of explanations for Nostromo's behavior
can be discovered through traditional character analysis. Some
readers have accepted, for example, Nostromo's deathbed rationalization that he could not return the silver after Decoud removed four ingots because suspicion would then tarnish his reputation as "the incorruptible Capataz."[67] Nostromo's decision
may also derive from a desire to avenge himself on the blancos,
those "fine people" who are "all betrayers of the poor" (N 453).
Probing deeper, we could find psychological consistency in Nostromo's impulse to withhold the silver as a response to feeling
that he has not received his due for the danger he survived in the
gulf. The text also states explicitly that Nostromo wishes to defeat Teresa's "spell of poverty and starvation" by getting rich
slowly (N 502). From this we might infer that for a man who ex-
pects a malign destiny, a small difficulty such as the mystery of
the missing ingots can become an impossible one. We could conclude, finally, that Nostromo, like Gould, is defeated by his de-

sire to assert his own power against the authority of an absent parent. But from Nostromo's desire to defy Teresa's "spell," a crucial complement to character analysis begins to emerge.

As the story of the silver unfolds, Nostromo's naturalistic motivations gradually become doubled by suggestions of the supernatural, and what results is a kind of supernatural naturalism.[68] Nostromo's first impulse after leaving Decoud on the island and discovering the necessity for anonymity is to seek out Giorgio Viola, a surrogate father who represents, through his connection with Garibaldi, the uncorrupted ideals of an earlier time and, through verbal links with Higuerota, the purity of a realm beyond the blood and mire of Costaguana. When instead he finds Monygham, who treats him like an errand boy, Nostromo impulsively withholds the secret of the cargo because he resents Monygham's suggestion that if the silver were "miraculously" to turn up ashore, he would hand it over to Sotillo as a bribe. The displacement of Viola by Monygham resembles the transformation of Descartes's God into the evil genius: the demonic author takes hold of a betrayed self.

The language of the supernatural then becomes insistent as Nostromo's story reaches its crisis. Returning with Barrios after his successful mission to Cayta, Nostromo spots an "empty boat, coming out to meet him mysteriously, as if rowed by an invisible spectre" (*N* 491). The boat exercises "the fascination of some sign, of some warning" that Nostromo cannot ignore. Instead of explaining the situation to Barrios, Nostromo leaps overboard to recover the dinghy and solve the mystery of its abandonment himself. As if in reply to the puzzle of why Nostromo has not told Barrios about Decoud, the narrator informs us that "the idea of secrecy had come to be connected with the treasure so closely that even to Barrios himself he had refrained from mentioning the existence of Decoud and of the silver on the island" (*N* 493). Despite Conrad's tendency to supply multiple and thus overdetermined motivations for behavior, in this instance he refrains, and the unlikelihood of Nostromo's reticence finds expression a few sentences later in the "indefinable form" of the "resentment and distrust" that prevents Nostromo from telling his story to Barrios.

Many readers probably do not stop to question the explanation (or lack of one) because their attention has been fixed by the grotesquely vivid picture of Nostromo sitting in the boat, "streaming from head to foot, with his hair and whiskers hanging lank and dripping and a lustreless stare fixed upon the bottom boards"; he resembles "a drowned corpse come up from the bottom to idle away the sunset hour in a small boat" (*N* 192). Just as Winnie "turns into" Stevie, Nostromo merges here with Decoud. The next passage symbolically registers the moment of betrayal before Nostromo even makes the decision.

[W]ith the means of gaining the Great Isabel thrown thus in his way at the earliest possible moment, his excitement had departed, as when the soul takes flight leaving the body inert upon an earth it knows no more. Nostromo did not seem to know the gulf. For a long time even his eyelids did not flutter once upon the glazed emptiness of his stare. Then slowly, without a limb having stirred, without a twitch of muscle or quiver of an eyelash, an expression, a living expression came upon the still features, deep thought crept into the empty stare—as if an outcast soul, a quiet, brooding soul, finding that untenanted body in its way, had come in stealthily to take possession. (*N* 493)

The imagery both anticipates Stevie's momentary possession of Winnie and repeats in a darker key the well-known description of Nostromo awaking:

Nostromo woke up from a fourteen hours' sleep, and arose full length from his lair in the long grass. He stood knee deep amongst the whispering undulations of the green blades with the lost air of a man just born into the world. Handsome, robust, and supple, he threw back his head, flung his arms open, and stretched himself with a slow twist of the waist and a leisurely growling yawn of white teeth, as natural and free from evil in the moment of waking as a magnificent and unconscious wild beast. Then, in the suddenly steadied glance fixed upon nothing from under a thoughtful frown, appeared the man. (*N* 411–12)

Possession and counterpossession. Immediately above, before consciousness returns him to his predicament, Nostromo enjoys a Rousseau-like moment of freedom in nature. In the previous passage he suffers a Dantesque loss of self in the moment of betrayal.[69] Both passages, like Stevie's possession of Winnie, can be read as allegories of the moment when authorial intention seizes hold of a character to supply a change in motivation.

Conrad himself was acutely sensitive to the fear that with inspiration may come possession: "I, too, would like to hold the magic wand giving that command over laughter and tears which is declared to be the highest achievement of imaginative literature. Only, to be a great magician one must surrender oneself to occult and irresponsible powers, either outside or within one's breast" (*PR* xviii–xix). When Nostromo's posture on the Great Isabel mirrors Decoud's, the moment of convergence is again described as a possession, and now it is the disembodied souls of the first chapter that come home to roost:

[Decoud's] sleepless, crouching figure was gone from the side of the San Tomé silver; and for a time the spirits of good and evil that hover near every concealed treasure of the earth might have thought that this one had been forgotten by all mankind. Then, after a few days, another form appeared striding away from the setting sun to sit motionless and awake in the narrow black gully all through the night, in nearly the same pose, in the same place in which had sat that other sleepless man who had gone away for ever so quietly in a small boat, about the time of sunset. (*N* 501)

Nostromo's counterpossession anticipates "the demon of perverse intention" that animates the characters in *The Secret Agent*. The crucial difference there, however, is that the potential humanity of the characters does not resist the willfulness of perverse intentions. In the thoughtfulness of Nostromo's features appears "the man"; Verloc's features lend him "the expression of a reflective beast" (*SA* 257).

The relationship between author and character inscribed into each novel is duplicated in the implied relationship between text and reader. In the last scene of *The Secret Agent*, Ossipon, reading over the newspaper account of Winnie's suicide, becomes "scientifically afraid of insanity lying in wait for him amongst these lines" and feels "his own brain pulsating to the rhythm" of the words on the page: "*This act of madness or despair*" (*SA* 307, 310). In a text that beckons us into its narrative secrets only to imply, as in Chapter Eight, that Winnie's mother is being sent to the glue factory or, as in Chapter Eleven, that the "piece of roast beef, laid out in the likeness of funereal baked meats for Stevie's obsequies" is to be associated with Stevie's corpse, a brain pulsating to the rhythm of madness and despair would seem to represent a fantasy of the desired response of the reader.

The painful comedy of Conrad's remarks about his reception in England jibes perfectly with a novel in which the English (as in "Amy Foster") are described as bland, stupid, and unimaginative. Conrad's hunger for approval invests his letters with both Professor-like resentment and childish glee. After a particularly good response from an anonymous reviewer early in his career, Conrad wrote to Garnett: "I wrote to the reviewer. I did!! And he wrote to me. He did!! And who do you think it is? . . . Guess. Can't tell?—I will tell you. It is H. G. Wells. May I be cremated alive like a miserable moth if I suspected it!"[70] Conrad's critical reception was essentially enthusiastic from the start, but only a few years later, in 1903, he sent some of his English reviews to a Polish friend: "I wished to give you an idea of what they say here about me. The newspapers are stupid!"[71] Whatever the role of newspapers, sales did not keep pace with critical and professional esteem. In 1907 Conrad permitted himself to believe that *The Secret Agent* had "an element of popularity in it," but soon after he had to pronounce it "an honourable failure. It brought me neither love nor promise of literary success."[72] Given its "grisly skeleton," *The Secret Agent* was a dubious *billet-doux* to send to the popular audience, and Conrad's long-thwarted desire for popularity underlies the disingenuousness of his remark to an aspiring writer who, some years after the commercial success of *Chance* (1914), sought out *his* approval: "I must confess that, in truth, I never did care what anybody said."[73]

Despite such affected insouciance, the writing of *The Secret Agent* deeply engaged Conrad's conflicted desire to please both the elite readership represented by Wells and the broader audience figured in the Professor's "mass of mankind. . . . swarm[ing] like locusts, industrious like ants, thoughtless like a natural force, pushing on blind and orderly and absorbed, impervious to sentiment, to logic, to terror, too, perhaps" (*SA* 81–82). Conrad, like the Professor, doubted his capacity to move this mass. In the wake of *The Secret Agent*'s disappointing sales Conrad wrote to Galsworthy: "Ah! my dear, you don't know what an inspiration-killing anxiety it is to think: 'Is it salable?'

There's nothing more cruel than to be caught between one's impulse and one's act."[74] Apart from the barely veiled condescension of the self-styled *artiste* writing to the more popular novelist and playwright, the letter accurately reflects the dilemma of a writer caught between rapidly diverging literary markets. Conrad's response to a 1907 review of *The Secret Agent* in the *Athenaeum* must have been bitterly mixed: "The subtlety of his mental processes, the keenness of the artistic senses, have placed him further away from the great reading public—if infinitely nearer to the select few who have trained faculties of literary appreciation—than many a writer of far less worth."[75] If, as Jessie Conrad reported, the reception of *Nostromo* was "perhaps the greatest disappointment—literary disappointment—Conrad ever had,"[76] it is easy to imagine that, caught "between impulse and act" in his next novel, Conrad felt like throwing a bomb in his audience's face.

In *Nostromo*, too, the reader is put on the defensive. For like the "privileged passenger" subjected to Mitchell's narration of Sulacan history, the unwary reader is likely to be "stunned and as it were annihilated mentally by a sudden surfeit of sights, sounds, names, facts, and complicated information imperfectly apprehended" (*N* 486–87).[77] Professional critics are not immune to this dynamic of imposition, though the temptation is to displace the violence onto "the common reader" at whose hands, according to Guerard, the novelist "maliciously chops" by "shifting scene, time, emphasis, focus, [and] post of observation."[78] The best introduction to the novel acknowledges that the novel's manipulations of chronology might make "us resent the apparently refractory, and sometimes even gratuitous, difficulties of the narrative," adding that *Nostromo* is "wayward, infuriating, complicated, and yet finally unique and acceptable."[79] The consensus seems to be that the novel is a guest one admits only with some reluctance. Or, turning the analogy inside out, those who enter Conrad's house of fiction may, as in *The Secret Agent*, suffer ill-treatment, but in *Nostromo* the violence is at least mitigated: we do not feel coerced into contemplating Conrad's version of the intolerable but rather frustrated in our attempt to see the world of the novel whole.[80]

The power of *The Secret Agent* lies precisely in Conrad's denial of readerly freedom, for its authoritative discourse forces the reader to experience the Swiftian dilemma of the impossible choice. From the standpoint of character, what is most interesting about *The Secret Agent* is the peculiar way in which its characters seem torn between competing paradigms: they are imprisoned by authorial intentions without simply becoming verbal nodes in a modernist text. As if Conrad were resisting the proto-modernist tendencies of his own textual practice, the shift from naturalistic character into verbal pattern entails violence, what I have called the violence of thematization. Heat's reflections on Stevie's remains becomes a comment on literary history: "it seemed impossible to believe that a human body could have reached that state of disintegration without passing through the pangs of inconceivable agony" (*SA* 87). Yet the novel reveals no simple nostalgia for the formal and social proprieties of the Victorian era. Indeed, throwing a bomb into the family may be read as hostility toward the kind of novelistic order typically established in the Dickensian novel.

In *Nostromo* the "sentencing" of Decoud anticipates the monological stance that distinguishes *The Secret Agent*. But where the complications of *The Secret Agent* mark significant divergences from the mimetic model of the urban novel, the difficulty of *Nostromo* remains more fundamentally novelistic in the dialogic tensions played out between characters and between the discourses of character and author. *Nostromo* is frequently punctuated by aphorisms that threaten to collapse competing interpretations of the story into the more unified monological order of *The Secret Agent*. Yet none of these aphoristic reductions offers an adequate reading of the novel. Sotillo's murder of Hirsch induces the narrator to universalize Sotillo's example in a dressed-up version of the proverb that money is the root of all evil: "there is no credulity so eager and blind as the credulity of covetousness, which, in its universal extent, measures the moral misery and the intellectual destitution of mankind" (*N* 450). Elsewhere the proximity of Emilia Gould produces a different moral: "Charles Gould's fits of abstraction depicted the energetic concentration of a will haunted by a fixed idea. A man haunted by a fixed idea is insane" (*N* 379). The example of Nostromo awakening from the magnificent freedom of a wild animal puts the blame on consciousness generally, whereas the dying Don José Avellanos suggests to the narrator, as Gould looks on, "the powers of moral darkness, whose stagnant depths breed monstrous crimes and monstrous illusions" (*N* 362). The examples could be multiplied. Under the influence of a particular character's moral perspective, the narrator suddenly tries to impose an order that the complexity of the surrounding narrative refuses to sanction—except in the narrowing of the story into Nostromo's romance with Giselle Viola, as if the need to end the story resulted in an overreaction against the impulse to expand it.

The threat (or the appeal) of aphoristic reduction is homologous with the potential imprisoning power of the moral fable rehearsed in the first chapter. Sometimes the homogenizing effect of thematic consonance even begins to undermine the integrity of distinct characters: in a sentence that could describe Nostromo on the lighter, *Gould*, we are told, has "the spirit of a buccaneer throwing a lighted match into the magazine rather than surrender his ship" (*N* 366). Yet the pull of abstraction and consolidation is always countered by a will to complication, whether in the form of rebellious characters or in the expansion of novelistic detail and incident.

The balancing of centripetal and centrifugal forces in *Nostromo* plays out a dialogical opposition between a moral skepticism that tends to contract the text into reductive formulas and a more inclusive skepticism that turns the perspective of the moral skeptic into just one more among many. Conrad politicizes the contraction to a dominant point of view by associating it with the cruel tyranny of Guzman Bento, who rules as the antithesis to Giorgio Viola's republican ideals. Expansion and the multiplication of narrative perspectives represent formal equivalents of Costaguana's various attempts to establish an authentic parliamentary government, which, like Bakhtin's ideal of polyphony, organizes competing perspectives into an inclusive system without denying their autonomy. In *Nostromo*, however, parliament and polyphony alike are under siege.

If the authorial perspective of *Nostromo* internalizes the dialogue of freedom and coercion played out in the narrative, we can imagine the debate having been silenced in *The Secret Agent* by the tyrannical power of a Bento, whose ruthless authority literalizes the power Conrad wields over Stevie and his fellow sufferers. In another novel Vladimir's bombing outrage might have represented resistance to centralized authority (as indeed another bombing will in *Under Western Eyes*); in *The Secret Agent* the explosion is designed to elicit an intensification of political repression. The monological features of *The Secret Agent* correspond to two forms of sheltering conception: the cruel and overbearing coercion of authorial intentionality represents a refuge from epistemological skepticism in the security of authority, and "the grisly skeleton" of Conrad's plot represents the calcifying of moral skepticism that Conrad resists in the more expansive form of *Nostromo*.

Viewed together, the monological features of *The Secret Agent* and the polyphony of *Nostromo* resemble the interplay between abstraction and dialogue at the end of *Women in Love*, where Birkin and Ursula retreat to Verona from the stark purity of Gerald's ice world in the Tyrol. Actualizing Birkin's apocalyptic reflections ("The white races . . . would fulfil a mystery of ice-destructive knowledge, snow-abstract annihilation"), Gerald, like Conrad's Stevie, suffers death by literalization when he freezes into an emblem of icy abstraction. The narrative ends by returning to a more traditionally novelistic scene of dialogue set in Birkin's home, and the "terrible look of cold, mute Matter" on Gerald's face is displaced by the vitality of a dialogue that promises no immediate end.[81] *Nostromo* too threatens to contract into a crystalline expression of the Conradian "idea," but, like Lawrence, Conrad conjures only to expel the monological perspective that he later embraces in *The Secret Agent*.

Skepticism and the Fiction of Betrayal

Like most of Conrad's stories, *Nostromo* and *The Secret Agent* turn on moments of betrayal. Betrayal of self, betrayal of others, betrayal of a cause: Conrad's great theme is also fundamental to the logic of skepticism. The stories of Nostromo and Decoud suggest that for Conrad betrayal names the relation between self and other in a world ungrounded by skepticism.

After leaving Decoud on the Great Isabel, Nostromo awakens from a long sleep to the necessity of lying low. Rather than accept that he has been left to his own devices, Nostromo feels the need of a clearly defined role within a larger network of relationships: "His imagination had seized upon the clear and simple notion of betrayal to account for the dazed feeling of enlightenment as to being done for, of having inadvertently gone out of his existence on an issue in which his personality had not been taken into account. A man betrayed is a man destroyed" (*N* 419–20). At this point Nostromo has no objective reason to feel betrayed: he has not yet spoken with Monygham and consequently has no reason to believe anyone has taken advantage of him. The sense of having "gone out of his existence" is produced by the realization that he will no longer be able to see himself reflected in the eyes of an adoring audience. Here we see the precariousness of a dialogic concept of the self in which every word is "half-ours and half-someone else's": Nostromo depends so much on what others think of him that he scarcely has a self when he has lost his reputation or when he is not seeing himself in others' eyes upon him. Stepping back a bit from the story, we can see that Nostromo's crisis requires some explanation beyond the diagnosis of paranoia, for the recourse to betrayal duplicates the deepest motive for skepticism as it emerges in Descartes and Hume: doubt about the existence of others covers the fear that we are partial and dependent, that we ourselves may be unknowable. Although doubting may allay these fears, Nostromo, unlike Decoud, is "incapable of scepticism" and turns instead to the saving fiction of betrayal.

Nostromo's "imagination" seizes on "the clear and simple notion of betrayal to *account* for the dazed feeling of enlightenment." The language underscores the pressing need to fabricate betrayal in order to screen out a deeper fear of absolute solitude and dependence. Though Nostromo's awakening to political isolation and, potentially, to class exploitation marks him as the most prominent of the text's dependent isolates, his defensive reaction is a common feature of the Costaguanan imagination. Monygham was imprisoned and tortured during the dictatorship of Guzman Bento because Bento believed him to be part of "the Great Conspiracy." But "it is admitted in Costaguana that there never had been a conspiracy except in the diseased imagination of the Tyrant; and, therefore, nothing and no one to betray"

(*N* 312). Alone in his authoritarian rule, Bento invents betrayal because he needs to. Bento's paranoia repeats in a more frightening register the comic mania of Sotillo's "old major," who, able to "smell a traitor a league off," extinguishes the steamer's binnacle light (which illuminates the compass) after mistaking it for a warning signal to Gould (*N* 289). Loyal to "the general proposition that 'the world was full of traitors,'" he later walks around Hirsch's body, relieved that "there was no need to guard against any future treacheries of that scoundrel" (*N* 444, 450). The "disease" of Bento's imagination, then, does not lie in his paranoid fear of betrayal, a fear shared by many, but rather in the desire to inflict pain.[82] For betrayal, Conrad's obsessive theme, can be considered a logical response to the threat of radical skepticism.

Conjuring the dependable existence of an undependable other, betrayal permits the grounding of a sense of self in one's relation to a consciousness other than one's own: if I can be betrayed, I am not alone. Nostromo's dying words underscore the point: "'I die betrayed—betrayed by—' But he did not say by whom or by what he was dying betrayed" (*N* 559). Nostromo himself soon fills in the blank with "Decoud," and we could easily see Nostromo as an ironic Christ-like figure by supplying, as Nostromo will not, the missing "silver." But to do so would be to mimic the dynamic of the narrative by betraying the absence Conrad so carefully draws to our attention. If the fiction of betrayal effectively fills such absences, it also provides a response to the realization that one has lost the power of self-determination: if I can be betrayed, I must have the capacity to betray others. As we might expect, then, after awakening to his solitude, Nostromo's later act of betrayal—the stealing of the silver—becomes the most important act in the novel.

Decoud, even when Nostromo does not return for ten days, does not invoke betrayal when marooned on the Great Isabel. But neither does Decoud's skepticism provide any solace because, passing beyond the limits set by a Humean naturalism, it prevents him even from believing in anyone to doubt. It is the violation of this philosophical naturalism that leads critics to question, in the literary sense of the word, the naturalistic status of Decoud's suicide. As Decoud's skepticism dissolves his individuality into "the world of cloud and water," the very category

of character disappears into the skeptic discourse of a monological author—but only momentarily. In *The Secret Agent* the author
does not release his grip. If Verloc, as the narrator speculates, is
"the victim of a philosophical unbelief in the effectiveness of
every human effort" (*SA* 12), the restriction on character enforced
by the narrative machinery of that novel both corroborates his
philosophy and subordinates the potential for psychological crisis to the requirements of comic form.

In both texts we find, as if a second story told simultaneously
with the fictional lives of the characters, the language and issues
that figure centrally in philosophical investigations of skepticism: Descartes's evil genius haunts Nostromo; human automa-
tons populate *The Secret Agent*; and betrayal emerges to prevent
separation from seeming utter isolation.

The more human and humane fictional embodiment of skepticism in *Nostromo* can be focused in Monygham, who, by the end
of the novel, overcoming cynicism and his own "ideal conception
of his disgrace" (*N* 375), achieves the kind of rehabilitation once
sought by Jim. We hear the full story of Monygham's past betrayal of others under torture—in the absence of actual conspir-
ators against Bento the pain apparently induced Monygham to
invent a conspiracy—only when he is on the verge of playing his
"game of betrayal with Sotillo" (*N* 410). Although Hirsch becomes a pawn sacrificed in this game, in Monygham's otherwise
successful effort to stall Sotillo and save Sulaco, Conrad begins
to sketch out the value of a mature capacity for role-playing that
does not, like Decoud's dandyism, come to seem the mere illusion of a fool. Whereas Jim is locked into a pattern of repetitions
that lead inevitably to his defeat, Monygham's second "betrayal"
constitutes a repetition conducive to the kind of psychic release
Freud called "working-through."[83] Once "the slave of a ghost,"
by the end of the novel Monygham has replaced Decoud as the
consciousness most attuned to the development of the narrative.
More than anyone else, for instance, Monygham is able to articulate the inherent amorality of material interests, which lack "the
continuity and force that can be found only in a moral principle"
(*N* 511). While Nostromo, whose enslavement to the silver finally
kills him, dies soon after telling Giselle that "there is something
that stands between us . . . and the freedom of the world"

(*N* 539), Monygham's devotion to Emilia Gould at least frees him enough to analyze the "inhuman" expediency of "material interests" that he himself predicts as Sulaco's future (*N* 511). Still, Monygham's conviction that Sulaco should annex Costaguana suggests that his powers of reflection do not enable him to resist implication in more encompassing patterns of historical determinism. The cycle of revolutions seems as fixed and regular as "the wasting edge of the cloud-bank [that] always strives for, but seldom wins, the middle of the gulf" (*N* 6).

In *Nostromo* Conrad permits limited freedom within the systole and diastole of Costaguana's authoritarian governments and democratic resistance. In the implication that history repeats itself Conrad's skepticism modulates into the pessimism characteristic of many early-twentieth-century intellectuals, who were often torn between the desire to affirm the freedom of the individual and a belief in various forms of determinism.[84] Benita Parry, however, has argued that *Nostromo* may also be read as "a radical political fiction mediated by a deeply conservative consciousness."[85] In this reading Nostromo's apotheosis as a *genius loci* in the last paragraph of the novel represents the muted possibility that his name may live on as an emblem, and perhaps a rallying cry, of the oppressed people already championed by Corbelàn, who declares "significantly, menacingly": "Let [the foreign capitalists] beware, then, lest the people, prevented from their aspirations, should rise and claim their share of the wealth and their share of the power" (*N* 510). That Parry's perhaps too hopeful interpretation of Linda's despairing cry cannot be ruled out suggests the extent to which Conrad refuses to cede absolute authority to any conceptual scheme that might lock his characters into the deterministic nightmare of his knitting machine.

After the tighter shackling of his characters in *The Secret Agent*, Conrad would again resist the potential disablement of pessimism in *Under Western Eyes*. For Razumov, the protagonist of Conrad's last great novel, struggles to shake off the burden that killed Decoud, a malady Haldin diagnoses early on as "philosophical scepticism."

Chapter Six

Under Western Eyes and
the Later Affirmations

> *Both at sea and on land my point of view is English, from*
> *which the conclusion should not be drawn that I have become an*
> *Englishman. That is not the case.* Homo duplex *has in my*
> *case more than one meaning.*   —Conrad to Waliszewski

My argument in the preceding chapters has been designed to
bring out the various ways in which Conrad's self-described status as *homo duplex* registers in the philosophical and formal intricacies of his fiction. As the letter to Waliszewski implies, this self-
division includes but is not limited to the opposition between Englishness and foreignness, an explicit concern of *Under Western
Eyes*. Skepticism too is a matter of division, and in *Under Western
Eyes* issues of nationality and politics, caught up in Conrad's discourse of skepticism, are stripped of the pathos that characterizes
the more sensational treatment of national identity in "Amy Foster" (1903). In Conrad's best work skepticism contests the consolations afforded by sheltered retreats; in much of his later writing shelters lock out skepticism with increasing effectiveness,
and his fiction becomes the worse for it. The story of Razumov,
narrated by a priggish teacher of languages, reprises the stron-
gest features of the skeptical tradition. It is, in consequence, the
last of Conrad's great fictions of skepticism.

   True to his logic of division, *Under Western Eyes* begins with the
assassination of a figure who incarnates an extreme version of
Conrad's investment in the shelter of centralized authority. The
Minister of State in Russia, Mr. de P——, once president of "the
notorious Repressive Commission" (*UWE* 7), is killed by bombs
thrown by two revolutionaries, one of whom, Victor Haldin,
later seeks refuge and aid from Razumov, a young scholar with

vaguely liberal yet unformed political beliefs. Before Haldin's sudden appearance in his rooms, "Razumov was one of those men who, living in a period of mental and political unrest, keep an instinctive hold on normal, practical, everyday life" (*UWE* 10). After Haldin turns to Razumov as one of those rare men who lead "unstained, lofty, and solitary existences" (*UWE* 135), Part One pivots on Razumov's dilemma: should he help the young idealist Haldin escape by notifying a sledge driver, or should he hand over Haldin the assassin to the authorities? Given Razumov's isolation, any kind of association with Haldin—as accomplice or betrayer—could destroy his career: the illegitimate son of a nobleman, he has no official standing in society and must seek a place for himself by writing a prize-winning essay. Razumov would like to maintain a self-image consonant with the idea of reason as an internally consistent discourse of the "normal," "practical," and "everyday"; his name even derives from the Russian for "reason." Skepticism, however, insists on the tendency of reason to subvert itself, and Razumov, forced into reflection, recognizes himself as *homo duplex*.

In novels after *Under Western Eyes* skepticism is still an issue, but, no longer a crucial force governing literary construction, it becomes rather an explicit topic of discussion within the text. The discourses of character and author alike directly engage skepticism as a "life issue," and these abstract philosophical reflections, as in the death of Decoud, tend to hover at some remove from the imagined life of the characters. But unlike in the analogous scenes from *Nostromo* or *The Secret Agent*, the abstract and concrete are less likely to become dialogically engaged. As theme, moreover, skepticism is usually reduced to the conflicting claims of detachment versus involvement; in *Victory* (1915) Conrad sometimes succeeds in ramifying the idea of detachment, but too often in the late fiction it is thematic reduction that manages the crises formerly mitigated by Conrad's sheltering conceptions.

If, as I believe, *Under Western Eyes* marks the last of Conrad's best work, any discussion of the later novels must inevitably be located in the context of Conrad's so-called decline. I am among those who see a clear falling off in much of Conrad's late work;

however, my concern here is not to rehearse the terms of the debate—others have already taken up that burden—but rather to redescribe Conrad's fiction and the course of his career in terms of shifting articulations of skepticism. No one, to my knowledge, has devoted sustained attention to the question of decline from the standpoint of authorial skepticism.[1] In this context Guerard's assertion that Conrad's fiction suffers from a "normalizing of attitude and method" coincides with my claims about the overly effective sheltering conceptions of the late work.[2] With *Chance* (1913) and after, Conrad achieves what Razumov could not: a firmer grip on "normal, practical, everyday life," as well as a rewarding audience for his writing.[3]

If my criticism of *Chance, Victory*, and other late work depends in part on Jamesian notions of the art of the novel, this is only because I am unwilling to read through awkward prose and uncertain handling of character and situation without relating such defects to articulations (or deflections) of authorial skepticism. To emphasize stylistic and structural criteria in this way is not necessarily to sacrifice historical resonance or political content to a modernist (or New Critical) privileging of irony and complexity. The skeptical dialogics I value in Conrad provide fictional adequation for the sense of inquiry that motivates what I take to be his most effective novels—those in which embodied vision is charged with the vigor of intellectual confrontation. Frequently the dialogue of ideas in Conrad returns to the ethics of authorship—the ethical status of descriptive vision in *Lord Jim*, the ethics of narrative form in *Nostromo* and *The Secret Agent*. By adding a few steps to these arguments, the formal process whereby the novel as genre tends to convert ideological issues into moral ones can be reversed. Because the narrative logic of *Under Western Eyes* is governed by the tension between individual ethics and political ideology, I will turn in later sections of this chapter to the ways in which Conrad's skeptical inquiry into models of political agency revises the analysis of power in *Nostromo*. Itself producing a species of doubleness, this complexly staged debate is situated within, though typically overshadowed by, the more generally discussed matrix of Conrad's response to Dostoevsky, Russia's occupation of Poland, and the virtual martyrdom of his parents to the Polish cause.[4]

Sheltering the Storm: Razumov and Haldin

Razumov, unlike Conrad, is unable to secure the normality of his life; nor is he able to realize the dream of writing his way out of encroaching poverty. Yet, failing where Conrad ultimately succeeds, Razumov lays the groundwork for the success of *Under Western Eyes*.[5]

Razumov seems to share a furtive, unspoken sympathy for Haldin's profound sense of devotion to an idea, but only his past silences, noncommittal and self-protective, have encouraged Haldin to project onto him the role of a secret sharer. (Conrad's most brilliant story of this period, "The Secret Sharer" [1910], was written as a break from *Under Western Eyes* and plays out the option Razumov ultimately rejects: loyalty to the outlaw.) The scenes of dramatic dialogue between Haldin and Razumov are among Conrad's best, and much of the intensity, as in the earlier fiction, derives from a complex narrative projection of fundamental issues explored in the skeptical tradition. The "philosophical scepticism" (*UWE* 22) Haldin attributes to Razumov is merely his way of accounting for Razumov's reserve; in Haldin's misreading and its consequences we find the more subtle and pervasive operations of authorial skepticism.

The mutual opacity of other minds dominates the exchanges between Haldin and Razumov. Though seething with resentment, Razumov consents to help, even as he continues to guard the "inner reality" of his deep revulsion. With Razumov's entry into the snowy streets of St. Petersburg, Haldin has literally and figuratively beckoned the solitary scholar out of the shelter he has made for himself in the concentrated routine of his studies. Once outside, however, Razumov soon discovers the need for a far deeper form of security. Having found old Ziemianitch in a dirty barn, Razumov viciously beats the drunk and unconscious driver before wandering back into the streets to ponder his predicament. The following paragraphs beautifully trace the gradual construction of a new refuge from the disruption embodied in Haldin.

Other men had somewhere a corner of the earth—some little house in the provinces where they had a right to take their troubles. A material refuge. He had nothing. He had not even a moral refuge—the refuge of confidence. To whom could he go with this tale—in all this great, great land?

Razumov stamped his foot—and under the soft carpet of snow felt the hard ground of Russia, inanimate, cold, inert, like a sullen and tragic mother hiding her face under a winding-sheet—his native soil!—his very own—without a fireside, without a heart!

He cast his eyes upwards and stood amazed. The snow had ceased to fall, and now, as if by a miracle, he saw above his head the clear black sky of the northern winter, decorated with the sumptuous fires of the stars. It was a canopy fit for the resplendent purity of the snows.

Razumov received an almost physical impression of endless space and of countless millions.

He responded to it with the readiness of a Russian who is born to an inheritance of space and numbers. Under the sumptuous immensity of the sky, the snow covered the endless forests, the frozen rivers, the plains of an immense country, obliterating the landmarks, the accidents of the ground, levelling everything under its uniform whiteness, like a monstrous blank page awaiting the record of an inconceivable history. It covered the passive land with its lives of countless people like Zie-mianitch and its handful of agitators like this Haldin—murdering foolishly.

It was a sort of sacred inertia. (*UWE* 32–33)

After a vivid rendering of external reality, the passage relocates the whole of Russia inside Razumov's mind—in a picture so immediate we may forget it is not composed of actual perceptions—and so anticipates his later exclamation that Russia cannot disown him because "I am *it*!" (*UWE* 209). Razumov has internalized Russia's "sacred inertia," the accumulated weight of her repressive history, figured in the snow, and the spirit of cynical resignation that attends it. Like Winnie Verloc, "who thought in images," Razumov literally sees what he must do. As one image gives way to another with a seductively persuasive rhythm, even the reader may be lulled into accepting Razumov's conversion into reactionary despotism as understandable, inevitable—even correct. The observation that he has no "little house in the provinces" or any "fireside" to escape to slips insensibly into the conclusion that he does not even have a "moral refuge." "A train of thought," the narrator remarks, "is never false. The falsehood lies deep in the necessities of existence." Casting around for someone to confide in, the orphaned Razumov stamps his foot "on the hard ground," and the slumbering landscape of Holy Mother Russia suggests to Razumov, now overwhelmed by his isolation, that what he and all Russia need is "a will strong and one . . . not the babble of many voices, but a man—strong and one!" (*UWE* 33). Razumov's train of thought runs precisely counter to Haldin's: he wishes to reinstate the central authority attacked in the opening pages of the novel. He does so by seeking out, for the first and last time, his father's help.

Beyond Razumov's more immediate emotional needs, his turn toward authority in the form of his father and the autocratic government his father represents resembles a desire for the authoritative discourse Bakhtin associates with the monological novel: "The authoritative word is located in a distanced zone, organically connected with a past that is felt to be hierarchically higher. It is, so to speak, the word of the fathers."[6] It is also a way of thinking that eases the pain of choice. Betraying Haldin to Councillor Mikulin, Razumov does not simply reenter the shelter of official authority: becoming a police spy in Geneva, he will extend it. Yet the narrative that springs from Razumov's conversion experience initiates a series of dialogical oppositions that mitigates the pull toward authority by juxtaposing it with opposing perspectives whose validity is allowed to stand. Conrad's own hatred for Russia—"from the very inception of her being the brutal destruction . . . of all that is faithful in human nature has been made the imperative condition of her existence"[7]—makes his sympathetic treatment of both Razumov and Haldin all the more impressive.

The very conception of Razumov's character and situation engages a profound dialogical tension. Conrad delays disclosing Razumov's new occupation for several chapters, letting it emerge slowly over a hundred pages or so, until we see that Razumov had no real alternative to a mission he, too, finds morally abhorrent.[8] It has often been noted that Razumov's statement of principles—"History not Theory . . . Evolution not Revolution . . . Unity not Disruption"—could easily be Conrad's. Yet because these pronouncements emerge as rationalizations of the betrayal of Haldin, some ironic distance opens between author and character. Given the contempt in which Conrad holds the anarchists of *The Secret Agent*, the dignity and authority he allows Haldin raises the stakes of Razumov's betrayal. A brilliant analyst of sham eloquence and political posturing, Conrad chooses to lend Haldin one of his most privileged tropes: "What will become of my soul when I die in the way I must die—soon—very soon perhaps? It shall not perish. . . . My spirit shall go on warring in some Russian body till all falsehood is swept out of the world. The modern civilization is false, but a new revelation shall come out of Russia" (*UWE* 22). Resonating with Conrad's own descriptions of artistic realization, the language of incarnation here implies that the author, unlike Razumov, is at least able to imagine Haldin's destructiveness as a form of creation, particularly if what Haldin destroys is the old Russia.[9] "You suppose that I am a terrorist," Haldin declaims to Razumov, "a destructor of what is. But consider that the true destroyers are they who destroy the spirit of progress and truth. . . . Men like me are necessary to make room for self-contained, thinking men like you" (*UWE* 19). Haldin becomes a kind of Prince Roman, the voice of one of Conrad's heroic ancestors who fought against Russia's tyranny over Poland. Underlying this is Conrad's inclination to defer, through Razumov, to the man of action whose unqualified commitment to liberty "makes room" for the reflective activity of the writer. (In *A Personal Record* Conrad works hard to overcome the anxiety and guilt associated with his own potentially marginalized and dependent relation to his more politically engaged countrymen.) But even if Haldin had not attacked a representative of the government largely responsible for the modern partitioning of Poland and the death of Conrad's parents, Razumov's betraying him, in Conrad's moral vision, would constitute a terrible breach of faith: when public and private duties collide, the greater guilt always lies in betraying the claim of the individual.

The conflict is internalized and sustained in Razumov, who eventually refuses to acquiesce to the authoritarian machine that dictates acceptable forms of the unity he endorses in his manifesto. Razumov's rebellion must be measured against the investment in authority Conrad reveals elsewhere in characters such as Allistoun in *The Nigger of the "Narcissus"* or MacWhirr in *Typhoon*—captains both. In these and other novels Conrad typically qualifies the potential authoritarianism of the surrounding fic-

tion by according some force (itself, of course, qualified) to opposing voices. Conrad himself, after all, was more often a crew
member than a captain. In the relationship between Razumov
and Haldin, Conrad articulates his most nuanced yet also his most
powerful response to the sovereignty of centralized power.[10] Later
in his career Conrad becomes less inclined to indulge in skeptical
attacks on authority,[11] and it will be useful to take a moment to
locate *Under Western Eyes* in the context of *Suspense* (1925) and *A
Personal Record*.

Skepticism and Authority

Published posthumously in its unfinished form, *Suspense* begins to transform the skeptical investigation of modern heroism
in *Lord Jim* and *Nostromo* into a relatively unqualified attraction
to authoritative power. The "offstage" presence of Napoleon in
Suspense can be usefully compared with the function of the same
figure in *A Personal Record*, written some sixteen years earlier,
when Conrad was in the midst of his most successful phase as a
writer.

Recounting the life of his grand-uncle, Nicholas B., who par-
ticipated in the Napoleonic invasion of Russia, Conrad returns
frequently to Napoleon, who, though a "great man," kindled "a
great illusion . . . like a false beacon . . . to lead astray the effort
of a brave nation" (*PR* 35). Although Conrad is clearly drawn to
the figure of a powerful man who can impose his dream on the
world, his skepticism, as in his novels of this period, also brings
into focus the tremendous costs of idealization: the fall of Napoleon entails "the ruin of national hopes" and, ultimately, of
Nicholas B. Conrad's ambivalence has the remarkable effect of
transforming Napoleon into a version of another figure who
dominates the pages of *A Personal Record*, Don Quixote, "the patron saint of all lives spoiled or saved by the irresistible grace of
imagination" (*PR* 37). That crucial equivocation—"spoiled *or*
saved"—is the sign of Conrad's dialogical response, and this inner division is what motivates the complex involutions and turns
of his subtle autobiographical narrative. The ambivalent Quixo-
tification of Napoleon also charts Conrad's distance from the
nineteenth-century novel, where Napoleon is typically associ-

ated with the fantasy of a solitary man able to effect rapid historical change through "a fierce assertion of will and the most cunning exercise of intelligence."[12] In this light we can see Charles Gould as a failed Napoleon, and Pedro Montero—inspired by historical romances, he styles himself a latter-day Duc de Morny—as a parody of the desire to dominate history. In *A Personal Record* "the thirst for domination through imagination"[13] associated with Napoleon is tempered with irony, and Napoleon himself is relegated to the background as an object of nostalgic yet skeptical fascination.

In *Suspense*, however, the irony has faded. The narrative begins with an Englishman, Cosmo Latham, and a mysterious Italian peering out across the Gulf of Genoa toward Napoleon's Elban exile; on the last pages of the fragment, Cosmo sets sail with a band of revolutionaries, their ultimate destination a rendezvous with Napoleon. Though Cosmo's admiration for Napoleon's "genius" is subjected early on to a bit of conversational cross fire, the narrative quickens only in Part Four, where, in a scene reminiscent of Decoud and Nostromo in the Golfo Placido, we are asked to thrill to the prospect of joining forces with the great man himself. Although it is impossible to know for certain what Conrad would have done with this fragment, evidence suggests that the narrative would have culminated in some scenes featuring Napoleon on Elba.[14] The shelter of authority can become as much a blind as a refuge.

In *Under Western Eyes* the authority of the narrator, an unnamed language teacher, is effectively drawn into the kind of dialogical network absent in *Suspense*. Razumov's final rebellion against Councillor Mikulin's commission to spy on Haldin's fellow revolutionaries, ostensibly motivated by guilt and the strain of prolonged dissimulation, also reads as a revolt against the teacher of languages, who seems to assume, from Razumov's point of view, the power of authorial control. Officious and obtuse, the narrator has a way of torturing Razumov with unintentionally "double-voiced" remarks about Haldin: "I believe myself authorized to speak. . . . There was something peculiar in the circumstances of his arrest. You no doubt know the whole truth." Razumov's response recalls Nostromo's resistance to Monygham in the Custom House: "'You spring up from the ground before me with this talk. Who the devil are you? This is not to be borne! Why! What for? What do you know what is or is not peculiar? What have you to do with any confounded circumstances, or with anything that happens in Russia, anyway?'" (*UWE* 186). Here again we encounter the *malin génie* of Descartes, and it is in this scene that Razumov is moved to exclaim that he is not "a young man in a novel." Later, writing in his journal (destined to be read by the narrator), Razumov describes the language teacher explicitly as the demonic author posited less directly by Nostromo: "Could he have been the devil himself in the shape of an old Englishman?" (*UWE* 360).[15] In the teacher of languages Conrad found the kind of narrator whose complex relationship with the protagonist generates the dialogic interest once associated with Marlow.

Despite Conrad's defense in the Author's Note, irritation with the language teacher's sometimes awkward presence persists in criticism to this day. Taking up the role of narrator while professing skepticism toward language, he sometimes resembles the titular hero of Iris Murdoch's *A Word Child* (1975), another linguist inclined to see empty structure where someone else might find the promise of communication. "To a teacher of languages," Conrad's narrator begins, "there comes a time when the world is but a place of many words and man appears a mere talking animal not much more wonderful than a parrot." But it is Razumov who holds the novel's most radically skeptical point of view; and the teacher of languages, like Marlow in *Lord Jim*, functions to hold that skepticism in check. Describing an effect of "double-detachment," Terry Eagleton notes that just as Razumov tries to detach himself from politics, so the narrator detaches himself from Razumov.

By doing so, he can protect the "sanity" of his own decent English empiricism from the risks of a corrosive scepticism; but having established that defensive margin between himself and scepticism, he can then, through the character of Razumov, indulge it to the full in a way which severely criticizes his own "decent" conventionality. The novel, by the use of its narrator-device, can therefore satirise the limits of English empiricism by the portrayal of passionate experience beyond its scope, without permitting that empirical position to be undermined; it can indulge, through Razumov, a wholly un-English nihilism without allowing that stance to be fully affirmed.[16]

I quote Eagleton with mixed feelings here, for while the terms of his argument seem to me exactly right, he uses them to accuse Conrad of a bad-faith defense of English conservatism. Although manuscript revisions indeed suggest that Conrad muted his criticism of the English in *Under Western Eyes*, unless one requires a bias *toward* the revolutionaries (instead of the reverse, which Eagleton finds), the double-edged ironies of Conrad's treatment of revolutionary, reformist, and conservative ideologies can be accepted as an intellectual strength of the novel. Even after revision, how many readers could fail to see England—particularly the London of *The Secret Agent*—reflected in the stultifying mediocrity of Conrad's Geneva?[17] And if the language teacher's cynical disquisition on the stages of violent revolution seems unfair ("Hopes grotesquely betrayed, ideals caricatured—that is the definition of revolutionary success"), Nathalie Haldin's response, part of which stands as the novel's epigraph, carries at least equal power: "I would take liberty from any hand as a hungry man would snatch at a piece of bread. The true progress must begin after" (*UWE* 135).[18] Soviet history through the 1930s, not to mention the political status of Poland to this day, has tended to vindicate the pessimism Conrad expresses through his narrator; but the integrity and fortitude of *Under Western Eyes* lie in Conrad's refusal, in the absence of any vision of a workable political solution, to write a more partisan novel. According to Ford, Conrad "agreed that the novel is absolutely the only vehicle for the thought of our day. . . . The one thing you can not do is to propagandize."[19] The interplay among the narrator, Nathalie, and Razumov is necessary to that suspension.[20]

Conrad's original conception for *Under Western Eyes*, then titled "Razumov," followed the contours of romantic melodrama and consequently was shot through with fewer dialogical complications. Writing to Galsworthy in 1908, Conrad laid out the projected second "movement" in which Razumov would meet and *marry* Nathalie: the "psychological developments leading to Razumov's betrayal of Haldin, to his confession of the fact to his wife and to the death of these people (brought about mainly by the resemblance of their child to the late Haldin), form the real subject of the story."[21] Mercifully, between conception and realization the alembic of Conrad's temperament removed Razumov's troublesome child, even though the more sensational treatment might have generated higher sales. Conrad's willingness (or perhaps more accurately, his capacity) to accommodate the market begins to change, however, and in later novels—*The Arrow of Gold* (1919), *The Rescue* (1920), and *The Rover* (1923)—he becomes more inclined to curtail skepticism by returning to what is generally considered the weakest part of *Lord Jim*, the romance conventions of Patusan.[22] *Victory* (1915) and *Chance* (1913) are particularly useful in charting the change in Conrad's career.

Romance, Skepticism, and the Criteria of Success

By 1912 Conrad was already becoming more immersed in the commercial aspects of his profession, and the pressures of commerce seem to have entered into the suppression of skepticism and his consequent normalizing of vision.[23] A new shrewdness in self-advertisement becomes evident in Conrad's correspondence around this time. Conrad had never blanched before the financial need to churn out short potboilers; nor had he ever been completely naive about the marketing of his fiction.[24] What is new is the way anguished commentary on his struggle to reach a broader audience gives way to almost parodic accounts of his developing work as a form of "easy listening" for the aspiring highbrow: "There is philosophy in it and also drama—lightly treated—meant for cultured people—a piece of literature before everything—and of course fit for general reading. Strictly proper."[25] Though Conrad is explicitly trying to sell *Victory* to his agent, the letter also gives a fairly accurate accounting of the novel. Like much of the late fiction, *Victory* often supplies unwitting parodies of Conrad's recurrent philosophical concerns, particularly his skeptical thought. Lena, for instance, travesties the instability of character when she is inclined to view herself as what we can recognize as a perfectly Berkeleyean object: "if you were to stop thinking of me," she says to Heyst, "I shouldn't be in the world at all" (*V* 187). Although the remark holds a certain

psychological interest, in context it reads as the kind of gratuitous philosophical shorthand that is easily consumed by a mass
audience.[26] In *Nostromo* moments of abstraction and compression
are subverted by the refractory materials of the narrative; in *Victory* aphoristic reductions sum up the narrative's moral fable all
too accurately all too often.

Those who admire Conrad's later work typically set aside the
formal component of the philosophical-formal criteria I employ
in this study in order to focus on the text's sociological dimension
or its *mythos*. The reception of *Victory* offers a case in point.[27] The
seductive power that the novel has held for critics and novelists
(such as Robert Stone, who rewrites *Victory* in his 1974 novel *Dog
Soldiers*) derives in part from the archetypal power of its romance
structure, which stirs the same yearnings for wholeness and
transcendence engaged by *The Tempest* and other versions of paradise lost and gained. More historically minded readers seize on
Victory and the late fiction for their commentary on issues of gen-
der, social structure, and the sociology of ideas. Thus Daniel
Schwarz, citing George Dangerfield's *The Strange Death of Liberal
England* (1935) and Samuel Hynes's *The Edwardian Turn of Mind*,
reads *Victory* as representing "the ennui, anxiety, and moral and
intellectual confusion of pre-War England"; and Tony Tanner, citing Schopenhauer and Darwin, meditates on the novel's semantic emptying out of the word "gentleman."[28] Such approaches are
valuable in their own right, though to my mind the kind of interest brought out does not always compensate for the decay in
Conrad's ability to combine verbal brilliance, as well as dialogical
complexities between characters and author, with the restless
probing of his philosophical imagination.

Surprisingly, Conrad's first great commercial success, *Chance*,
outstrips even *Lord Jim* and *Nostromo* in its structural complexity.
Far from being marketed as an "art novel," however, the story of
Flora de Barral benefited enormously from enthusiastic promo-
tion targeted directly at the large audience of women Conrad had
never before reached.[29] For the most part, *Chance*'s elaborate narrative scaffolding seems an empty formalism.

Marlow returns in *Chance* after a thirteen-year sabbatical, apparently having discovered that his passing remark in *Lord Jim*—
"The marital relations of seamen would make an interesting sub-

ject" (*LJ* 156)—deserves more than casual dismissal within a digression. In that novel Marlow's early account of Jim introduces authorial skepticism as a dynamic principle of structure; but his presence in *Chance* does not produce the restless, charged language of *Lord Jim*, where the irresolutions and hesitancies of Marlow's skeptical regard register in the ellipses, suspensions, and obsessive qualifications of his address. Although much of Marlow's narration in *Chance* advances by means of an explicit dialogue with the narrating "I," their exchanges are largely perfunctory, as in the characteristic interruption, "How do you know all this?" Occasionally their exchanges become quite charged, usually around Marlow's tendentious remarks about women; but more often the narrator betrays none of the intense involvement necessary to catalyze the skeptical crises that erupt from Marlow's troubled relationships with Kurtz and Jim.[30] Conrad's need for distancing devices has long been recognized; but it was equally important for him to enter into, consciously or not, an intense dialogical engagement, and in *Chance* Marlow no longer fulfills that need.

Yet the novel does achieve moments of true power, and in the best of these—the account of Flora's traumatic loss of innocence at the hands of her governess—even the complicated narrative situation contributes to the dramatic effect. Like Razumov's encounter with Haldin, Flora's "fall" turns on the mystery of other minds. In the governess we recognize the familiar trope of shelter: "The woman before her had been the wisdom, the authority, the protection of life, security embodied and visible and undisputed" (*C* 117). Flora, in her ignorance of "the evil which lives in the secret thoughts . . . of mankind," loses "all her hold on reality" as the governess angrily pours out the pent fury of her resentment while Charley, a young man posing as Flora's suitor, stands by watching. Once Flora's most intimate acquaintances, Charley and the governess become "amazing and familiar strangers," uncanny threats to her security and identity (*C* 99, 118, 116). The scene comes to us from at least three removes: Marlow is telling the story to the "I" as we listen in, and he first heard it from neighbors, the Fyneses, who saw some of the action from a distance and heard the rest from Flora herself. Often in *Chance* these distancing devices amount to little more than the quotation marks within quotation marks that clutter the page;[31] but in this scene Marlow's conjectural narration, filling in the gaps of his sources, sees into, with the advantage of hindsight, all that Flora cannot. The contrast between Flora's horrified incredulity and Marlow's level-headed attempt to fathom the "subterfuges" of the governess's "menaced passion" links up with the Fyneses' slowly dawning comprehension of the spectacle they witness through their window to bring out with startling vividness the anguish of unforeseen betrayal.[32] As in *Lord Jim*, the opacity of other minds motivates a psychologically complex and technically sophisticated scene without sacrificing the virtues of embodied philosophical form. In *Chance* as a whole, however, the interest generated by Marlow's sexual politics and the sometimes moving story of Flora's life competes unsuccessfully with architectonic excess, verbal bathos, and sentimentality.

Always a danger for Conrad, sentimentality represents only one of the ways in which skepticism may be suppressed.[33] In *Under Western Eyes* Conrad is more successful than in most of the later work in sustaining a vitally dynamic relation between his various sheltering conceptions and authorial skepticism. This is particularly true of the novel's inquiry into the nature of politics in modern life.

Skeptical Politics: The Ideology of Ghosts

Momentarily forgetting about his complex characterization of Razumov, Conrad announced an important half-truth to Garnett: "in this book I am concerned with nothing but ideas, to the exclusion of everything else."[34] More accurately, *Under Western Eyes*, like most of the middle fiction, dramatizes the refusal of "everything else" to acquiesce in its own exclusion. As in *Nostromo*, Conrad's conservative distrust of political motivation per se invokes personal motives in order to discredit the idealism of public goals. Yet looking beyond individuals, Conrad also articulates the political as the systemic influence of ideology.[35] These competing models of political agency position the novel somewhere between an ideological critique of autocracy and a "mystified" account of the exigencies of individual consciousness. Tropes of the ghostly and the material again come into play: not just a projection of conscience, the distinct specter of Haldin's prostrate body over which Razumov walks in the first part becomes, in the later sections, a "featureless . . . component of mental discourse," one that provides implicit commentary on the operations of political power.[36]

A paradigm of the first model of political agency can be located in the satiric treatment of Peter Ivanovitch, in which political abstraction is subordinated to the dubious particularity of the individual. After his death, Haldin's revolutionary idealism finds expression in his sister, Nathalie, and in Peter Ivanovitch, who, modeled loosely on Tolstoy and Bakunin, is described as a visionary thinker—but also as a bedraggled bear lumbering naked through the woods, a cynical manipulator bilking a former aristocratic lover out of her fortune, and a tyrannical author exploiting the labor of his amanuensis, Tekla. Similarly, General T——, Razumov's first contact in the government, is presented as a professional defender of autocracy whose commitment is so ferociously instinctual that Razumov inwardly complains that the man is "simply unable to understand a reasonable adherence to the doctrine of absolutism" (*UWE* 84). In both cases a wedge is driven between the human individual, characterized chiefly in terms of his baser drives, and more sublimated manifestations of consciousness, which are made to seem weaker and less authentic. Peter Ivanovitch is again paradigmatic, here as an escaped convict: "it was as though there had been two human beings indissolubly joined in that enterprise. The civilized man, the enthusiast of advanced humanitarian ideals thirsting for the triumph of spiritual love and political liberty; and the stealthy primeval savage, pitilessly cunning in the preservation of his freedom from day to day, like a tracked wild beast" (*UWE* 122). When mocking treatment of *homo duplex* later slides into more vituperative satire, Conrad himself, as in the satiric reductions of *The Secret Agent*, may exemplify the failing the teacher of languages attributes to "modern" man generally, "always dazzled by the base glitter of mixed motives, everlastingly betrayed by a shortsighted wisdom" (*UWE* 305).

Yet together with man as a (barely) political animal, Conrad also projects a more subtle understanding of political motivations and their effects. In Sophia Antonovna, Conrad imagines a

woman whose commitment to revolution is unsullied by impu-
tations of selfishness; and in the coercive pressure of the scrutiny
to which Razumov feels subjected, Conrad acknowledges the in-
sidious reach of ideological control.

As Razumov struggles to maintain his composure, the novel
begins to display twin rhetorical obsessions: with ghosts, souls,
and the demonic and with eyes, seeing, and supervision. Waiting three weeks for the expected summons from Mikulin, Razumov (whose cover will soon be a visit to "an oculist") is tempted
to flee: "But a retreat was big with shadowy dangers. The eye of
the social revolution was on him, and Razumov for a moment felt
an unnamed and despairing dread, mingled with an odious sense
of humiliation. Was it possible that he no longer belonged to himself?" (*UWE* 301). Recasting the Gothicism of his earlier work,
Conrad suggests that no refuge, even the solitary musing of the
writer, is proof against the shadowy invasions of unwanted supervision. Vainly asserting his autonomy, Razumov imagines
winning the essay competition as a step toward becoming "a
great reforming servant of the greatest of States." But, suddenly
striking out at Haldin's absent figure, Razumov catches "for an
instant in the air, like a vivid detail in a dissolving view of two
heads, the eyes of General T—— and of Privy-Councillor Mikulin
side by side fixed upon him, quite different in character, but with
the same unflinching and weary and yet purposeful expression"
(*UWE* 302). As Razumov's fantasy of idealized servitude gives
way to the disciplinary power of surveillance, *Under Western Eyes*
transforms the imagery of the ghostly, found throughout Conrad's
work, into an expression of the invisible operations of ideology.

The tension between egocentric and systemic models of
agency comes to the foreground in an exchange between the
teacher of languages and Nathalie Haldin prompted by the newspaper report of de P——'s assassination. When the narrator argues that "antagonistic ideas" will never be reconciled into a
"concord" through "blood and violence," Nathalie responds in
what the teacher of languages understands as purely mystical
terms: "The whole world is inconceivable to the strict logic of
ideas" (*UWE* 104–6). At one level their disagreement is about the
relative value of compromise versus utopianism; Nathalie condemns the "artificial conflict" of the English parliamentary sys-

tem, preferring the "better way" of revolutionary idealism (*UWE* 106). At another level their disagreement recasts the tension between abstraction, now registered as the irrational grip of the ideological, and the concrete, associated with the pragmatism of the English system. Though we exist in the sensible world, says Nathalie, "there must be a necessity superior to our conceptions." With this statement she tries to seize both the political and the spiritual high ground; and insofar as the West is reduced to the material complacency of the Swiss and the bland obtuseness of the narrator himself, her claim carries some force. The teacher of languages responds as if he were compounded of a bourgeois politician and a nineteenth-century novelist, the former asserting the primacy of the individual, the latter affirming an aesthetic of the material: "what can be this era of disembodied concord you are looking forward to? Life is a thing of form. It has its plastic shape and a definite intellectual aspect. The most idealistic conceptions of love and forebearance must be clothed in flesh as it were before they can be made understandable" (*UWE* 106). The narrator fails to see that the very story he tells suggests that "conceptions" need not be incarnated to be understandable or effective in the world. Unwilling or unable to bracket the individual for the purposes of analysis, the teacher of languages cannot apprehend political power as a decentered system. At the same time, by providing the mediation of conventionally novelistic eyes, he ensures that the narrative's conceptions, unlike Nathalie's, will, to the best of his ability, be "clothed in flesh."

Razumov, in contrast, is quick to intuit the impersonal nature of the political machinery that has caught him up. In a sudden vision during his talks with Mikulin, "Razumov beheld his own brain suffering on the rack—a long pale figure drawn asunder horizontally with terrific force in the darkness of a vault, whose face he could not see. . . . The solitude of the racked victim was particularly horrible to behold. The mysterious impossibility to see the face . . . inspired a sort of terror" (*UWE* 88). "Brain . . . figure . . . face . . . victim": the fleeting fantasy oddly conflates and confuses the mental and the physical. (Any effort to visualize the "dark print of the Inquisition" in Razumov's mind must hesitate over the idea of a brain on a rack—a careless literalization of the English idiom?) Anticipations and echoes of the passage suggest that Razumov's mental torture revises an earlier description of an innocent victim of Haldin's bombing, "the only one whose identity was never established," a peasant whose "face was unrecognizable" (*UWE* 10). Like the dissolving and dispersed figure of Haldin, whose spectral presence is strategically redeployed throughout the text, the materiality of the victim is gradually refined out of existence until the fantasy of corporeal punishment is displaced by the vague yet unnerving effect of the narrator's Western eyes: having crossed paths with the ubiquitous teacher of languages, "Razumov felt a faint chill run down his spine. It was not fear. He was certain that it was not fear—not fear for himself—but it was, all the same, a sort of apprehension as if for another, for someone he knew without being able to put a name to the personality" (*UWE* 199). Razumov's subjective experience thus compresses into the narrative space of an individual life what Foucault has analyzed as an epistemic shift from punishment to discipline: surveillance supersedes torture.[37] While Conrad probably would have associated "the empire of the gaze" with paternal power, thirty-eight years later Orwell would name it Big Brother.[38]

Conrad's fantasy of the knitting machine evinces his fear that the individual is wholly powerless within larger structures, whether those structures are construed as illusions fabricated by a *malin génie* or as ideological mechanisms designed to regulate human behavior.[39] In this light the focus on individual consciousness in *Under Western Eyes*—the brooding violence of Razumov's wayward thoughts, the venality of Peter Ivanovitch's ulterior motives, the inwardness of Haldin's reaction to the bombing—has the effect of hollowing out a private space behind the blank wall of the bureaucratic or the doctrinal. Resentment, anger, and despair assert the (absent) place of the individual within the impersonal political networks that otherwise dominate the novel. The individual subject may yield to politics, but the political cannot *erase* the subjectivity of the individual.

Stuck in Geneva as a police spy, Razumov responds to his "prison of lies" (*UWE* 363) with ironic detachment, a defensive posture denounced by Sophia Antonovna, whose rebuke reads like a strangely mocking, even comic, defense of Conradian pieties: "Remember Razumov, that women, children, and revolutionists hate irony, which is the negation of all saving instincts, of all faith, of all devotion, of all action" (*UWE* 279). Yet irony competes with affirmation as one of Conrad's chief comforts: though the knitting machine has "knitted time space, pain, death, corruption, despair and the illusions—and nothing matters"—irony provides a detached view of the gears: "I'll admit however that to look at the remorseless process is sometimes amusing."[40] The thematics of coercion are thus inseparable from Conrad's (and Razumov's) addiction to irony, which claims to lever the individual into a vantage beyond the grasp of constraint. Challenged in his detachment by Antonovna, Razumov seeks relief from the taint of "direct lying" in silence and writing. Though he is compelled to write spy reports for Mikulin, Razumov's autobiographical journal constitutes a rebellion against that necessity, inasmuch as the very existence of the document imperils the covert operation installed by the state. Yet confession has its own compulsion—Razumov confesses openly to the assembled revolutionaries as soon as the death of Ziemianitch virtually ensures his safety—and the solitary scene of writing, however rebellious, cannot grant Razumov the autonomy he seeks. Rebellion, after all, requires a target, and will create one where necessary.

Sitting alone on his tiny island under a bronze effigy of Rousseau, Razumov as writer contrasts sharply with what we know of the second most prominent writer in the novel, Peter Ivanovitch, who, dictating to the much-abused Tekla, hardly permits her to breathe. Dictation turns the act of writing into an explicitly social activity, and Ivanovitch's virtual mechanization of Tekla replicates the coerciveness of all social relations in the novel. Hoping to escape the contamination of social existence, Razumov positions himself as if to reappropriate the power of surveillance exercised by the state: "If solitude could ever be secured in the open air in the middle of a town, he would have it there on this absurd island, together with the faculty of watching the only approach" (*UWE* 290). Yet in miming the power of the state Razumov is still subject to it, and the scene of his writing bears multiple witness to the impossibility of his dream of autonomy. Though seemingly free from the constraints of dictation and all it implies, Razumov cannot remain inviolate within his "mental soliloquy." Like Decoud writing to his sister ("In the most sceptical heart there lurks . . . a desire to leave a correct impression of the feelings"), or like Descartes at his writing desk and Hume at his, Razumov in his solitude both resists and solicits the presence of others: "the idea of writing evoked the thought of a place to write in, of shelter, of privacy, and naturally of his lodgings, mingled with a distaste for the necessary exertion of getting there, with a mistrust as of some hostile influence awaiting him within those odious four walls" (*UWE* 289). Conrad has already embodied this "hostile influence" as Haldin; Descartes imagined it as a demon; Hume's anxiety in the midst of engulfing doubt is somewhat less Gothic: "From what causes do I derive my existence, and to what condition shall I return? Whose favour shall I court, and whose anger must I dread? What beings surround me? and on whom have I any influence, or who have any influence on me?" (*THN* 269). Skepticism may dissolve the grounds for establishing the reality of others, but in the consequent emptiness anxieties about agency restore the presence of others in the fear of their malign influence. The action of the narrative dramatizes this dynamic: the words Razumov initially intended only for his own eyes will ultimately be turned over to Nathalie, who passes them on to the narrator, a man he sardonically considers "the devil himself" (*UWE* 360).

The recourse to polarized language of good and evil here and elsewhere in Conrad defends against a more troubling perception of nothingness. In "Autocracy and War" Conrad described Russia as "Le Néant" (*NLL* 99); in *Under Western Eyes* it is figured as the "monstrous blank page awaiting the record of an inconceivable history." That people act as the agents of their own destruction—that they make their own history—is a fact Conrad simultaneously asserts and denies. Describing Nathalie's sorrowful gesture in response to Razumov's confession, the narrator remarks that it was "so far-reaching in its human distress that one could not believe that it pointed out merely the ruthless working of political institutions" (*UWE* 355). Yet the novel does not simply demystify the causes of human suffering by ironizing "Russian obscurantism."[41] The demystification of, say, Mikulin's power, which is "not obscure, not occult, but simply inconspicuous" (*UWE* 305), is partially remystified by the way Razumov's subjectivity dominates the novel: his mode of seeing survives trial by irony. Surrounded by revolutionaries, "[Razumov] felt, bizarre as it may seem, as though another self, an independent sharer of his mind, had been able to view his whole person very distinctly indeed" (*UWE* 230). For the reader with a distinct view of Razumov's whole person, to accede entirely to the language teacher's "proprieties" ("In the conduct of an invented story," he remarks, "there are, no doubt, certain proprieties to be observed for the sake of clearness and effect"—*UWE* 100) is to translate Razumov's sensations exclusively into the ideological terms discussed earlier. To accept the mysticism at face value is to ignore the narrative attention devoted to the parody of Madame de S——'s spiritualism. Between these positions is something closer to what I called in Chapter Five the supernatural naturalism of *Nostromo.* Just as Conrad's "moments of vision," unlike Joyce's epiphanies, retain a residual sense of the holy, so his parodic spiritualism, "bizarre as it may seem," sustains a genuine feel for the uncanny, one that cannot be wholly resolved into "the ruthless working of political institutions."

Shelter from the Storm: Atoning for Duplicity

Under Western Eyes ends with an act of atonement that Razumov, unlike many of Conrad's heroes, is permitted to survive. I use the word advisedly, for "atonement" derives from the phrase "at one" and so suggests the act of transforming the many into the one. Razumov's conversion to autocracy early in the novel takes precisely this form, as "a will strong and one" seems to him the antidote to "the babble of many voices." Razumov ends the novel neither as a reactionary nor as a revolutionary; he is a sage apparently, though one unlikely to be consulted by agents of the state. Razumov's atonement is presented as a kind of serenity, but he arrives there at a cost.

Publicly confessing before the revolutionaries gathered at Laspara's, Razumov feels released from his past: "To-day, of all days since I came amongst you, I was made safe [by the death of Ziemianitch], and to-day I made myself free from falsehood, from remorse—independent of every single human being on this earth" (*UWE* 368). The desire for an escape into autonomy recalls Jim, Kurtz, and other Conradian dreamers; the motivation of each represents an attempt to overcome, as in Descartes and Hume, the sense of dependency that underlies and motivates doubt of other minds. To an extent Razumov's singular survival comes at the expense of human connectedness, for Nikita, the professional killer, bursts his eardrums in revenge. Stumbling into the street, Razumov is sealed in the silence of what may be a cleansing storm—or perhaps only a negative version of the autonomy he has sought all along: "lightning waved and darted round him its silent flames, the water of the deluge fell, ran, leaped, drove—noiseless like the drift of mist" (*UWE* 369). The beauty of this carefully crafted impressionism makes it all the more poignant as an ultimately untenable refuge from the sounds, political or otherwise, of everyday life. Though deaf, Razumov is later released from this lyrical void, becoming, Sophia Antonovna tells the narrator, a thinker highly respected in Geneva's revolutionary circles. Solipsistic aestheticism (initially Razumov experiences the world as a series of heightened visual moments) thus gives way to the claims of the political.

In the denouement, as in the early counterpoise established between Haldin and Razumov, Conrad strikes a surprisingly generous attitude toward all concerned. Razumov is forgiven his crime against Haldin, and the revolutionaries are forgiven the violence that occasioned it. Mikulin too is treated lightly: he had never wanted to employ Nikita in the first place, and during a chance meeting with Peter Ivanovitch, he betrays the double agent to the revolutionary. And the narrator's skeptical remarks about the mystery of Russian idealism and mysticism are undercut no more than Sophia Antonovna's closing declaration that Peter Ivanovitch—who abandons the cause to marry a peasant girl—"is an inspired man" (*UWE* 382). Conrad gives us no reason to accept the description of Ivanovitch but every reason to admire the fortitude and clear-sightedness that permit Antonovna to distinguish between the corrupt individual and his ideal role. Inspiration and skepticism achieve a standoff.

Razumov, meanwhile, the erstwhile *homo duplex* against whom the parodic treatment of Ivanovitch could be gauged, has retired to "a little two-roomed wooden house, in the suburb of some very small town, hiding within the high plank-fence of a yard overgrown with nettles" (*UWE* 379). Secure in the shelter of Tekla's care, he "talks well," according to Sophia Antonovna, though there is no indication that he continues to write.

Epilogue

In all the incidents of life we ought to preserve our
scepticism. —David Hume, *A Treatise of Human Nature*

I cannot say I had ever seen him distinctly . . . but it seemed to
me that the less I understood the more I was bound to him in
the name of that doubt which is the inseparable part of our
knowledge. —Lord Jim

"Words," according to the teacher of languages, "are the great foes of reality" (*UWE* 3). Consonant with the tradition of philosophical skepticism, Conrad in his best fiction meticulously assesses our verbal constructions of the world.[1] Within the terms of such a project, the affirmations of the late romances can supply only spurious closure—a false version of "that full utterance" sought by Marlow—to a career whose central fictions explore even as they struggle to deny the insights generated by authorial skepticism. Traditional themes of the novel enter the skeptical medium of Conrad's fiction and are intensified, refracted, and distorted, like objects seen through the irregular facets of cut glass.

Since *Tristram Shandy* the English novel has been centered in the family; in *The Secret Agent* Conrad throws a bomb into it. Raymond Williams has argued more generally that community has always been the central focus of the nineteenth-century novel.[2] In Conrad the issue takes on an obsessive intensity, with communal norms and institutional codes understood as both crucial systems of order and oppressive threats to individuality. Ian Watt has established the importance of English empiricism to the rise of the novel.[3] Conrad conjures the demon of radical skepticism latent in that tradition. Bakhtin has argued that the dominance of the novel as genre marks the transition from theology to psychology, from metaphysics to epistemology.[4] The extremity of the skeptical dialogics in Conrad pulls him in opposing directions: no matter how much he yearns for the prior terms, for the consolations of theology and the stability of metaphysics, Conrad is forced to acknowledge, without fully accepting, that the attempt "to render the highest kind of justice to the visible universe, by bringing to light the truth, manifold and one, underlying its every aspect" can only return him to the conflicted crosscurrents of psychology, the ambiguities and *aporias* of epistemology, the "truths of skepticism."[5] By studying Conrad in this light, I hope to have defined more precisely the interrelation of skepticism and representation in his fiction and, in so doing, to have established a more sharply focused understanding of the nature of his distinctive achievement. Conrad is, in the best sense, a philosophical novelist; for rather than espousing a definite school of thought, he advances a particular style of thinking.

Notes

Notes

Preface

Epigraph: Conrad to Galsworthy, November 11, 1901, in *LL*, I: 301.

1. *Sunday Times*, October 20, 1907. Quoted in Sherry, ed., *The Critical Heritage*, 28–29.

2. The literature on Conrad's skepticism has grown considerably in recent years. I have learned from the following articles: Widmer, "Conrad's Pyrrhonistic Conservativism" (1974); Park, "Conrad's *Victory*: The Anatomy of a Pose" (1976); and Raval, "Conrad's *Victory*: Skepticism and Experience" (1980). Raval's *The Art of Failure* incorporates a modestly revised version of his *Victory* essay; see also his chapter on *Nostromo*, 79–83, and his conclusion, 166–69, for more on skepticism as a social and cultural stance. Raval's arguments are considerably more informed and sophisticated than Park's, but neither critic shows much familiarity with the tradition of philosophical skepticism, and each tends to reduce skepticism to detachment from the social world. Widmer's antipathy toward Conrad produces outright factual blunders even as it generates considerable insight into the troubled relation between skepticism and morality in Conrad. For a fine discussion of Conrad's own idiosyncratic use of the words "skepticism" and "cynicism" and their relation to his pessimism, see Kertzer, "'The bitterness of our wisdom'" (1983). Kertzer rightly recognizes that skepticism should be the prior term in any analysis of cynicism or pessimism in Conrad. For a bibliography on philosophical skepticism see n. 13 below.

3. I borrow the formulation from Rorty, "The Philosophy of the Oddball," a review of Cavell's *In Quest of the Ordinary*.

4. Camus, *Notebooks, 1935–1942*, 10.

5. Lawrence, "Surgery for the Novel—Or a Bomb," in *Phoenix*, 520.

6. On the relation between skepticism and Derridean deconstruction, see Cavell, *In Quest of the Ordinary*, 130–36. Cavell argues persuasively that the deconstructive concept of "undecidability" trivializes the skeptic's claim that we cannot know by stripping the agent of responsibility for meaning something one way rather than another. For a sustained discussion of Cavell's understanding of skepticism in relation to

poststructuralist literary theory, see Fischer, *Stanley Cavell and Literary Skepticism*.

7. Forster, "Joseph Conrad: A Note," in *Abinger Harvest*, 137. Forster nicely catches Conrad's evasive irony.

8. Warren, "'The Great Mirage': Conrad and *Nostromo*," in *Selected Essays*, 58. Warren also has some useful remarks about Conrad's skepticism.

9. Though Conrad would have read Schopenhauer in the Haldane and Kemp edition of 1883–86, I will be referring to the more easily accessible Payne edition.

10. Bakhtin, *Problems of Dostoevsky's Poetics*, 25–26. For Bakhtin's most comprehensive exposition of "dialogism," see *The Dialogic Imagination*. In *Coercion to Speak*, Fogel sees Bakhtin as providing only one model among many for an analysis of dialogue in Conrad. Fogel discounts the importance of the philosophical dialogic in Conrad, focusing instead on a Foucauldian vision of disproportionate power relations as they are expressed in forms of dialogue. Our analyses converge in a shared interest in Conrad's thematics of coercion, but, as I argue in Chapter Five, I see the operations of authorial skepticism as crucially involved in the coercive relations represented in Conrad's fiction. For a reading claiming to find a "dialectic" between belief and unbelief in Conrad, see Gekoski, *The Moral World of the Novelist*, especially the first chapter.

11. Cavell, *The Claim of Reason*, 391.

12. Hardy's skepticism may make his fiction especially amenable to the method I employ here. For the interpenetration of the social and metaphysical in Forster, see Burke, "Social and Cosmic Mystery: *A Passage to India*," in *Language as Symbolic Action*, 223–39. For a reading of representation in *To the Lighthouse* in terms of the subject-object relations studied by Mr. Ramsay, see Beer, "Hume, Stephen, and Elegy in *To the Lighthouse*" (1984).

13. Once thought to have been dispelled by Wittgenstein and ordinary language philosophy, skepticism has returned to the scene of philosophy in recent years as an important issue. For Cavell's contribution to thinking about skepticism, see his seminal study, *The Claim of Reason*, as well as "Knowing and Acknowledging," in *Must We Mean What We Say?* and his latest collection of essays, *In Quest of the Ordinary*. For Kripke, see *Wittgenstein on Rules and Private Language*. Also important is *The Skeptical Tradition*, edited by Burnyeat, which features articles on particular philosophers and specific issues. For an excellent historical survey of the skeptical tradition, see Popkin, *The History of Scepticism from Erasmus to Spinoza*. Having spilled over into literary studies, the resurgence of interest in skepticism has informed several recent philosophical

studies of fiction and poetry. See, for instance, Cascardi, *The Bounds of Reason: Cervantes, Dostoevsky, and Flaubert*, and Benfey, *Emily Dickinson and the Problem of Others*. My understanding of skepticism has also been sharpened by my participation in a special session on Skepticism and Literary Theory at the 1989 MLA Convention in New Orleans. The panel featured papers by Gary Wihl, Jules Law, Alan Kennedy, and myself.

14. Arguing for a poetics of utterance, Said applies the slogan to Derridean deconstruction. Said is revising the phrase coined by Blackmur, *A Primer of Ignorance*, who uses "techniques of trouble" to describe the responses of art to the new troubles of modernity, not the troubling of art *by* new critical techniques. Said's preference for voice over the purely scriptive status of writing (and thus for Foucault over Derrida) probably accounts in part (a Palestinian no doubt feels other affinities with an exiled Pole) for the considerable attention he has devoted to Conrad and his loquacious narrators. See "The Problem of Textuality" (1978), 684.

Chapter One

1. Eliot, *Middlemarch*, 272.

2. "A Familiar Preface" to *A Personal Record*, xxi. For relevant material on Conrad's Polish heritage, see Najder, "Conrad and the Idea of Honor," in Zyla and Aycock, eds., *Theory and World Fiction*, 103–14, who traces the history of the concept of honor and its enduring importance to the Polish nobility. For a more comprehensive attempt to place Conrad's sense of commitment in the history of ideas, see Watt, "Joseph Conrad: Alienation and Commitment," in Davies and Watson, eds., *The English Mind*, 257–78.

3. January 14, 1898, in Watts, ed., *Letters to Graham*, 65. As Watts points out, it is characteristic of Conrad that his most radically skeptical letters are elicited in response to the idealism of Graham.

4. Huxley, "On Descartes' 'Discourse Touching the Method of Using One's Reason Rightly and of Seeking Scientific Truth'" [1870], in *Methods and Results*, 171. Hume often uses the same word. See, for instance, *THN* 186, 264.

5. To Graham, December 20, 1897, in Watts, ed., *Letters to Graham*, 56–57.

6. Putnam, *Reason, Truth, and History*, 6, 12.

7. Conrad refers to Descartes only in passing in his correspondence; no doubt he was familiar, however, with Huxley's essays on Descartes and the skeptical tradition.

8. In Sherry, ed., *The Critical Heritage*, 127.

9. Jameson, *The Political Unconscious*, 219.

10. Ibid., 243.

11. For the interidentity of ideology and individual subjectivity, see Althusser's discussion of the "interpellation" of subjects in "Ideology and Ideological State Apparatuses," in *Lenin and Philosophy*, 170–83. For my discussion of representations of ideology in *Under Western Eyes*, see Chapter Six, 184–91. For Conrad's sensitivity to language as control, see, for instance, *The Secret Agent*, in which the Professor scorns Ossipon's characterization of the Greenwich bombing as "criminal": "How am I to express myself?" Ossipon responds, "One must use the current words" (*SA* 71).

12. Thus Beerbohm's superb job of it in "The Feast" (1912), 126: "Within the hut the form of the white man, corpulent and pale, was covered with a mosquito-net that was itself illusory like everything else, only more so."

13. To Meldrum, August 10, 1898, in Wright, ed., *Conrad on Fiction*, 15–16.

14. To Graham, August 15, 1897, in Watts, ed., *Letters to Graham*, 45.

15. Undated letter of October 1907, in Najder, *Conrad's Polish Background*, 25.

16. The most notorious allegorizing of Conrad's Polish past was undertaken by Morf, who reads "Poland" for *Patna* in the course of arguing that *Lord Jim* reflects Conrad's guilt over abandoning the sinking ship of his countrymen. At some level Morf is clearly "right," though his reading greatly oversimplifies both the novel and Conrad's relation to his past. See *The Polish Heritage of Joseph Conrad*, 149–66. Rather than sifting the fiction for allegories of Conrad's personal history, I am interested in more encompassing contexts for the skepticism that informs his best work.

17. Houghton, *The Victorian Frame of Mind*, 14. On the expression in British literature of the growing sense of cultural crisis during the transition from the Victorian to the modern era, see Lester, *Journey Through Despair, 1880–1914*.

18. Amid the profusion of biographical materials, the most reliable accounts in English of Conrad's life in Poland and his Polish heritage are Najder's: *A Chronicle*, *Conrad Under Familial Eyes*, and *Conrad's Polish Background*. Baines, *A Critical Biography*, is better on the fiction itself.

19. The classic Renaissance examples are Montaigne's "Of Cannibals," which praises the nobility of cannibals, and *The Tempest*, which implicitly criticizes the idealization of "brave new worlds." Compare Ruthven, "The Savage God" (1968), who locates "Heart of Darkness" in turn-of-the-century primitivism as a Romantic revolt against civilization. Like Marlow's response to Kurtz, however, Conrad's attitude toward the primitive is deeply ambivalent.

20. A representative piece is Nicoll's pamphlet "Stanley's Exploits" (1891), which denounces Stanley's "brutal carelessness of human life." Since Conrad appears to have used Nicoll's penny pamphlet "The Greenwich Mystery" (1897, reprinted in Sherry, *Conrad's Western World*) for *The Secret Agent*, it is possible that he was also familiar with the earlier essay.

21. For the quoted phrase, see the letter to Graham, February 8, 1899, in Watts, ed., *Letters to Graham*, 116. The letter does not specify what these ideas are. For a powerful reading of the contradictions produced by the conjunction of ideological demystification and mythopoetic narrative in "Heart of Darkness," see Parry, *Conrad and Imperialism*, 20–39.

22. A. N. Whitehead here echoes a letter from William James to his brother Henry in *Science and the Modern World*, 3. On the scientific in Conrad, see Levine's fine discussion in "George Eliot, Conrad, and the Invisible World," Chapter Twelve in *The Realistic Imagination*. For a provocative, if overstated, argument about the influence of contemporary science on Conrad, particularly physics, see the first chapter of O'Hanlon's *Joseph Conrad and Charles Darwin*. O'Hanlon largely restricts his discussion of the fiction to intensive study of *Lord Jim*. For a comprehensive treatment of "Heart of Darkness" and the history of ideas, see Watt, *Conrad in the Nineteenth Century*, 147–68.

23. For a fine account of Conrad's use of Nordau's *Degeneration* (1895), see Ray, "Conrad, Nordau, and Other Degenerates" (1984). On Lombroso, see Hunter, *The Ethics of Darwinism*, 153–219.

24. To Garnett, September 29, 1898, in Garnett, ed., *Letters from Joseph Conrad*, 143.

25. *Works of H. G. Wells*, 607. Wells's *The Plattner Story, and Other Stories* (1897) was among the books sold from Conrad's personal library after his death. See *A Catalogue of Books, Manuscripts from the Library of the Late Joseph Conrad* (1925). For more on Conrad's indebtedness to Wells, see McCarthy, "*Heart of Darkness* and the Early Novels of H. G. Wells" (1986).

26. March 18, 1917, in *LL*, II: 185. For further discussion of this important letter, see Chapter Two, 49–50.

27. Woolf, "Mr. Conrad" (1923), in *The Captain's Death Bed*, 80.

28. Young, *The Writings of Walter Pater*, 20. For more on Pater's philosophical skepticism, see Inman, "The Organic Structure of *Marius the Epicurean*" (1962).

29. The depth of Conrad's investment can be gauged by the rhythmic intensity of the writing: "On the main deck, men . . . splashed, dashing aimlessly here and there with the foam swirling up to their waists. Apart, far aft, and alone by the helm, old Singleton had deliberately tucked his white beard under the top button of his glistening coat. Sway-

ing upon the din and tumult of the seas, with the whole battered length of the ship launched forward in a rolling rush before his steady old eyes, he stood rigidly still, forgotten by all, and with an attentive face. In front of his erect figure only the two arms moved crosswise with a swift and sudden readiness, to check or urge again the rapid stir of circling spokes. He steered with care" (*NN* 89).

30. To Graham, December 14, 1897, in Watts, ed., *Letters to Graham*, 53.

31. Huxley, *Methods and Results*, 226–29.

32. Cavell, *The Claim of Reason*, 20.

33. I intend "aesthetic" to refer to the heightened visual perception described by Baumgarten when he coined the term. See *Reflections on Poetry*, 78. I owe this reference to Jonathan Freedman.

34. See *The Basic Writings of Bertrand Russell, 1903–1959*, 67. For Conrad's familiarity with the essay, see Najder, *A Chronicle*, 389, 579 n.

35. Although Paterson, *The Novel as Faith*, remarks on Conrad's novelistic career as "a religious enterprise" (p. 105), he does not actually pursue the point, and his commentary on Conrad is generally unreliable. Too recent to be incorporated here is Lester's *Conrad and Religion* (1988), which analyzes Conrad's use of religious imagery and offers historical information on the Polish Catholic church. For a representative treatment of Conrad in the context of existentialism, see Gillon, "Conrad and Sartre" (1960). For what promises to be a more philosophically informed study, see Bohlmann, *Conrad's Existentialism*, forthcoming. Given the distinctions supplied by Jonas, Conrad can be understood as more gnostic than existentialist: "Gnostic man is thrown into an antagonistic, anti-divine, and therefore anti-human nature, modern man into an indifferent one. . . . In the gnostic conception the hostile, the demonic, is still anthropomorphic, familiar even in its foreignness, and the contrast gives direction to existence—a negative direction, to be sure, but one that has behind it the sanction of the negative transcendence to which the positivity of the world is the qualitative counterpart. Not even this antagonistic quality is granted to the indifferent nature of modern science." See *The Gnostic Religion*, 338–39.

36. Joyce, *A Portrait of the Artist as a Young Man*, 243.

37. To Graham, January 31, 1898, in Watts, ed., *Letters to Graham*, 71.

38. Though Purdy's detection of the lineaments of the mass in the Preface suggests the importance of incarnation to Conrad's ideal conception of art, Conrad never appropriates Christian theology as artistic trope in the self-conscious manner of Joyce's "Scylla and Charybdis" episode in *Ulysses*. At the same time, Conrad is often closer to the Catholic sense of mystery. For the Preface, see *Joseph Conrad's Bible*, 25.

39. See Chapter Four, 84–96.

40. For a more hypnotic example, see the first paragraph of the third chapter of *Lord Jim*, in which Conrad's prose poem asserts and enacts a fullness of meaning soon ruptured by the *Patna*'s collision with an unseen obstacle.

41. For Conrad on action in his novels, see the letter to Blackwood, May 31, 1902, in Blackburn, ed., *Letters to Blackwood*, 156. On the development of Conrad's evasive narrative strategies, see Chapter Two in Guerard, *Conrad the Novelist*, and my discussion in Chapter Four.

42. I thank Francesco Rognoni, who read an earlier version of this chapter, for suggesting the exemplary value of Stein's remark.

43. Conrad's ambivalence toward the moral order enforced by institutions resembles the classic debate between Erasmus and Luther about the problem of religious skepticism. Erasmus contended that many theological and scriptural problems were beyond human understanding and so counseled a suspension of individual judgment in favor of accepting the views of the Church. Luther rejected the refuge of institutional controls on skepticism and advocated the private dictates of one's conscience. Recapitulating this debate, Conrad never overcomes his self-division.

44. Bakhtin, *Problems of Dostoevsky's Poetics*, 16–18.

45. Ibid., 70, 72.

46. See Foucault's "The Discourse on Language," an appendix to *The Archaeology of Knowledge*.

47. My reading here is indebted to Price, "Conrad" (1984), who uses Dickens as a foil for analyzing the relation between the satiric and the novelistic in "An Outpost of Progress," "The Return," and *The Secret Agent*.

48. Brooks, *Reading for the Plot*, 249.

49. January 14, 1898, in Watts, ed., *Letters to Graham*, 65.

50. November 11, 1901, in *LL*, I, 301.

Chapter Two

Epigraphs: *WWR*, I: 185; Preface, 147.

1. Huxley, *Methods and Results*, 190.

2. See Burnyeat, "Can the Skeptic Live His Skepticism?" in Burnyeat, ed., *The Skeptical Tradition*, 121.

3. For an attempt to define the metaphysical novel as a species of romance, see Eigner, *The Metaphysical Novel in England and America*, 1–12. Oddly, Eigner tends to cite Conrad as a realist, even though his definitions of the metaphysical novel could have been derived from *Lord Jim*.

4. In what follows I am mainly concerned with presenting an expos-

itory account of Schopenhauer's thought, not a philosophical critique. I
will therefore discuss the contradictions and inconsistencies of his system (and there are many) only when they are relevant to my reading of
Conrad.

5. Here only I follow the older translations of *Vorstellung* as "idea"
rather than "representation."

6. Although Freud would later reconstitute this "endless striving"
within the individual as the unconscious, Schopenhauer's will is not to
be identified with individual volition because the individual will is itself
a phenomenon or representation of the metaphysical will.

7. January 14, 1898, in Watts, ed., *Letters to Graham*, 65.

8. Royce, *The Spirit of Modern Philosophy*, 228; quoted from the first
edition by Gardiner in his *Schopenhauer*, 21. Despite more recent books,
Gardiner's remains the best general commentary on Schopenhauer
available in English. On late-century interest in Schopenhauer, see Lester, *Journey Through Despair*, 62–65.

9. Axel Heyst's father, a philosopher who counsels withdrawal and
resignation, is clearly modeled on Schopenhauer. Whether or not Conrad's characters are burdened, as Heyst is, with the paternal injunction
to "Look on—make no sound" (*V* 175), frequently they are torn between
desire for detachment and the imperative of action. In *Victory*, Heyst's
simple movement from emotional isolation to a belated recognition of
the need for involvement offers a distinct paradigm of Conrad's equivocal attitude toward Schopenhauer's philosophical justification for re-
nouncing the claims of the world. Ambivalence toward the father in
Conrad is never a matter of philosophy alone. In characters such as
Heyst's father, Stein, even the French lieutenant, Conrad struggles with
his conflicted response to the antithetical legacies left by the radical ac-
tivism of his father, Apollo Korzeniowski, and the conservatism of his
uncle *cum* guardian, Tadeuz Bobrowski. Conrad works through his most
direct confrontation with the conflict in *A Personal Record*, where he anx-
iously responds to the charge that his "desertion" of Poland has transformed him into a mere spectator to his country's woes.

10. Galsworthy, *Castles in Spain and Other Screeds*, 91. If Conrad read
any English commentary, very likely it would have been in James Sully's
Pessimism (1877), 74–105. According to Said, Conrad may have discovered Schopenhauer by way of Ferdinand Brunetière. See *The Fiction of
Autobiography*, 102. Schopenhauer's thought would have come to Conrad from many sources in any case—Maupassant, Pater, and Hardy, to
name only a few. For a brief survey of creative writers influenced by
Schopenhauer, see Magee, *The Philosophy of Schopenhauer*, appendix 7.
Magee discusses Tolstoy, Turgenev, Zola, Proust, Hardy, Mann, Maupassant, and Conrad.

11. Grim physical comedy in Conrad's work may draw on the difficulties caused by Jessie's unsuccessful knee surgery in 1904. The operation left her permanently lame and made the Conrads' travels very arduous. See Najder, *A Chronicle*, 304.

12. To Sir Hugh Clifford, October 9, 1899, in Wright, ed., *Conrad on Fiction*, 20, emphasis added.

13. Here only I follow the Haldane and Kemp translation, *The World as Will and Idea*, I: 153.

14. Thomas Moser makes a similar point in psychoanalytic terms when he quotes this passage as evidence of the sexual anxiety Conrad feels as he describes Dain and Nina's first kiss. *Achievement and Decline*, 53–54. Compare Hardy's suggestion of an inherent cruelty in the fertility of nature: "The outskirt of the garden in which Tess found herself had been left uncultivated for some years, and was now damp and rank with juicy grass which sent up mists of pollen at a touch; and with tall blooming weeds emitting offensive smells—weeds whose red and yellow and purple hues formed a polychrome as dazzling as that of cultivated flowers. She went stealthily as a cat through this profusion of growth, gathering cuckoo-spittle on her skirts, cracking snails that were underfoot, staining her hands with thistle-milk and slug-slime, and rubbing off upon her naked arms sticky blights which, though snow white on the apple-tree trunks, made madder stains on her skin." *Tess of the D'Urbervilles*, 178–79. Considering that Tess creeps through this seething garden toward Angel Clare, Hardy too seems to associate the destructive energy of nature with sexual desire.

15. The best discussion is Kirschner's in *The Psychologist as Artist*, 266–75. Green, "Diabolism, Pessimism, and Democracy" (1962), also has some interesting remarks on Schopenhauer and skepticism. Comparisons between Conrad and Schopenhauer usually focus on several themes held in common: resignation, the blind striving of the will, or the veil of appearances screening us from the void. On Jim's resignation and Schopenhauer's concept of tragedy in *Lord Jim*, see Watt's brief remarks in *Conrad in the Nineteenth Century*, 350; on the hunger of the will in *Falk*, see Kirschner, *The Psychologist as Artist*, 267–69; on appearances and the void, see Bonney, *Thorns and Arabesques*, 3–30. Bonney reduces Schopenhauer to a synecdoche for Eastern thought and Eastern thought to an unblinking awareness of the "abyss." Schopenhauer has also been linked to Conrad's general vision of the world. Watts cites Schopenhauer as probably "the most direct literary contribution to Conrad's pessimism," and one of Conrad's biographers has tried to sharpen the claim by suggesting that Conrad found in "Schopenhauer, Darwin, and Nietzsche . . . metaphors for his own sense of doom." Watts, ed., *Letters to Graham*, 25; Karl, *The Three Lives*, 194.

16. Kirschner also cites this parallel. One of Conrad's descriptive techniques virtually enacts this process, as he frequently will move—in what film critics call an "eyeline shot"—from the eyes of a character to a vivid description of what it is he or she sees.

17. *WWR*, I: 69: "perception is the first source of all evidence [and] immediate or mediate reference to this alone is absolute truth." See also Chapters II and VII in Volume II. Not long before composing the Preface, Conrad wrote to a friend about *The Nigger*: "I tried to get through the veil of details at the essence of life." To Helen Watson, January 27, 1897, in Karl and Davies, eds., *Collected Letters*, I: 334. The "veil of Maya," a favorite allusion of Schopenhauer's, was later taken up by the French Symbolists, particularly in the poetry and theoretical writings of Mallarmé. Conrad also uses the image frequently. For Conrad and French symbolism, see Yelton, *Mimesis and Metaphor*.

18. Pater, "The School of Giorgione," in *The Renaissance*, 111. See also Yelton, *Mimesis and Metaphor*, 54 n., 94–96.

19. For the trope of the rescued fragment, see Conrad's Preface, 147, and *WWR*, I: 185, the epigraphs for this chapter. For the aesthetic as release, see Conrad's "Henry James: An Appreciation" (*NLL* 13), and *WWR*, I: 198.

20. Watt, *Conrad in the Nineteenth Century*, 86–87. On Conrad's Romantic heritage see Thorburn, *Conrad's Romanticism*. Although Thorburn focuses on the theme of community as a Romantic inheritance, one can also detect the outlines of an internalized quest in the "lonely region of stress and strife" where the artist-errant seeks his grail, "the terms of his appeal" (*P* 145). Thorburn downplays the relevance of the school of criticism that emphasizes the apocalyptic strain in Romanticism. Yet regardless of whether or not "the unmediated vision," to borrow Geoffrey Hartman's phrase, has been exaggerated in Romantic studies generally, visionary experience is clearly important to Conrad's early fiction.

21. The following from a letter to Edward Garnett, the man most responsible for encouraging Conrad's writing, is typical of the period of his literary apprenticeship: "I am sending you MS. already [*The Rescuer*]—if it's only twenty-four pages. But I must let you see it. I am so afraid of myself, of my likes and dislikes, of my thought and of my expression that I must fly to you for relief—or condemnation—for anything to kill the doubt with. For without doubt I cannot live—at least—not for long." April 13, 1896, in Garnett, ed., *Letters from Joseph Conrad*, 49.

22. This conjecture finds support in the fact that Schopenhauer's presence in Conrad's writing is most evident not only in the early novels but also in *Victory* (1915), the first new novel Conrad conceived after the severe emotional breakdown that followed his completion of *Under*

Western Eyes (1911). Though *Chance* (1913) was published between *Under Western Eyes* and *Victory*, it was conceived as early as 1898 and was at least partially drafted by 1905. See Karl, *The Three Lives*, 426. On Conrad's debt to Flaubert see Yelton, who focuses on the "musical structure" of their symbolic procedures in Chapter Four of *Mimesis and Metaphor*. More interesting, however, would be an account of the influence on Conrad of Flaubertian irony.

23. Katharine Gilbert has argued that Schopenhauer can be considered an early precursor of aestheticism because he relocated the idea of contemplation in art, where "a refined idea of esthetic pleasure" replaces the philosophical and theological ideal of contemplating the rational order of the world for its own sake. Gilbert and Kuhn, *A History of Esthetics*, 472. Gardiner notes the debt of French symbolism to Schopenhauer and speculates that it might have been the very vagueness of Schopenhauer's theory of the Platonic Ideas that appealed to such theorists of symbolism as Moréas. *Schopenhauer*, 212.

24. For a discussion of Schopenhauer's neoclassicism see Wellek, *A History of Modern Criticism*, II: 313–15.

25. See Gilbert and Kuhn, *A History of Esthetics*, 464–65.

26. "Ulysses, Order, and Myth," in Kermode, ed., *Selected Prose of T. S. Eliot*, 177. The article first appeared in *The Dial* in 1923.

27. Simmel, *Schopenhauer and Nietzsche*, 5.

28. The following is representative of the understanding of the will overturned in Schopenhauer's theory of music: "the will must live on itself, since nothing exists besides it, and it is a hungry will" (*WWR* I: 154). This version resonates in Conrad's Falk, who resorts to cannibalism when adrift in a disabled ship.

29. Robert Caserio has discussed "the determining reality of what is ghostly" in "Joseph Conrad, Dickensian Novelist of the Nineteenth Century" (1981). Eloquently pugnacious, Caserio faults Watt's *Conrad in the Nineteenth Century* for underplaying the importance of Victorian literature as a context for Conrad, especially the Dickensian focus on "the romantic side of familiar things." Caserio has some excellent pages, to which I am indebted, on the aim of so-called Dickensian fiction "to make the novel haunt life with meanings not glimpsed in other modes of reflection" (p. 344). But to associate this intention almost exclusively with Dickens is unwarranted. See my discussion of ghosts and skepticism on pp. 41–42.

30. See Todorov, *The Fantastic*, esp. 33, for whom this suspension constitutes the defining feature of the "fantastic." For a discussion of the tremendous resurgence of ghost stories at the turn of the century, see Sullivan, *Elegant Nightmares*.

31. The story was first collected in the posthumous *Tales of Hearsay*

(1925). For the complications of dating the story—it was written early and later revised—and a brief commentary, see Graver, "Conrad's First Story" (1965).

32. See my discussions in Chapters Five and Six, 155–60, 188–91.

33. Gekoski, *The Moral World of the Novelist*, 44.

34. To Garnett, June 19, 1896, in Garnett, ed., *Letters from Joseph Conrad*, 59.

35. Cavell, *In Quest of the Ordinary*, 108.

36. October 16, 1891, in Gee and Sturm, eds., *Letters to Poradowska*, 38.

37. See Cavell, *In Quest of the Ordinary*, 110: The idea of "self-authorizing . . . asks us, in effect, to move from the consideration that we may sensibly disclaim certain actions as ours . . . to the possibility that none of my actions and thoughts are mine—as if, if I am not a ghost, I am, I would like to say, *worked*, from inside or outside."

38. Although the narrative situation of "The Idiots" appears at first to have the kind of complexity found in *Lord Jim*, the narrator's collation of sources for the narrative never emerges as a significant dimension of the story. A later story, "Amy Foster" (1903), is also presented as a kind of *bricolage*, but in both stories the most important feature of their structure is that each narrative departs retrospectively from an initial visual impression (some idiot children, Amy Foster's face), which is then invested with significance by the ensuing sequence of events. This structure thus repeats on the level of narrative the closing of the gap between perception and understanding that is a prominent feature of Conrad's descriptive technique.

39. In actualizing the evocative potential of the newspaper in his own prose, Conrad does his part to uphold the side of literature in the contemporary debate about the literary merits of journalism. More self-conscious about such matters, Joyce ironically plays the game the other way in "A Little Cloud," where the "poetical" clerk, Little Chandler, tries pathetically to assert himself against his old friend and successful journalist, Ignatius Gallaher. On the growth and influence of the popular press late in the century, see Williams, *The Long Revolution*, 173–213.

40. Graver, *Conrad's Short Fiction*, 33. Although in the following pages I will be criticizing Graver's reading of "Karain," I am happy to acknowledge my indebtedness to his insights. I focus on his treatment because by denying the validity of his own points, Graver exemplifies an important blind spot within the critical response to the story.

41. To Graham, April 14, 1898, in Watts, ed., *Letters to Graham*, 82.

42. Graver, *Conrad's Short Fiction*, 33.

43. To Garnett, August 14, 1896, in Garnett, ed., *Letters from Joseph Conrad*, 67–68.

44. Though Conrad's description of "The Lagoon" as a concatenation of scenic conventions does not take too much away from the story, a few years later he indulged his penchant for hyperbolic self-deprecation and preemptive self-criticism in the claim that "the *Outcast* is a heap of sand, the *Nigger* a splash of water, *Jim* a lump of clay." To Garnett, November 12, 1900, in ibid., 172.

45. The verbal effect sometimes recalls the opening of *Little Dorrit*, but Dickens's play between the "glare" and "stare" of the sun's relentless intensity suggests a bifurcation whose transcendental serenity is distinctly unlike Conrad's version of Schopenhauer's will and representation. The cool shade of the prison contrasts with the outer world of Marseilles, and transcending both is an ideal realm to which Conrad is drawn but whose existence he cannot accept as readily as Dickens does: "The wide stare stared itself out for one while; the sun went down . . . the stars came out in the heavens and the fireflies mimicked them in the lower air, as men may feebly imitate the goodness of a better order of beings" (p. 53).

46. The best general discussion of the meaning of Conrad's "darkness" is in the first section of Miller's chapter on Conrad in *Poets of Reality*. While my understanding of the interplay of unintelligible spectacle and the comprehensible in Conrad, as well as many other matters, has been enriched by Miller's interpretation, he often attributes to "darkness" a more univocal meaning than the range and complexity of Conrad's canon warrants. See also Roussel, *The Metaphysics of Darkness*, in which phenomenological assumptions tend to emphasize unity over development: "The *presence* of darkness at the *source of all things* is a *constant* reminder for Conrad of the insubstantiality of creation, of the ephemeral nature of what we accept as reality" (p. 8, emphasis added).

47. Karain possesses "a fidelity to his purpose" and a "steadfastness of which I would have thought him racially incapable." "We . . . failed to discourage his eagerness to strike a blow for his own primitive ideas. He did not understand us, and replied by arguments that almost drove one to desperation by their childish shrewdness." "[We] caught glimpses of . . . a concentrated lust of violence which is dangerous in a native" (*TU* 18).

48. Guerard argues that it is "as though Conrad did not yet want to admit that Lord Jim with his crime was 'one of us'" (p. 91). Johnson counters Guerard's claim that to Conrad, "Karain is only a superstitious native" by showing that "Karain" is as close to *Lord Jim* thematically as it is formally. Johnson, "Conrad's 'Karain' and *Lord Jim*" (1963), 18.

49. Though Marlow, who is far closer to Conrad than this narrator is, often shows an interest in something resembling the philosophical problem of other minds, the issue concerns how one consciousness can seem

real to another, not to itself. For Conrad resentment may be the lowest common denominator of humanity. Jameson, whose ideological critique does not cancel his evident pleasure in Conrad, has described him in *The Political Unconscious*, 268, as "the epic poet" of "*ressentiment*."

50. See Graver, *Conrad's Short Fiction*, 29.

51. Said, *The Fiction of Autobiography*, 149, sees only one side of the issue, but he makes the point effectively: Conrad is a version of "the Schopenhauerian artist who, with artistic imagery," resists "the invasion of darkness," the formless flux of the world as will.

52. From an unpublished letter of dedication, October 16, 1896, inscribed in *An Outcast of the Islands*; quoted by Watt, *Conrad in the Nineteenth Century*, 202–3.

53. March 18, 1917, in *LL*, II: 185. The letter is motivated by Conrad's desire to shape Colvin's second review of *The Shadow Line*, the literalism of the first having disappointed him. For further commentary on the nature of Conrad's Platonism here, see Watt, "Story and Idea in Conrad's *The Shadow-Line*," in Schorer, ed., *Modern British Fiction*, esp. 133–35.

54. Quoted in Schwab, "Joseph Conrad's American Friend" (1955), 224.

55. Johnson, "Conrad's 'Karain,'" 17.

56. Long after writing these words, I came across the following from Cavell: "If some image of marriage, as an interpretation of domestication [in Emerson and Poe], is the fictional equivalent of what [Austin and Wittgenstein] understand to be the ordinary or the everyday, then the threat to the ordinary named skepticism should show up in fiction's favorite threat to forms of marriage, namely, in forms of melodrama." See *In Quest of the Ordinary*, 129–30. For more on the philosophical underpinnings of melodrama, see my discussion of "Heart of Darkness" in the next chapter.

57. Guerard's treatment is representative of this approach: "The Return" is "the most troubled expression of Conrad's confused misogyny and the extreme example of his creative bewilderment in the presence of a sexual situation" (p. 96). Following Guerard is Moser, whose book is devoted to the thesis that the decline in Conrad's writing later in his career is directly related to his attempts to write about love. On "The Return," see *Achievement and Decline*, 71–78.

58. Tanner, "'Gnawed Bones' and 'Artless Tales,'" in Sherry, ed., *A Commemoration*, 18.

59. See Gekoski, *The Moral World of the Novelist*, 53.

60. The verb "bind" also appears in an earlier articulation of the aims of art: the artist speaks to "the subtle but invincible conviction of solidarity that knits together the loneliness of innumerable hearts: to that

solidarity . . . which binds men to each other, which binds together all humanity—the dead to the living, and the living to the unborn" (P 146).

61. See, for example, *WWR*, II: 339–41, where Schopenhauer refutes the charge that positing a teleology in nature necessarily implies a theology.

62. For O'Connor's own commentary on the religious dimension of her fiction, see Chapter Five of her *Mystery and Manners*.

63. *The Idea of the Holy*, 5–7. Despite the phonemic resemblance, "numinous" and "noumenal" are not etymologically related. "Noumenal" derives from the Greek *nooùmenon*, a noun derived from the past participle of *noein*, to apprehend or conceive. Kant introduced the English word "noumenon" as the opposite of phenomenon. "Numinous" derives from the Latin *nuere*, to nod, which has a derivative *numen*, a divine nod, thus divine power. The *OED* cites "numinous," used of a king's power, in 1647, but the word did not gain currency until *The Idea of the Holy*, published in German in 1917 and translated into English in 1923.

64. The phrase is Hulme's from "Romanticism and Classicism," in *Speculations*, 118.

65. Burke, *The Rhetoric of Religion*, 22. See also Edwards, ed., *The Encyclopedia of Philosophy*: "According to this doctrine, nothing positive can be known about God, who has nothing in common with any other being. No predicate or descriptive term can legitimately be applied to him unless it is given a meaning which is wholly different from the one the term has in common usage and is purely negative"; *supra* "Maimonides."

66. Miller, *Poets of Reality*, 5.

Chapter Three

1. Quoting Marlow, I will include quotation marks only when the context does not make clear who is speaking. "Heart of Darkness" appears in the Doubleday volume entitled *Youth and Two Other Stories*, but for the sake of clarity I will cite it as *HD*.

2. Leavis, *The Great Tradition*, is the *locus classicus* for complaints about Conrad's melodrama. Although Wilt, *Ghosts of the Gothic*, xi, quotes the well-known description of Marlow's mode of narration in "Heart of Darkness" as an exemplary account of Gothic conventions, the citation is used only to legitimate the wanderings of her own narrative. Wilt eventually returns to "Heart of Darkness," but only to introduce her treatment of the Gothic in Lawrence. Brooks, who writes brilliantly about melodrama in *The Melodramatic Imagination* and about Conrad in *Reading for the Plot*, does *not* discuss melodrama when analyzing "Heart of Darkness." Conrad himself described *The Secret Agent* as an attempt

to sustain an ironic melodrama. See To Poradowska, June 20, 1912, in Gee and Sturm, eds., *Letters to Poradowska*, 116. Although Conrad never characterized his writing as Gothic, much of his fiction participates in the tradition. *The Secret Agent* clearly picks up Gothic elements from Dickens—particularly from *Bleak House*—in the sordid vision of London. The shared symbolism of exploding a character in the middle of a novel may be considered a form of Gothic melodrama, though the explosion in Dickens is far more mysterious than the bombing in Conrad. In *Lord Jim* one can detect the Gothic in Stein's dark, mysterious house, where Marlow is met by "an elderly, grim Javanese servant," who, before vanishing like "a ghost only momentarily embodied for that particular purpose," guides him through the shadowy interior, where Stein awaits him, oracular, in a circle of light. The pure evil of Gentleman Brown and the spectral intensity of Jones in *Victory* also draw on Gothic conventions.

3. Miller, *Poets of Reality*, 7.

4. Ibid., 37.

5. Watt, *Conrad in the Nineteenth Century*, 33.

6. Schopenhauer is quick to point out that his largely traditional ethical system is also consonant with Indian theology. Although Schopenhauer never accepted any of the radical ethical transvaluations that his metaphysics might imply, he inscribes within *The World as Will and Representation*, as Karsten Harries pointed out in a Yale lecture (February 20, 1983), the possibility of a Nietzschean response to his metaphysical pessimism. See *WWR*, I: 273. Lee M. Whitehead, in "Conrad's 'Pessimism' Re-examined" (1969–70), makes some perceptive remarks about Schopenhauer's concept of aesthetic contemplation but then argues unpersuasively that Conrad exhibits a Nietzschean response to Schopenhauer.

7. I am aware that this is only one dimension of a complex literary phenomenon, for the Gothic tradition can also be traced back through Gray and Collins to Richardson. To explain the Gothic revival is to account for the development of the Romantic movement itself. On the connection between Otto's concept of the holy and Gothic fiction, see Varnado, "The Idea of the Numinous in Gothic Literature," in Thompson, ed., *The Gothic Imagination*. For a more historically minded treatment of Gothic terror as "a genuine expression of religious malaise" rooted in Protestant theology, see in the same volume Porte, "In the Hands of an Angry God."

8. Varma, *The Gothic Flame*, 211.

9. Ruins were also seen as the mysterious work of great forces or eternal processes. For a useful compendium of Gothic conventions which

locates them in various Romantic traditions, see Railo, *The Haunted Castle*.

10. Varma, *The Gothic Flame*, 211.

11. See Otto, *The Idea of the Holy*, 12–24.

12. Brooks, *The Melodramatic Imagination*, 20. Succeeding quotations are from pages 20–21. Although Brooks does not mean to assert that the moral occult constitutes a metaphysical reality, for Conrad it does, and I will adapt the concept accordingly.

13. Wilt, *Ghosts of the Gothic*, xi. Wilt analyzes the incorporation of Gothic elements and procedures into what F. R. Leavis canonized as "the great tradition."

14. The *Ms.* reads "not inside like a kernel but outside *in the unseen*" (emphasis added). *Heart of Darkness*, Norton Critical Edition, 9. For the symbolist and impressionist background of this well-known passage, see Watt, *Conrad in the Nineteenth Century*, 169–200. For a rhetorical reading, see Miller, "*Heart of Darkness* Revisited" (1985).

15. Brooks, *The Melodramatic Imagination*, 4.

16. Leavis, *The Great Tradition*, 180. And from the same passage: "Conrad must . . . stand convicted of borrowing the arts of the magazine-writer . . . in order to impose on his readers and on himself, for thrilled response, a 'significance' that is merely an emotional insistence on the presence of what he can't produce."

17. Guetti, *The Limits of Metaphor*, has argued that "the emphasis shifts in 'Heart of Darkness' from the idea of a 'reality' beyond language to the limitations within language that were seen as evidence for the existence of such a reality" (p. 3). Although I am largely in agreement with Guetti's critique of Leavis (pp. 4–6), I cannot wholly accept his interpretation of the problem of the ineffable in exclusively linguistic terms, for this approach underestimates Conrad's investment in an absolute realm beyond language.

18. Compare Brooks, *The Melodramatic Imagination*, 77. He argues that gestural signification in the nineteenth-century novel represents a transformation of the hyperbolic gestures of theatrical melodrama: "Gesture appears as a way to make available certain occulted perceptions and relationships, to render, with the audacity of an as-if proposition, a world of significant shadows."

19. Compare Conrad's essay on Anatole France, in Wright, ed., *Conrad on Fiction*, 63: "only in the continuity of effort there is a refuge from danger for minds less clear-seeing and philosophic than his own." In *Lord Jim* Marlow defines "the wisdom of life" more explicitly as a kind of repression: the "putting out of sight all the reminders of our folly, of our weakness, of our mortality" (*LJ* 174).

20. For a lucid new historical critique of the ideology of work in "Heart of Darkness," see Thomas, "Preserving and Keeping Order by Killing Time in *Heart of Darkness*," in Murfin, ed., *Joseph Conrad: "Heart of Darkness*," esp. 252–55.

21. Beer, *Darwin's Plots*, 74–76. See also pp. 53–62 on metaphor as an expression of man's need to tame the "thisness" of a reality that resists interpretation.

22. Compare Levenson, *A Genealogy of Modernism*, discussing Pater's legacy to English modernism as promoting "a bifurcation into a realm of fact and a realm of subjective consciousness. Value was to reside within consciousness, and all other value became derivative" (p. 18).

23. Burke, *The Rhetoric of Religion*, 16. Conrad will later insist on the symbol-body duality in his satiric treatment of Peter Ivanovitch's escape from prison in *Under Western Eyes*.

24. Gilliam, "Undeciphered Hieroglyphs" (1980), is very interesting on this scene, and her conclusion essentially accords with my understanding of the metaphysical in "Heart of Darkness": Conrad's "complex ambivalence anticipates a full-blown modern attitude toward language, but despite his intense scepticism he does not foreclose on the possibility of linguistic signification, as a post-modernist might. . . . He hoped for and feared *both* possibilities—that the paleography of Russian character might indicate either that language is ultimately empty or that it bears a profound metaphysical meaningfulness" (p. 49).

25. Simmel, *Schopenhauer and Nietzsche*, 9–10.

26. For a surprisingly persuasive attempt to write out the unspeakable, see Reid, "The 'Unspeakable Rites' in *Heart of Darkness*" (1963–64). Reid uses *The Golden Bough* to argue for the hidden presence of human sacrifice and cannibalism.

27. The classic treatment of this theme is Miller's *The Disappearance of God*, which analyzes "heroic attempts to recover immanence in a world of transcendence" (p. 15).

28. In *Bleak House*, Tulkinghorn, much to his misfortune, does not have eyes to see. As he walks out on the leads, Tulkinghorn's absorption in the futile legal documents on his writing table blinds him to the signs that portend his own death: "The time was when men as knowing as Mr Tulkinghorn would walk on turret-tops in the starlight, and look up into the sky to read their fortunes there." *Bleak House*, 631. The Eliot anecdote is quoted in Haight, *George Eliot*, 464. In *Women in Love*, Gerald asks, ". . . you mean if there isn't the woman, there's nothing?", to which Birkin replies, "Pretty well that—seeing there's no God" (p. 51).

29. Watt, *Conrad in the Nineteenth Century*, 222, compares "Marlow's persistent description of the company agents as 'pilgrims'" with Eliot's

ironic echoing of the Grail legend in *The Waste Land* and Joyce's use of the *Odyssey* in *Ulysses*. The Moslem passengers of the *Patna* are also called "pilgrims," and it is their "exacting faith" and "unconscious belief" that seem to carry them safely to port in a leaking ship. Watt's discussion recalls Brooks's theory of melodrama as a response to the loss of "social glue."

30. Burke, "Four Master Tropes," Appendix D in *A Grammar of Motives*, 514.

31. For a sustained treatment of this theme, see Gillon, *The Eternal Solitary*.

32. Cavell, *The Claim of Reason*, 470.

33. James, *Notes on Novelists*, 351.

34. Bakhtin, *Problems of Dostoevsky's Poetics*, 9–13, 27.

35. For the classic reading of "Heart of Darkness" as an expression of "the disenchantment of our culture with culture itself," see Trilling, "On the Teaching of Modern Literature," in his *Beyond Culture*. He elaborates the argument, now cast as the rebellion of the Romantic self against the inauthenticity of society, in *Sincerity and Authenticity*, 106–11, 133.

36. On the mind's resistance to the private redefinition of language, see Quigley, "Wittgenstein's Philosophizing and Literary Philosophizing" (1988), esp. 220–21.

37. Cavell, *The Claim of Reason*, 369.

38. Houghton, *The Victorian Frame of Mind*, 277.

39. The scene has been one of the most widely discussed in Conrad. For a concise review of the critical controversy, see Martin, "The Function of the Intended in Conrad's *Heart of Darkness*" (1974). Stark, "Kurtz's Intended" (1974), offers a more comprehensive survey, but his own reading is very odd. For a more recent and critically sophisticated meditation on "the taint of mortality" Marlow finds in lies, see Stewart, "Lying as Dying in *Heart of Darkness*" (1980). The essay has since been revised and expanded in his *Death Sentences*.

40. A standard joke about oral examinations: What is the name of Kurtz's fiancée? The horror. Like most jokes, this one works on a variety of levels, and the comic conjunction of the (ideal) Intended and the horrifying fits nicely with my argument. The ambivalence registers also as a sexual one: "the whore" resonates in "the horror."

41. Felperin, "Romance and Romanticism" (1980), 704.

42. On this dimension of women in Conrad, see Bross, "The Unextinguishable Light of Belief" (1969–70). For a very rich discussion of the novelistic appropriation of the traditional iconography of truth as a woman, including a few pages on "Heart of Darkness," see Welsh, "The Allegory of Truth in English Fiction" (1965).

43. See Chapter One, pp. 8–9, n. 21.

44. See Guerard on evil, *Conrad*, 37.

45. To Graham, December 20, 1897, in Watts, ed., *Letters to Graham*, 56–57. The letter is frequently read as expression of proto-existentialism, though Said devotes a more interesting chapter to the machine in *The Fiction of Autobiography*. The letter also recalls Pip's dream near the end of *Great Expectations*, when he imagines himself as "a steel beam of a vast engine, clashing and whirling over a gulf" and begs to have his part hammered off (471–72). Pip wakes from his dream to forgive Magwitch for placing him where he does not belong. Marlow, in contrast, cannot escape his nightmare, nor will Conrad extend his forgiveness to God.

46. To Graham, January 14, 1898, in Watts, ed., *Letters to Graham*, 65.

47. Brooks, *Reading for the Plot*, 255: "Marlow's narrative has revealed the central motive that compelled his act of narration. . . . He must re-tell a story, that of Kurtz, mistold the first time."

48. Raval, "Narrative and Authority in *Lord Jim*" (1981), advances a similar argument. The essay is revised and expanded in Raval's *The Art of Failure*.

Chapter Four

1. Freud first used the term "repressed" in 1893. See "The Mechanism of Hysterical Phenomena," 10 n. 1. Although Freud may well have derived the theory independently, he notes in "On the History of the Psychoanalytic Movement," in Strachey, ed., *The Standard Edition*, XIV: 15, that Schopenhauer anticipates the concept in *The World as Will and Representation*.

2. See *The Dialogic Imagination*, 263. For the incorporation of genres in particular, see 320–24.

3. To Norman Douglas, February 29, 1908, in *LL*, II: 68.

4. Cavell, *The Claim of Reason*, 141.

5. "The Secret Sharer" (1910) demonstrates most explicitly Conrad's interest in sympathetic identification, yet critical commentary has erred in understanding Marlow's sympathy for the outcast as the *origin* of his attentiveness.

6. Ford, *The English Novel*, 124, comments on what he sees as a paradigm shift occurring in late Victorian fiction: "the story of a novel should be the history of an Affair and not a tale in which a central character with an attendant female should be followed through a certain space of time until the book comes to a happy end on a note of matrimony or to an unhappy end—represented by a death." Compare Said, *Beginnings*, Chapter Two, where Said describes the shift in narrative conventions as a movement from "relationships linked together by familial

analogy" to a privileging of concepts of discontinuity in which "complementarity and adjacency" supplant the logic of paternity and succession. Said associates the former with a mimetic model of fiction and the latter with an understanding of the novel as "construction."

7. I borrow the first phrase from Bailin, "'An Extraordinarily Safe Castle'" (1984), 623. For the second, see Conrad, *Last Essays*, 136, and my discussion in Chapter One, pp. 16–17.

8. Marcus, *Dickens*, was the first to recognize that analogy constitutes the main principle of organization to Dickens, an idea Daleski explores more fully in *Dickens and the Art of Analogy*.

9. The structure of *The Secret Agent* shows that Conrad's analogical ordering is not limited to first-person narration. For the "uncanny" presence of Dickens in that novel, see Daleski, *The Way of Dispossession*, 150–51.

10. Garrett, *The Victorian Multiplot Novel*, 11. Seeking a middle ground between programmatic univocality and the unlimited play of signification, Garrett uses Bakhtin's concept of the dialogical novel to define and delimit the range of meanings generated by the tension between centering and decentering structures in multiple narratives.

11. Ibid., 68.

12. Introduction to the Penguin edition of *Bleak House*, 32.

13. A recent essay on law in the *New York Times* suggests that to this day a desire for absolute laws runs deeper than one might expect: "Openness of interpretation is a threatening idea. Commenting on Oliver Wendell Holmes's famous work, *The Common Law*, the Oxford legal scholar Patrick Atiyah notes that 'it is necessary for the law to retain some mystique, some mystery, and some permanence, if it is to hold its persuasive power and emotive force over the public. Demystification of the law is all very well, but the power of the law over the minds of men will surely collapse if the process goes too far, and the public comes to see the law as a purely man-made instrument.'" Frug, "Henry James, Lee Marvin, and the Law," *New York Times Book Review*, February 16, 1986.

14. Nietzsche, "On Truth and Lies in a Nonmoral Sense," in Breazeale, trans. and ed., *Philosophy and Truth*, 84. For affinities between Conrad and Nietzsche, particularly their hyperconsciousness of the limitations of language in representing experience, see Said, "Conrad and Nietzsche," in Sherry, ed., *A Commemoration*.

15. Compare Miller, *Fiction and Repetition*, who focuses his discussion of indeterminacy in *Lord Jim* in the concept of "ungrounded" repetition as a subversion of the ideal of organic form.

16. Conrad provides comic commentary on the potential inhumanity

of the lieutenant's unyielding stance through a verbal link with the "yellow cur," which, outside the court of inquiry, suddenly snaps "like a piece of mechanism" (*LJ* 74).

17. For example, "The Duel" (1907), a story whose brilliant comedy deserves acknowledgment and in which Conrad pushes the idea of honor into the realm of the absurd.

18. But see Guerard, *Conrad the Novelist*, 157–59, who reads the same details as unequivocally positive signs and claims that only Marlow, who in a second reading "clearly diverges from Conrad" in these chapters, wishes to criticize the French lieutenant. I would simply take this as confirmation of the inherent ambiguity of Conrad's analogies, but Guerard also fails to persuade me of the clear line he draws here between Conrad and Marlow. Guerard believes, on the same grounds, that the helmsman and Bob Stanton offer purely damning commentary on Jim.

19. *Middlemarch*, 226. See also Conrad to Graham, August 27, 1898, in *LL*, I: 246: "If this miserable planet had perception, a soul, a heart, it would burst with indignation or fly to pieces from sheer pity." Such is precisely the fate of the most sensitive character in *The Secret Agent*, Stevie. Beer, "Myth and the Single Consciousness," in Adam, ed., *This Particular Web*, 100, argues that "hyperaesthesia" was "the particular disease of the Victorian consciousness. . . . The ethic of realism—paying respect to things as they are, accepting the objectivity of objects—combined with the ethic of sympathy descending from the Romantics, resulted in near intolerable pressure on the receptive or penetrating consciousness from the external world."

20. To Garnett, February 13, 1897, in Garnett, ed., *Letters from Joseph Conrad*, 89.

21. Early on the anonymous narrator introduces a long evocation of "the anger of the sea" with the remark that "That *truth* is not so often made apparent as people might think": "now and then . . . there appears on the face of facts a sinister violence of intention—that indefinable something which forces it upon the mind and the heart of a man, that this complication of accidents or these elemental furies are coming at him with a purpose of malice" (emphasis added). Gaining passion, the sentence culminates in nature's mad attempt to sweep "the whole precious world utterly away" (*LJ* 10–11).

22. For all the brilliance of her chapter on *Lord Jim* in *The English Novel*, Van Ghent greatly underestimates the degree of rationalization and moral evasion in the novel by claiming that "the apparent 'collusion' between external nature and the soul, that gives to Conrad's work its quality of the marvelous and its religious temper, is thus, really, only the inevitable working out of character through circumstance" (p. 234).

23. To E. L. Sanderson, October 12, 1899, in *LL*, I: 283.

24. Mégroz, *Joseph Conrad's Mind and Method*, 41. Conrad's early difficulty with dramatic scenes probably derived, as Guerard argues (see his *Conrad the Novelist*, Chapter Two, "Discovery of a Fictional World," esp. p. 76), from the temperamental evasiveness that also manifests itself as a need for the distancing effects achieved through multiple narrators and retrospective narration.

25. Aristotle cites analogy in the *Poetics* as the exemplary case of metaphor, and subsequent discussions have largely concurred. Burke, "Four Master Tropes," in *A Grammar of Motives*, 503, associates metaphor with perspective because we can understand the trope as asking us to see one thing under the aspect of another: it "brings out the thisness of a that, or the thatness of a this."

26. Hawkes, *Metaphor*, 2–3.

27. The problem of providing for Jim has become much more acute than it was when Marlow encountered Chester. As Jim flees from job to job in a vain attempt to hide from his guilt, he both tests Marlow's ability as a self-appointed guardian and threatens Marlow's role as narrator, for Marlow's narration will collapse into sterile repetition if Jim exhausts the fictional world Conrad has provided for him. As Egström, one of Jim's erstwhile employers, remarks: "I told him the earth wouldn't be big enough to hold his caper" (*LJ* 196).

28. That the tangled language of Stein's famous injunction "in the destructive element immerse" presents unresolvable ambiguities has been acknowledged and accounted for by Newell. His survey of the critical literature and restoration of the original manuscript reading reveal the nature of the contradictions introduced at a later stage of revision. See Newell, "The Destructive Element and Related 'Dream' Passages in the *Lord Jim* Manuscript" (1970). Watt, *Conrad in the Nineteenth Century*, 325–31, drawing on Newell, gives a more detailed reading and also shows how critical commentary has typically read into the ambiguities of the passage the concerns of its own cultural moment. Nor does Stein's diagnosis of Jim as a romantic require much comment: Jim seeks human perfection in a world intrinsically imperfect; he wishes to close the gap between an idealized conception of himself and the lesser self his actions have shown him to be. Stein's advice apparently amounts, as Watt has shown, to a recommendation that Jim render his romantic ideals self-supporting by persevering in his high aspirations.

29. Translation by Anna Swanwick, quoted from the Norton Critical Edition of *Lord Jim*, ed. Moser, 128 n.

30. Tanner, "Butterflies and Beetles—Conrad's Two Truths" (1963), reprinted in the Norton Critical Edition of *Lord Jim*, Moser, ed.

31. For discussion of the quoted phrase, see Chapters One and Two, pp. 10–11, 49–50.

32. See, for example, Chapter Twenty-One, where the scene in which Marlow and Jim look out over the hills of Patusan fades into an excursus on, among other things, homecoming, the relationship between knowledge of others and of self, the capacity for introspection, the binding power of community, and Jim's status within Marlow's discourse.

33. For an excellent exposition of the negative axis of the ethics of Conrad's narration, see Perry, "Action, Vision, or Voice" (1964). My analysis emphasizes the recuperative aim of narration in Conrad.

34. Compare Palmer, *Joseph Conrad's Fiction*, 42–43. The reliquary encloses the butterfly that has come to represent Stein's ideal past.

35. See Newell, "The Destructive Element," 41–42. The scene recalls the vision of the narrator in "Karain," who glimpses a formless, haunted realm where ideal values have come to reside after their banishment from the modern world. As in the earlier story, darkness becomes a refuge from the "concrete and perplexed world," the empirical reality that resists Jim's pursuit of his ideal self-image.

36. To Graham, January 14, 1898, in Watts, ed., *Letters to Graham*, 65.

37. Quoted at greater length by Watts in ibid., 67.

38. This, I take it, is one of the implications of Cavell's argument in *The Claim of Reason* that we "live [our] skepticism" with respect to other minds (p. 437). For the classic argument that skepticism cannot provide a viable way to live, see Burnyeat, "Can the Skeptic Live His Skepticism?" in *The Skeptical Tradition*. Burnyeat essentially confirms Hume's claim that there are inherent limits to *radical* skepticism.

39. See Pascal, *The Dual Voice*, 2–32. On the danger of one discourse swallowing up or dissolving another in the novel, see Bakhtin, *Problems of Dostoevsky's Poetics*, 63–64.

40. Despite the tendency of many readers to accept Leavis's judgment that the romance of Patusan, "though plausibly offered as a continued exhibition of Jim's case, has no inevitability as that," the inevitability lies not in a logic inherent in Jim's fictional life history but in Conrad's *presentation* of that life. See *The Great Tradition*, 190. Responding to Garnett's criticism, Conrad himself described "the division of the book into two parts" as a "plague spot." To Garnett, November 12, 1900, in Garnett, ed., *Letters from Joseph Conrad*, 171. Yet Conrad's deference to Garnett's opinion sometimes seems disingenuous.

41. See Gordon, *The Making of a Novelist*, 64–73. For more on the historical sources for *Lord Jim*, see Sherry, *Conrad's Eastern World*, esp. 41–64.

42. Since Conrad alludes to Homer elsewhere, I assume that here he

borrows from L. Bigge-Wither's translation of *The Odyssey* (1869), which, to my knowledge, is unique among nineteenth-century translations in rendering Homer's epithet for Odysseus—*polytropos*—as "many-sided" (p. 1).

43. Unlike Jim, however, we may still find Patusan "strangely barren of adventure," for widespread criticism of Jim's triumph over Sherif Ali responds to a very real falling off in the imaginative power of Conrad's narrative. To the extent that Patusan emanates from Jim, we may wonder whether the enigmatic quality Marlow insistently attributes to Jim derives (to reapply the subtitle of *The Rescue*) from a "romance of the shallows." Lack of consciousness may be as puzzling as complexity of consciousness.

44. Van Ghent, *The English Novel*, 236–37, also reads the landscape of Patusan as an allegory of Jim's inner state, though she sees it not as an expression of Jim's romantic imagination but as a sign of his spiritual self-division.

45. For sustained attention to the tension in Conrad between language as inherently deceptive and perfectly transparent, see Hawthorn, *Language and Fictional Self-Consciousness*. For Conrad's narrative technique as an attempt to negate its status as writing—to become, that is, a *voice* of pure communication—see Said, "Conrad: The Presentation of Narrative" (1974), 130–32.

46. Conrad repeats the scene in *The Secret Agent*, where Winnie Verloc also holds the door against her father's violent efforts to break in. For an interpretation of the literary significance of the incestuous subtext there, see Caserio, *Plot, Story, and the Novel*, 264–74.

47. Compare Crews, *Out of My System*, who observes in a hilariously iconoclastic essay that "Conrad indulges our fears of isolation, neglect, and victimization by malign higher powers—the fears of an anxious infant—without locating their source" (p. 49). Crews has since renounced his psychoanalytic vows generally, and his Freudian analysis of Conrad in particular, in *Skeptical Engagements*, 223–35.

48. ". . . again [Jukes] heard a man's voice—the frail and indomitable sound that can be made to carry an infinity of thought, resolution and purpose, that shall be pronouncing confident words on the last day, when heavens fall, and justice is done—again he heard it, and it was crying to him, as if from very, very far—'All right'" (*T* 44). Here Conrad characteristically undermines the initial affirmation with a glance at the more powerful voice of God before reaffirming the limited value of the human voice.

49. Momentarily worrying over his past, Jim remarks to Marlow: "I've got to look only at the face of the first man that comes along, to

regain my confidence" (*LJ* 306). Compare the letter to E. L. Sanderson, October 12, 1899, in *LL*, I: 282: "I fear I have not the capacity and the power to go on,—to satisfy the just expectations of those who are dependent on my exertions."

50. Conrad's letters provide an astonishing array of such fears. Consider only two examples from early in his career, when a return to the sea still seemed possible: "I am appalled at the absurdity of my situation. . . . Most appalled to feel that all the doors behind me are shut and that I must remain where I have come blundering in the dark"; "I am haunted by the idea that I cannot write,—I dare say a very correct idea too. The harm is in its haunting me." To Garnett [August 1898], in Garnett, ed., *Letters from Joseph Conrad*, 142; To Mrs. Bontine, October 16, 1898, in *LL*, I: 252.

51. But see Seidel, *Exile and the Narrative Imagination*, 69. He has noted a parallel "reordering effort" in *A Passage to India*, where Forster's Fielding "crosses back into the precision and perspective of the Mediterranean after the sounded but senseless horror of the Ou-Boum in India's Marabar Caves."

52. Though not the skeptic Marlow is, Jim's subjective self-enclosure represents a logical consequence of skepticism. While Stein diagnoses Jim as a romantic, Cornelius comes closer to naming Jim's narcissism in his refrain that Jim is a "child." As a narcissist, Jim resembles the rigorous skeptic in having "no dealings but with himself" (*LJ* 339).

53. Schopenhauer's anticipations of repression, in contrast, emerge directly from his reflections on insanity. See *WWR*, I: 192–93 and II: 400–401.

54. Cavell, *The Claim of Reason*, 129.

55. I should distinguish here, following Cavell, ibid., 111, between convention as convenience and convention as an expression of "those exigencies of conduct and feeling which all humans share." Jim's father dwells in a shelter of convenience; Marlow is carried beyond even "natural" conventions before returning to their shelter.

56. Daleski, *The Way of Dispossession*, traces the language of possession and dispossession over Conrad's career in order to investigate Conrad's gradual acceptance of the value of "losing oneself in order to find oneself." But Daleski's fine psychological interpretation cannot account for passages in which the language of embodiment involves not psychology but the articulation of elusive meanings and values—"those who return not to a dwelling but to the land itself, to meet its disembodied, eternal, and unchangeable spirit—it is those who understand best its severity, its saving power, the grace of its secular right to our fidelity, to our obedience" (*LJ* 222). Nor can it account for the trope as

the expression of a kind of spiritual dislocation: "a native policeman . . . looked up at me . . . as though his migrating spirit were suffering exceedingly from that unforeseen—what d'ye call 'em—avatar—incarnation" (*LJ* 157). The negative axis of this pattern appears in an early description of the inquiry: "The facts those men were so eager to know had been visible, tangible, open to the senses, occupying their place in space and time . . . they made a whole that had features, shades of expression, a complicated aspect that could be remembered by the eye, and something else besides, something invisible, a directing spirit of perdition that dwelt within, like a malevolent soul in a detestable body" (*LJ* 30–31).

57. Simpson, *Fetishism and Imagination*, 102.

58. Though Conrad could not yet have read Joyce, he would have been familiar with the idea, like most writers at the time, from the four volumes of Flaubert's letters that had been published by 1893. "The artist in his work must be like God in his creation—invisible and all-powerful: he must be everywhere felt, but never seen." To Mme. Leroyer de Chantepie, March 18, 1857, in Steegmuller, ed., *Letters of Gustave Flaubert*, I: 230.

59. Conrad's deep attraction to the idea of an action that perfectly realizes its intention helps account for Marlow's Nietzschean justification of Brown's massacre: "Notice that even in this awful outbreak there is a superiority as of a man who carries right—the abstract thing—within the envelope of his common desires" (*LJ* 404).

60. Some disagreement exists regarding Jim's confrontation with Brown. A tradition of psychological criticism arguing for the paralyzing effect of Jim's guilty identification with the outlaw begins in Morf, *The Polish Heritage of Joseph Conrad*, 156–59, and extends through Meyer, *A Psychoanalytic Biography*, 161–62; Van Ghent, *The English Novel*, 243; and Guerard, *Conrad the Novelist*, 149–51. Watt, *Conrad in the Nineteenth Century*, 341–45, attempts to overturn this tradition, which he describes as a Freudian version of original sin, and to exculpate Jim by arguing that Jim feels not guilt but shame. My reading attempts to connect the psychological argument with the significance of the shift from romance to tragedy.

61. Watt, *Conrad in the Nineteenth Century*, 349. After surveying the various senses in which Jim's death can be considered tragic, Watt settles on Schopenhauer's theory of tragedy as a revelation of the essential misery of the world and on Miguel de Unamuno's formulation of the tragic sense of life as deriving, in part, from the feeling that consciousness is a curse. These versions of tragedy account very well for Jim's resignation, if we assume he has reconciled himself to something like Scho-

penhauer's will; they harmonize also with Conrad's deep distrust of consciousness. For a different understanding of tragedy in *Lord Jim*, see Krieger, *The Tragic Vision*, 165–79.

62. Cavell, *The Claim of Reason*, 478. See also p. 493 for passages informing the rest of this paragraph.

63. From an undated letter to Neil Munro quoted in Keating, ed., *A Conrad Memorial Library*, 292.

Chapter Five

1. For an introduction to the evolution of Marlow in these works, see Tindall, "Apology for Marlow," in Rathburn and Steinmann, eds., *From Jane Austen to Conrad*. For a provocative treatment of Marlow as a developing character, see Friedman, "Conrad's Picaresque Narrator," in *Theory and World Fiction*. See my Chapter Six for a more detailed discussion of *Chance*.

2. Cavell, *The Claim of Reason*, 493. "Knowing and Acknowledging," in *Must We Mean What We Say?*, 263.

3. Descartes, *Discourse on Method*, 60.

4. For commentary on the demon hypothesis as the ultimate conclusion of Pyrrhonism, see Popkin, *The History of Scepticism from Erasmus to Spinoza*, 178–88.

5. See, for instance, Putnam, Chapter One in *Reason, Truth, and History*, and the discussion in my first chapter, pp. 2–3.

6. Descartes, *Discourse on Method*, 78.

7. Marten, "Conrad's Skeptic Reconsidered" (1972), surveys the critical controversy surrounding Decoud and attempts to resolve it by arguing for the primacy of Decoud's egotism. But Marten's fine character analysis fails to address the issue of fictional adequacy (e.g., the abstractness of philosophy versus the concreteness of the novel) and reveals only a partial understanding of skepticism as a philosophical problem. Rather than separating Decoud's skepticism from his egotism by calling it "a pose, an affectation," we should recognize Decoud's radical skepticism on the Great Isabel as a deeply motivated psychological response to a metaphysical insight of the kind described by Cavell.

8. Chapter Twenty, "The Brown Stocking," in Auerbach, *Mimesis*.

9. I borrow the word from Meyer, *A Psychoanalytic Biography*, 162. My discussion in this paragraph is also indebted to Daleski, *The Way of Dispossession*, 104–12, who has several fine things to say about the relationship between the two texts and, more particularly, between Jukes and Jim.

10. To Conrad, November 22, 1912, in Jean-Aubry, ed., *Twenty Letters to Joseph Conrad*.

11. Compare *The Secret Agent*: "a man must identify himself with something more tangible than his own personality, and establish his pride somewhere, either in his social position, or in the quality of the work he is obliged to do, or in the superiority of the idleness he may be fortunate enough to enjoy" (*SA* 116–17). Decoud dies when deprived of his superiority in idleness and the supports of society and work.

12. See, for instance, p. 156. Antonia's attraction for Decoud, moreover, derives in part from her readiness to challenge his ironic detachment from life.

13. Guerard, *Conrad the Novelist*, 199–200. I have removed the italics from the original.

14. Although like many others Leavis, *The Great Tradition*, 195, 197, considers Hirsch, a stowaway on the lighter, a purely allegorical figure of fear, the paradoxically vivid details of "the featureless night" push the allegory into the background.

15. See pp. 6–7, where the moral skepticism of the novel is again evoked in terms of the natural setting: "Sky, land, and sea disappear together out of the world when the Placido—as the saying is—goes to sleep under its black poncho. The few stars left below the seaward frown of the vault shine feebly as into the mouth of a black cavern. In its vastness your ship floats unseen under your feet, her sails flutter invisible above your head. The eye of God Himself—they add with grim profanity—could not find out what work a man's hand is doing in there; and you would be free to call the devil to your aid if even his malice were not defeated by such a blind darkness."

16. Like Jim in Patusan, Decoud's sense of self depends on the regard of others, though not to the extent that Nostromo's does. Decoud's insight into Nostromo, moreover, ironically prefigures his own predicament: "I wonder . . . how he would behave if I were not here" (*N* 275). Yet Decoud's more articulate self-awareness distinguishes him from Nostromo and contributes to the disabling recognition of his own dependence.

17. Strawson, *Skepticism and Naturalism*, 40.

18. Murdoch, "The Sublime and the Beautiful Revisited" (1960), 265. Though Murdoch focuses on the mixed legacy of Kant and Hegel as it is represented in the development of the novel, her most fundamental concern is with the potential triumph of skepticism in modern fiction. In this respect her critique resembles Auerbach's criticism of Woolf's epistemological skepticism.

19. See "Extracts from 'Notes' (1970–1971)," in Morson, ed., *Bakhtin*, 181. The concept is related to Wayne Booth's "implied author," but in contrast to the formalism of Booth's immanent reconstruction of the au-

thor's implied norms and attitudes, Bakhtin's intentionalist concept does not bracket out the historical author. For Booth's implied author see *The Rhetoric of Fiction*.

20. In Bakhtin's own words, "ultimate semantic authority—the author's intention—is [sometimes] realized not in his direct discourse but with the help of other people's words, created and distributed specifically as the words of others." *Problems of Dostoevsky's Poetics*, 188.

21. See Bakhtin, *The Dialogic Imagination*, 399–400, 419–20, and *Problems of Dostoevsky's Poetics*, 9–16.

22. For a view affirming Guerard see, for instance, Price, *Forms of Life*, 265. For the objectification of characters in the monologic novel, see Chapter Two, "The Hero, and the Position of Author with Regard to the Hero, in Dostoevsky's Art," in Bakhtin, *Problems of Dostoevsky's Poetics*, esp. 51–52, 56.

23. Murdoch, "The Sublime and the Beautiful Revisited," 267.

24. Freedman, *The Lyrical Novel*, 2, analyzes the way in which the "lyrical novel" deemphasizes traditional character by absorbing action and refashioning it "as a pattern of imagery." Docherty, *Reading (Absent) Character*, aims to supplant classical theories of character with one that takes into account the dissolution of character in the New Novel. Bersani discusses "the process of violently deconstructing the self" in *A Future for Astyanax*, xi. Jameson incorporates Greimas's structuralist model of character into a Marxist analysis of *Lord Jim* and *Nostromo* in *The Political Unconscious*. Jameson's Althusserian structuralism essentially mimics the problem of agency in these texts by dispensing altogether with the category of the subject.

25. Although several critics have noticed the connection, including Friedman, *The Turn of the Novel*, 91, and Cox, *The Modern Imagination*, 81, only Davidson, *Conrad's Endings*, 37–41, has understood it within the broader patterns of the text. But Davidson finds that the connection *increases* the verisimilitude of Decoud's suicide, whereas I see it as a subversion of the mimetic dimension of the text.

26. The geography of Costaguana is so important to the story that one can understand (and be thankful for) Watt's decision to include a contoured relief map of the country in his book, *Joseph Conrad: Nostromo*. The decision to include elevations (Higuerota evidently soars beyond 13,000 feet, Punta Mala a mere 3,000 plus) offers testimony to the vividness of Conrad's pictorial imagination.

27. Gould and Nostromo meet face to face only after Sulaco has been safely established as an independent republic; Mitchell, the only person present, reports that only a few inconsequential words were exchanged.

28. Said, *Beginnings*, 118. I consider Said's brilliant pages to be the best available on *Nostromo*, and my discussion here is indebted to his.

Holquist's "Answering as Authoring," in Morson, ed., *Bakhtin*, is also useful when thinking about characters as potential authors. For a reading that reflects more interest in the historical fiction and its politics, including Conrad's historical sources, see Fleishman, *Conrad's Politics*.

29. The author's note responds to his concern: "I can safely assure my readers that [Jim] is not the product of coldly perverted thinking. . . . One sunny morning in the commonplace surroundings of an Eastern roadstead, I saw his form pass by" (*LJ* ix). We are asked to see Jim, through Marlow, as an encountered "form," not a contrived or manipulated fictional construct.

30. Watts, *A Preface to Conrad*, points out, in a list of symbolic names in Conrad, that "nostromo" is also Italian for "bosun" (p. 178).

31. On the types of "double-voiced" and "unmediated" discourses, see Bakhtin, *Problems of Dostoevsky's Poetics*, 181–204.

32. Joyce, *Ulysses*, 126. On omission in *Ulysses* see Kenner, *Ulysses*, 15.

33. One can easily imagine, for instance, a profitable analysis of fetishism in *Nostromo* (the word surfaces several times in relation to the mine) as an instance of "reification." In such an approach the "spell" associated with the silver would be read as a mystification of commodity relations, as if the laws governing the value of the silver constituted an autonomous, invisible, self-begotten force. See Lukács, *History and Class Consciousness*, esp. 83–87.

34. Said, *Beginnings*, 133–37.

35. To Wells, November 30, 1903, in Wright, ed., *Conrad on Fiction*, 30. The letter-writing scene I discussed in *Lord Jim* also gets at the involuntary in Conrad's writing, as does the fact that most of his novels began as short stories.

36. Conrad's source for Hirsch's torture adds weight to the claim that Hirsch must be seen as more than an abject victim: the scene with Sotillo is modeled on Garibaldi's autobiographical account of his own torture at the hands of Don Leonardo Milan. Garibaldi is Giorgio Viola's patron saint. See Sherry, *Conrad's Western World*, 158–61.

37. See, for instance, Widmer, "Conrad's Pyrrhonistic Conservativism" (1974), 137–42; Price, *Forms of Life*, 358–59 n. 30.

38. Kermode, "Secrets and Narrative Sequence" (1980). The essay, which interprets some of the puzzling imagery in *Under Western Eyes*, is reprinted in Kermode's *The Art of Telling*.

39. Swift, *Gulliver's Travels and Other Writings*, ed. Landa, 332. Succeeding quotations are from pages 332–33.

40. For a review of this crux in Swift, see Clark, *Form and Frenzy in Swift's Tale of a Tub*, 3–35.

41. See, in addition to those cited below, Gekoski, *The Moral World of*

the Novelist, 142: *The Secret Agent* "creates a group of unworthy and contemptible characters—and then brilliantly castigates them for their unworthiness and contemptibility." And see Watt, ed., *The Secret Agent Casebook*, 77–80, who finds that "the tension between what is seen and how it is presented betokens an admirable elasticity of spirit."

42. June 20, 1912, in Gee and Sturm, eds., *Letters to Poradowska*, 116.

43. Howe, *Politics and the Novel*, 96.

44. See Price, "Conrad: Satire and Fiction," who surveys the relevant commentaries and shows that critical response makes clear "the way in which the irony seems to effect a moral levelling of all the characters and the way in which the aloofness or comic distance of the novelist makes us associate our feelings more with his virtuosity than with the minds of his characters" (p. 234). The book, Price concludes, succeeds neither as satire nor as fiction: "We are not allowed the full detachment which might allow us to scorn the shams and bunglers alike. Nor are we allowed to entertain very long or far the sympathy which the more complex characters awaken" (p. 242).

45. Bakhtin, *The Dialogic Imagination*, 342, 345; idem, *Problems of Dostoevsky's Poetics*, 63. For Ford's claim that he and Conrad agreed that characters should *never* respond to each other, see Ford, *A Personal Remembrance*, 188.

46. See Miller's reading in *Poets of Reality* for an excellent account of this dimension of the text.

47. Compare Conroy, *Modernism and Authority*, 150, who analyzes this scene in the course of a fine discussion of Foucault's "panopticism" and "the imprisonment of the characters" in *The Secret Agent*.

48. The association between the "evil freedom" of the foreign-looking Assistant Commissioner and the denationalizing effect of the restaurant may also derive from Conrad's ambivalent desire to assimilate. Defensively disdainful of the English audience, Conrad nevertheless worried that his Polishness kept him from being more popular. The evil would lie in denying the claims of his Polish ancestry. Writing to Galsworthy (at the time a *very* popular novelist) about the commercial failure of *The Secret Agent*, Conrad lamented: "I suppose there is something in me that is unsympathetic to the general public,—because the novels of Hardy, for instance, are generally tragic enough and gloomily written too,—and yet they have sold in their time and are selling to the present day." At this point in the letter we can imagine Conrad pausing to reflect further on what distinguished him from Galsworthy and Hardy before going on to write a one-sentence paragraph: "Foreignness, I suppose." January 6, 1908, in *LL*, II: 65. For the pathos of Conrad's self-division, see "Amy Foster," where foreignness becomes fatal.

49. The attempt to destroy the observatory, the seat of Greenwich mean time, is only the most obvious expression of the theme. The classic analysis is Stallman, "Time and *The Secret Agent*," in Stallman, ed., *The Art of Joseph Conrad*.

50. It is also unwise to try to escape from them. Clearly Winnie commits suicide because Ossipon betrays her, yet her death by drowning in the English Channel also coincides with her aborted attempt to escape from the "insular nature of Great Britain," which had "obtruded itself upon [Ossipon's] notice in an odious form" as he planned their flight (*SA* 282).

51. See Cavell, *The Claim of Reason*, 369.

52. Nietzsche, *Beyond Good and Evil*, 66.

53. Likewise with the motivation borrowed from "Heart of Darkness," which could be taken as the half-mocking ironic evocation of primeval feelings and archaic energies: "Into that plunging blow . . . Mrs. Verloc had put all the inheritance of her immemorial and obscure descent, the simple ferocity of the age of caverns, and the unbalanced nervous fury of the age of bar-rooms" (*SA* 263).

54. The connection survives Conrad's professed loathing for this kind of romantic self-indulgence and for the kind of Rousseau-like self-justification Michaelis would write. Conrad's excessive denunciations of Rousseau, like his condemnation of Dostoevsky, represent refusals to acknowledge the confessional dimension of his own fiction, as well as the project of self-justification undertaken in *A Personal Record*. It has been widely recognized, moreover, that *Under Western Eyes* is indebted to *Crime and Punishment*.

55. To Poradowska, March 29 or April 5, 1894, in Gee and Sturm, eds., *Letters to Poradowska*, 64.

56. On the other hand, life (as we read of it in a short pamphlet by Jessie Conrad) imitated Conrad's art on this score. Several years after Conrad's death, Jessie decided to lay to rest various rumors that he had returned from the dead to chat with Stephen Crane (also a spirit, which makes the trip seem rather unnecessary), Lord Northcliffe, and Arthur Conan Doyle, who wrote to the bereaved widow informing her that during a séance conducted by a Mrs. Dean, Conrad had returned to imprint his face on a plate. Jessie suspects forgery and is relieved to report that she has found a photograph of her husband that looks remarkably like the plate. See Mrs. Joseph Conrad [Jessie George], *Did Joseph Conrad Return as a Spirit?*

57. Cavell, *The Claim of Reason*, meditates on the question in response to Putnam's classic articulation of the issue in "Robots: Machines or Artificially Created Life?" (1964).

58. Thomas, *Man and the Natural World*, 33.

59. See Vartanian, "Man-Machine from the Greeks to the Computer," in *Dictionary of the History of Ideas*, ed. Weiner, as well as my discussion of Cavell on other minds in Chapter Three.

60. Huxley, *Man's Place in Nature*, v.

61. Huxley, "On the Hypothesis that Animals Are Automata," in *Methods and Results*, 244.

62. Thomas, *Man and the Natural World*, 30–36, 122–23.

63. Cross-cultural psychology offers yet another perspective on Conrad's overdetermined language of wandering souls. Shweder, "Menstrual Pollution, Soul Loss, and the Comparative Study of Emotions" (1985), describes the phenomenology of depression: "When you feel depressed you feel as though your soul has left your body. What you feel is empty, and a body emptied of its soul loses interest in things, except perhaps its own physical malfunctioning as a thing. The phenomenon of soul wandering is widely acknowledged among the world's cultures, and the phenomenology of soul loss has, for millennia, been a topic of theoretical and practical concern" (p. 193). One thinks of Winnie after Stevie's death, and of Nostromo on discovering Decoud's death (see below, pp. 158–59). Conrad himself suffered from numerous depressive episodes, and his correspondence provides a great deal of support for Shweder's claims: "Under the stress of physical suffering the mind sees falsely, the heart errs, the soul unguided wanders in an abyss." To Poradowska, March 23, 1890, in Gee and Sturm, eds., *Letters to Poradowska*, 8. For Conrad's depressed self-image as a malfunctioning thing—a broken doll—see the letter to Poradowska, October 16, 1891, in ibid., 38. See also the biographies by Meyer and Najder for discussion of Conrad's depression.

Turning to another depressive, we can compare Woolf on the melancholia of Lily Briscoe's experience of the artistic process: "before she exchanged the fluidity of life for the concentration of painting she had a few moments of nakedness when she seemed like an unborn soul, a soul reft of body, hesitating on some windy pinnacle and exposed without protection to all the blasts of doubt." *To the Lighthouse*, 237.

64. For provocative meditations on the mechanical in modernist aesthetics, see Kenner's anecdotal approach in *The Mechanic Muse*.

65. The most important exception is Daleski, *The Way of Dispossession*, who precedes me in interpreting the language of possession and counterpossession in *Nostromo*. But because Daleski's interest remains in the psychology of the characters (see my pp. 222–23, n. 56), he does not see the imagery in relation to the larger patterns of superstition I interpret.

66. Only Tillyard, *The Epic Strain in the English Novel*, has considered

this dimension of the story, though he does little more than chart the fairy tale features.

67. Hewitt, *A Reassessment*, 56–57, accepts this as one motive, supplies a second—greed—and recognizes superstition as a third, though not in relation to Teresa's "curse." Like Daleski, Hewitt notices only one facet of a more inclusive pattern.

68. In his author's note (1920) to *The Shadow Line*, Conrad devotes considerable energy to rebutting those who read the story as a tale of the supernatural, and the terms of his response effectively characterize the quality I single out in *Nostromo*: "The world of the living contains enough marvels and mysteries as it is; marvels and mysteries acting upon our emotions and intelligence in ways so inexplicable that it would almost justify the conception of life as an enchanted state" (*SL* vii).

69. The analogy with Dante is close enough to suggest the possibility of allusion. In Canto 33 of the *Inferno*, the souls of those who betray their guests plunge into hell, leaving behind the body on earth as a kind of zombie inhabited by a demon. The subdivision of Cocytus is named for Ptolemy, who murdered his father-in-law, and the sinners Dante describes both betrayed their own relatives, one of them his father-in-law. Nostromo's theft of the silver symbolically betrays the ideals associated with Viola, who, as his future father-in-law, is later made to exact retribution by mistakenly shooting Nostromo dead.

70. To Garnett, May 22, 1896, in Karl and Davies, eds., *Collected Letters of Joseph Conrad*, I: 281. The review was published in the *Saturday Review*.

71. To Waliszewski, December 1903, in Najder, *Conrad's Polish Background*, 241.

72. To Pinker, May 18, 1907; To Galsworthy, January 6, 1908, in *LL*, II: 49, 65.

73. To Cumberland, November 20, 1919, in ibid., II: 235.

74. To Galsworthy, January 6, 1908, in ibid., II: 65. Conrad's son, Borys, was ill during the writing of *The Secret Agent*, and his wife, Jessie, became sick after its release. Some of the weight of these worries seems to have found its way into Verloc's worries about supporting his family after Vladimir's ultimatum.

75. In Sherry, ed., *The Critical Heritage*, 29.

76. Jessie Conrad, *Joseph Conrad as I Knew Him*, 120.

77. Compare Moser, *Achievement and Decline*, 43.

78. Guerard, *Conrad the Novelist*, 215.

79. Watt, "*Nostromo*," 42, 47.

80. Compare Daleski, *The Way of Dispossession*, 116.

81. Lawrence, *Women in Love*, 246, 472.

82. Consistent with my reading of authorial complicity in Hirsch's

torture, Bento, like Vladimir, must be seen as another instance of the demonized author surrogate.

83. See Freud, "Remembering, Repeating and Working-Through," in Strachey, ed., *The Standard Edition*, XII: 147–56.

84. See Wohl, *The Generation of 1914*, 213: "the very intellectuals who prided themselves on being liberated from the illusions of progress and the mystique of science remained strangely indentured to determinisms of various kinds, determinisms, furthermore, that were themselves inspired by scientific theories. For some, it was the determinism of biology; for others, the determinism of geography; for still others, the determinism of history or race. Whatever the determinism chosen, however, it led toward the acknowledgement of a painful contradiction: that man was free to create his own life, as the novelist creates a fiction; and yet was a slave to the material conditions of his existence. Most European intellectuals of the late nineteenth century sought escape from this dilemma by asserting that man could master the determinisms that bound him only by raising them to consciousness, accepting them, and living life with vitality and passion."

85. Parry, *Conrad and Imperialism*, 102. For her reading of Nostromo as a *genius loci*, see p. 127.

Chapter Six

Epigraph: Conrad to Waliszewski, December 5, 1903, in Najder, *Conrad's Polish Background*, 240.

1. Of the many genetic explanations for the decline in Conrad's work, Moser's somewhat dated yet perceptive psychoanalytic interpretation of the "uncongenial subject"—romantic love—in *Achievement and Decline*, and Guerard's last chapter in *Conrad the Novelist*, remain the most persuasive. For an argument linking the decline to Conrad's suppression of evil in the later novels, see Hewitt, *A Reassessment*. Karl, "Three Problematical Areas in Conrad Biography," in *Conrad Revisited*, offers a provocative theory about Conrad's collaboration on the French translation of his works with Gide, who began with the early Malayan romances and thus may have influenced Conrad to return to these earlier materials. In his biography, however, Karl does not quite accept arguments that Conrad's late work suffers in comparison with the earlier. See *The Three Lives*, 680–86. For arguments that the decline does not exist, see Palmer, *Joseph Conrad's Fiction*, especially his "'Achievement and Decline': A Bibliographical Note," 260–68; Geddes, *Conrad's Later Novels*; and Schwarz, *The Later Fiction*. Valiant as these are, none can counter the power of Guerard's critique. Schwarz's book may be representative in its tendency to make claims for the value of Conrad's later work which are

belied by his own commentary. See, for instance, his remarks on Marlow in *Chance*, 42–45.

2. Guerard, *Conrad the Novelist*, 255.

3. Najder points out that Conrad's heavy manuscript revisions were designed in part to obscure "similarities between Razumov's dilemmas and the author's own perplexities." Najder, *A Chronicle*, 361.

4. Conrad's overdetermined ambivalence toward "*Cosas de Russia*" draws from various wells. For the quoted phrase in relation to *Under Western Eyes*, see the letter to Galsworthy, January 6, 1908; for Conrad's dismissal of *The Brothers Karamazov* as "fierce mouthings from prehistoric ages," see the letter to Garnett, May 27, 1912, in *LL*, II: 64, 140. For Conrad's most sustained response to Russia and the idea of autocracy, see "Autocracy and War" (1905) in *NLL*. For general commentary on Conrad and Russia, together with an excellent bibliography, see Lewitter, "Conrad, Dostoyevsky, and the Russo-Polish Antagonism" (1984). For the best analysis of Conrad's revisions of *Crime and Punishment* in *Under Western Eyes*, see Fogel, *Coercion to Speak*, 196–98, 199–207; for the biographical facts, see, as always, Najder, *A Chronicle*.

5. This is the governing theme of Raval's *The Art of Failure*.

6. Bakhtin, *The Dialogic Imagination*, 342.

7. "Autocracy and War," in *NLL*, 99.

8. Guerard, *Conrad the Novelist*, 236.

9. See also my earlier discussions of incarnation, pp. 19–20, 98–99, 113–19, 153–55. But see also Hay, *The Political Novels of Joseph Conrad*, 284, who argues that in passages such as this Conrad aims to demystify the national messianic myth of "the mystic body" of Mother Russia. See also note 36 below.

10. Najder notes that *Under Western Eyes* caused Conrad "more anguish than anything else he ever wrote," and speculates that "he must have felt an intensified conflict between his antipathy to the revolutionaries, and his awareness that only they could dislodge the fossilized autocratic system and its power." Najder, *A Chronicle*, 356, 354.

11. Exceptions must be made for *The Rescue* and *The Shadow Line* (1917). *The Rescue*, begun in 1896 but not completed until 1920, deals explicitly with insurrection; in *The Shadow Line* Conrad returns to the formation of his own authority as captain of his first ship, the *Otago*. In the former, the insurrection plot begun early in Conrad's career culminates much later in an explosive failure; in the latter, the narrator's self-doubt about his capacity to assume command is not so much exorcized as confronted and accepted.

12. Alter, *Partial Magic*, 101.

13. Ibid., 100.

14. Basing his remarks on recollected conversations with Conrad and on extant notes for the novel, Jean-Aubry offers corroboration for my sense of the narrative direction. See "The Inner History of Conrad's *Suspense*" (1925).

15. Hay, *The Political Novels of Joseph Conrad*, historicizes the idea of the demonic author by calling attention to the echo of Mickiewicz's *Dziady* in Conrad's description of the snowy landscape as "a monstrous blank page awaiting the record of an inconceivable history" (*UWE* 33). The question raised by Mickiewicz, it has been argued, is "will Satan cover the page before God has a chance to?" (p. 288).

16. Eagleton, *Exiles and Émigrés*, 27, 28. Although I accept Eagleton's basic claim about the antirevolutionary bias of the novel, my following text details reservations about his argument.

17. A representative remark: "I observed a solitary Swiss couple, whose fate was made secure from the cradle to the grave by the perfected mechanism of democratic institutions in a republic that could almost be held in the palm of one's hand" (*UWE* 175).

18. Fleishman, "Speech and Writing in *Under Western Eyes*," in *A Commemoration*, suggests that the oddness of the epigraph's misquotation of Miss Haldin (it omits the word "at") must be "counted among those linguistic devices by which the author of the novel establishes . . . that he is not an inventor but only the conveyor of an authoritative document written by another, the narrator" (p. 120). The article is more interesting as an introduction to the other side of the coin—the self-conscious architectonics of *Under Western Eyes* as construction as opposed to mimesis—and as a very early American attempt (1976) to appropriate Derrida for criticism of the novel.

19. Ford, *A Personal Remembrance*, 208.

20. Eagleton faults *Under Western Eyes* for failing to achieve "transcendence" (historical self-consciousness) through a dialectical exchange between Englishness and foreignness. Eagleton's Marxism motivates his preference for a more dialectical work, yet since none of Conrad's novels, with the possible exception of "Heart of Darkness," transforms dialogue into dialectics, the negative evaluation of *Under Western Eyes* in the context of other *unspecified* Conrad novels carries little authority. See *Exiles and Émigrés*, 10 n. 1, 31–32.

21. To Galsworthy, January 6, 1908, in *LL*, II: 65.

22. For a strong challenge to my negative remarks on Conradian romance, see Caserio's insistence on the need to suspend evaluation of these works in order to interpret what might be called the political economy of romance in relation to Conrad's understanding of the art of the novel. See "*The Rescue* and the Ring of Meaning," in Murfin, ed., *Conrad*

Revisited, esp. 176–77, n. 1. Caserio's argument is powerful, original, historically informed, though at times quite obscure.

23. For details about Conrad's "growing reputation in England and America, contractual complications, sale of his manuscripts and type-scripts, courtship by a wider circle of friends and admirers," see Karl, *The Three Lives*, 715.

24. For the economics of Conrad's career, see Watts, *A Literary Life*, one of the first volumes in the new Macmillan Literary Lives series under the general editorship of Richard Dutton. Watts's study is an excellent contribution to a series that focuses on "the publishing context" (e.g., patronage, subscription, periodical publication) and intellectual backgrounds of British authors.

25. Here is a fuller quotation from the letter to Pinker, his agent, about upcoming negotiations for the possible serialization of *Victory*, then titled, fittingly enough, "Dollars": "it has a tropical Malay setting—an unconventional man and a girl on an island under peculiar circumstances to whom enters a gang of three ruffians also of a rather unconventional sort—this intrusion producing certain psychological developments and effects. There is philosophy in it and also drama—lightly treated—meant for cultured people—a piece of literature before everything—and of course fit for general reading. Strictly proper. Nothing to shock the magazine public." (October 7, 1912, Henry W. and Albert A. Berg Collection, New York Public Library. Quoted with permission.) The letter also ranges over financial questions regarding future translations and Conrad's contracts with Methuen and his American publishers, as well as strategy for a prospective interview by James Huneker for the *New York Times*.

26. Along the same lines, I would reverse Leavis's preference for Heyst in the parallel he draws to Decoud in *The Great Tradition*, 199–202. The melodramatic villains who arrive to persecute Heyst on his island hermitage seem to punish him for having violated his father's philosophy of skeptical detachment by rescuing Lena from the lecherous grasp of Schomberg. Or is Heyst punished for his former withdrawal? The difference hardly matters. Decoud's "death by skepticism" is reprised with the difference that Heyst is permitted to see the light, though too late: "woe to the man whose heart has not learned while young to hope, to love—and to put its trust in life" (*V* 410). The simple theme of skepticism as withdrawal from life binds Heyst as tightly as Winnie Verloc is bound by the narrative logic of *The Secret Agent* (Heyst loses either way), but the novel lacks the earlier work's interest in skepticism as a challenge to the traditional status of novelistic character. Heyst represents the dead end of skepticism and not enough more to become very interesting.

27. *Victory* may occupy the most controversial place in Conrad's canon. Some readers accept Leavis's argument that the novel justifies Conrad's claims to "classical standing," whereas others subscribe to Guerard's judgment that it is "one of the worst novels for which high claims have ever been made by critics of standing." I incline to the latter view. See Leavis, *The Great Tradition*, 209; Guerard, *Conrad the Novelist*, 272.

28. Schwarz, *The Later Fiction*, 73; Tanner, "Joseph Conrad and the Last Gentleman" (1986). One admirer has claimed that *Victory* is "Conrad's test of the nature of fiction: in general, of the ability of drama to move towards allegory while retaining intact its dramatic form and essence; and in particular, the ability of fiction to move towards drama while retaining its identity as fictional narrative." See Lewis, "The Current of Conrad's *Victory*," in Shapiro, ed., *Twelve Original Essays on Great English Novels*, 207. Although the formulation certainly gets at some of the peculiarities of the novel, if there is any experiment here, I believe it fails, and *Victory* should be taken as an example of the progressive disjunction of the philosophical and the novelistic in Conrad's later fiction. For an analogous attempt to recuperate the elaborate architectonics of *Chance*, see Boyd, *The Reflexive Novel*, who argues that the text is really about the making of a novel. The arguments of Lewis and Boyd impose an order (and assume an intention) foreign to the texts by willfully construing awkward constructions and uneasily yoked allegorical and mimetic modes as evidence of self-conscious fictions. For a perceptive discussion of the critical confusion generated by the allegory in *Victory*, see Raval, "Conrad's *Victory*" (1980), 414–21.

29. See Watts, *A Literary Life*, 114–22. Watts quotes from an interview-article with Conrad (in fact based on a letter from Conrad to the newspaper) bearing the subheading: "World's Most Famous Author of Sea Stories Has Written 'Chance,' a Deliciously Characteristic Tale in Which, He Says, He Aimed to Interest Women Particularly . . ." (p. 115). To Pinker Conrad wrote: "It's the sort of stuff that *may* have a chance with the public. All of it about a girl with a steady run of references to women in general all along." Baines, *A Critical Biography*, 381.

30. For a more promising version of the sociological approach referred to earlier, see Luftig, "Representing Friendship Between the Sexes in England, 1850–1940" (1987), who argues persuasively that beginning with *Under Western Eyes* and more so in *Chance*, Conrad "epitomizes the adjustments undertaken by English writers confronted with women's increasingly visible participation in their world . . . of mental commerce" (p. 180).

31. James put the problem of Conrad's method well in a series of

backhanded compliments which culminated in a notorious trope describing Conrad's subordinate narrators: "the sense and the interest of the subject have to be passed on together, in the manner of the buckets of water for the improvised extinction of a fire, before reaching our apprehension: all with whatever the result, to this apprehension, of a quantity to be allowed for as spilt by the way." To my mind, in *Chance* Conrad could afford to spill very little. James, *Notes on Novelists*, 350.

32. "This evening confabulation," Marlow remarks of the consultation between the governess and Charley, "is a dark, inscrutable spot. And we may conjecture what we like." Having heard Marlow begin to do so, the narrator responds, "with a cheerfully sceptical smile," "'You have a ghastly imagination'" (*C* 101–2). The skepticism of the narrator's smile is of the inconsequential sort that characterizes much of the late fiction.

33. One minor triumph in *Victory* lies in Conrad's resistance to an excessively sentimental treatment of the fire that finally unites Heyst and Lena in death. Had Conrad reached for the romantic grandeur of Shelley's "Epipsychidion," he might well have fallen into the kind of sentimental bathos that mars the treatment of romantic love in *The Arrow of Gold* and *The Rescue*. Instead, the flames are not described at all, and the mingling of the lovers' ashes receives only glancing acknowledgment from Davidson, the stoical witness who happens upon the closing scene of the catastrophe.

34. October 20, 1911, in Garnett, ed., *Letters from Joseph Conrad*, 233.

35. I understand "ideology" to mean coherent systems of belief and practice that inform and influence the individual subject's lived relation to the world. Rather than link this definition to a particular account of ideology, such as Althusser's, I find a sympathetic context in the work of John B. Thompson, who argues for a critical conception of ideology that makes use of discourse analysis and sociohistorical conditions in order to analyze strategies of domination. See *Studies in the Theory of Ideology*, Chapter Three.

36. Guerard, *Conrad the Novelist*, 237, who is picking up Conrad's language: "[Razumov] had made for himself a mental atmosphere of gloomy and sardonic reverie, a sort of murky medium through which the event appeared like a featureless shadow having vaguely the shape of a man; a shape extremely familiar, yet utterly inexpressive, except for its air of discreet waiting in the dark" (*UWE* 246). For a brilliant meditation on the spectral imagery and the critical response (and nonresponse) to it, including Guerard's, see Kermode, "Secrets and Narrative Sequence." Kermode actively resists the temptation to dispense with the odd details by means of a psychological reading. He also resists a polit-

ical reading, but not the sort I engage in here, before focusing on the text's articulation of Conrad's ambivalent attitude toward an inattentive (or improperly attentive) audience.

37. See Foucault's *Discipline and Punish* for the transformation of the prison's punitive procedures into the penitentiary's disciplinary technologies and the importation of these techniques into the social body.

38. I borrow the quoted phrase from Jay, "In the Empire of the Gaze," in Hoy, ed., *Foucault: A Critical Reader*.

39. The thematics of coercion in Conrad have been analyzed brilliantly by Fogel, who argues persuasively that in *Under Western Eyes* Conrad finally finds "the pure story of forced dialogue for which he had been looking." *Coercion to Speak*, 184. My line of thought in the following pages is indebted to his remarks on Nathalie's mystification of silence as freedom.

40. To Graham, December 20, 1897, in Watts, ed., *Letters to Graham*, 56–57.

41. Fleishman, *Conrad's Politics*, 224. Hay and Fogel also take up this line, as does Busza in his analysis of Conrad's relation to Dostoevsky. Busza, "Rhetoric and Ideology in Conrad's *Under Western Eyes*," in Sherry, ed., *A Commemoration*.

Epilogue

Epigraph: *THN*, 270; *LJ* 221.

1. "The skeptic is assessing our constructions of the world; constructions after the fact; sorts of imaginations of it." Cavell, *The Claim of Reason*, 391.

2. Williams, *The English Novel*, 9–27.

3. See Watt, *The Rise of the Novel*.

4. See Bakhtin, "Epic and Novel," in *The Dialogic Imagination*.

5. Cavell explores the incontrovertible truths discovered by radical doubts about the existence of external reality in Parts One and Two of *The Claim of Reason*.

Works Cited

Primary Works: Fiction

Conrad, Joseph. *Joseph Conrad: Complete Works*. 24 vols. Garden City, N.Y.: Doubleday, Page, 1924. This edition, despite its subtitle, is not complete, and supplementary volumes, along with some critical editions, are cited below.

————. *Heart of Darkness*. 3d ed. Ed. Robert Kimbrough. The Norton Critical Edition. New York: Norton, 1988.

————. *Lord Jim: A Tale*. Ed. Thomas C. Moser. The Norton Critical Edition. New York: Norton, 1968.

————. *The Nigger of the "Narcissus"*. Ed. Robert Kimbrough. The Norton Critical Edition. New York: Norton, 1979.

————. *Tales of Hearsay*. Garden City, N.Y.: Doubleday, Page, 1925.

Primary Works: Letters and Essays

Blackburn, William, ed. *Joseph Conrad: Letters to William Blackwood and David S. Meldrum*. Durham, N.C.: Duke Univ. Press, 1958.

Conrad, Joseph. *Last Essays*. Garden City, N.Y.: Doubleday, Page, 1926.

Garnett, Edward, ed. *Letters from Joseph Conrad, 1895–1924*. Indianapolis: Bobbs-Merrill, 1928.

Gee, John A., and Paul J. Sturm, trans. and eds. *Letters of Joseph Conrad to Marguerite Poradowska, 1890–1920*. New Haven, Conn.: Yale Univ. Press, 1940.

Jean-Aubry, G., ed. *Joseph Conrad: Life and Letters*. 2 vols. Garden City, N.Y.: Doubleday, Page, 1927.

Karl, Frederick R., and Laurence Davies, eds. *The Collected Letters of Joseph Conrad*. 2 vols. Cambridge: Cambridge Univ. Press, 1983.

Watts, C. T., ed. *Letters to R. B. Cunninghame Graham*. Cambridge: Cambridge Univ. Press, 1969.

Wright, Walter F., ed. *Joseph Conrad on Fiction*. Lincoln: Univ. of Nebraska Press, 1964.

Secondary Works

Alter, Robert. *Partial Magic: The Novel as a Self-Conscious Genre*. Berkeley: Univ. of California Press, 1975.

Althusser, Louis. *Lenin and Philosophy and Other Essays*. Trans. Ben Brewster. New York: Monthly Review Press, 1971.

Auerbach, Erich. *Mimesis: The Representation of Reality in Western Literature*. Trans. Willard R. Trask. Princeton: Princeton Univ. Press, 1953.

Bailin, Miriam. "'An Extraordinarily Safe Castle': Aesthetics as Refuge in *The Good Soldier*." *Modern Fiction Studies* 30 (1984): 621–36.

Baines, Jocelyn. *Joseph Conrad: A Critical Biography*. London: Weidenfeld, 1960.

Bakhtin, Mikhail. *The Dialogic Imagination*. Trans. Caryl Emerson and Michael Holquist. Austin: Univ. of Texas Press, 1981.

———. "Extracts from 'Notes' (1970–1971)." In Gary Saul Morson, ed., *Bakhtin: Essays and Dialogues on His Work*, 179–82.

———. *Problems of Dostoevsky's Poetics*. Ed. and trans. Caryl Emerson. Minneapolis: Univ. of Minnesota Press, 1984.

Baumgarten, Alexander. *Reflections on Poetry*. Trans. Karl Aschenbrenner and William B. Holther. Berkeley: Univ. of California Press, 1954.

Beer, Gillian. *Darwin's Plots: Evolutionary Narrative in Darwin, George Eliot and Nineteenth-Century Fiction*. London: Routledge and Kegan Paul, 1983.

———. "Hume, Stephen, and Elegy in *To the Lighthouse*." *Essays in Criticism* 34 (1984): 33–55.

———. "Myth and the Single Consciousness: *Middlemarch* and *The Lifted Veil*." In Ian Adam, ed., *This Particular Web: Essays on Middlemarch*. Toronto: Univ. of Toronto Press, 1975.

Beerbohm, Max. "The Feast." In *A Christmas Garland*. London: Heinemann, 1912.

Benfey, Christopher. *Emily Dickinson and the Problem of Others*. Amherst: Univ. of Massachusetts Press, 1984.

Bersani, Leo. *A Future for Astyanax: Character and Desire in Literature*. Boston: Little, Brown, 1976.

Bigge-Wither, L., trans. *A Nearly Literal Translation of Homer's "Odyssey" into Accentuated Dramatic Verse*. Oxford: James Parker, 1869.

Blackmur, R. P. *A Primer of Ignorance*. Ed. Joseph Frank. New York: Harcourt, Brace and World, 1967.

Bohlmann, Otto. *Conrad's Existentialism*. Forthcoming from Macmillan.

Bonney, William. *Thorns and Arabesques*. Baltimore, Md.: Johns Hopkins Univ. Press, 1980.

Booth, Wayne. *The Rhetoric of Fiction*. 2d ed. Chicago: Univ. of Chicago Press, 1983.

Boyd, Michael. *The Reflexive Novel: Fiction as Critique*. Lewisburg, Pa.: Bucknell Univ. Press, 1983.

Brooks, Peter. *The Melodramatic Imagination: Balzac, Henry James, Melo-*

drama, and the Mode of Excess. 1976. Reprint. New York: Columbia Univ. Press, 1985.

————. *Reading for the Plot: Design and Intention in Narrative.* New York: Knopf, 1984.

Bross, Addison C. "The Unextinguishable Light of Belief: Conrad's Attitude Toward Women." *Conradiana* 2, no. 3 (1969–70): 39–46.

Burke, Kenneth. *A Grammar of Motives.* 1945. Reprint. Berkeley: Univ. of California Press, 1969.

————. *Language as Symbolic Action: Essays on Life, Literature and Method.* Berkeley: Univ. of California Press, 1966.

————. *The Rhetoric of Religion: Studies in Logology.* Boston: Beacon, 1961.

Burnyeat, Myles. "Can the Skeptic Live His Skepticism?" in Miles Burnyeat, ed., *The Skeptical Tradition,* 117–48. Berkeley: Univ. of California Press, 1983.

Busza, Andrzej. "Rhetoric and Ideology in Conrad's *Under Western Eyes,*" in Norman Sherry, ed., *Joseph Conrad: A Commemoration.* London: Macmillan, 1976.

Camus, Albert. *Notebooks, 1935–1942.* Trans. Philip Thody. New York: Modern Library, 1965.

Cascardi, Anthony J. *The Bounds of Reason: Cervantes, Dostoevsky, and Flaubert.* New York: Columbia Univ. Press, 1986.

Caserio, Robert L. "Joseph Conrad, Dickensian Novelist of the Nineteenth Century: A Dissent from Ian Watt." *Nineteenth-Century Fiction* 36 (1981): 337–47.

————. *Plot, Story, and the Novel: From Dickens and Poe to the Modern Period.* Princeton: Princeton Univ. Press, 1979.

————. "*The Rescue* and the Ring of Meaning." In Ross C. Murfin, ed., *Conrad Revisited,* 125–49.

A Catalogue of Books, Manuscripts from the Library of the Late Joseph Conrad. To be Sold by Auction by Messrs. Hodgson & Co., March 13, 1925.

Cavell, Stanley. *The Claim of Reason: Wittgenstein, Skepticism, Morality, and Tragedy.* Oxford: Oxford Univ. Press, 1979.

————. *In Quest of the Ordinary: Lines of Skepticism and Romanticism.* Chicago: Univ. of Chicago Press, 1988.

————. "Knowing and Acknowledging." In *Must We Mean What We Say? A Book of Essays,* 238–66. Cambridge: Cambridge Univ. Press, 1976.

Clark, John R. *Form and Frenzy in Swift's Tale of a Tub.* Ithaca, N.Y.: Cornell Univ. Press, 1970.

Conrad, Mrs. Joseph. [Jessie George.] *Did Joseph Conrad Return as a Spirit?* Webster Groves, Mo.: International Mark Twain Society, 1932.

Conrad, Jessie. *Joseph Conrad as I Knew Him.* Garden City, N.Y.: Doubleday, Page, 1926.

Conroy, Mark. *Modernism and Authority: Strategies of Legitimation in Flaubert and Conrad*. Baltimore, Md.: Johns Hopkins Univ. Press, 1985.

Cox, C. B. *Joseph Conrad: The Modern Imagination*. London: J. M. Dent, 1974.

Crews, Frederick. *Out of My System: Psychoanalysis, Ideology, and Critical Method*. New York: Oxford Univ. Press, 1975.

———. *Skeptical Engagements*. New York: Oxford Univ. Press, 1986.

Daleski, H. M. *Dickens and the Art of Analogy*. London: Faber and Faber, 1970.

———. *Joseph Conrad: The Way of Dispossession*. London: Faber and Faber, 1977.

Davidson, Arnold E. *Conrad's Endings: A Study of the Five Major Novels*. Ann Arbor: UMI Research Press, 1984.

Descartes, René. *Discourse on Method and Meditations on First Philosophy*. Trans. Donald A. Cress. Indianapolis: Hackett, 1980.

Dickens, Charles. *Bleak House*. 1853. Reprint. Harmondsworth, Eng.: Penguin, 1971.

———. *Great Expectations*. 1861. Reprint. Harmondsworth, Eng.: Penguin, 1965.

———. *Little Dorrit*. 1857. Reprint. Harmondsworth, Eng.: Penguin, 1967.

Docherty, Thomas. *Reading (Absent) Character: Towards a Theory of Characterization in Fiction*. Oxford: Clarendon Press, 1983.

Eagleton, Terry. *Exiles and Émigrés: Studies in Modern Literature*. New York: Schocken Books, 1970.

Eigner, Edwin M. *The Metaphysical Novel in England and America: Dickens, Bulwer, Melville, and Hawthorne*. Berkeley: Univ. of California Press, 1978.

Eliot, George. *Middlemarch*. 1871–72. Reprint. Harmondsworth, Eng.: Penguin, 1965.

Eliot, T. S. "Ulysses, Order, and Myth." In Frank Kermode, ed., *Selected Prose of T. S. Eliot*, 175–78. New York: Harcourt, 1975.

Felperin, Howard. "Romance and Romanticism." *Critical Inquiry* 6 (1980): 691–706.

Fischer, Michael. *Stanley Cavell and Literary Skepticism*. Chicago: Univ. of Chicago Press, 1989.

Fleishman, Avrom. *Conrad's Politics: Community and Anarchy in the Fiction of Joseph Conrad*. Baltimore, Md.: Johns Hopkins Univ. Press, 1967.

———. "Speech and Writing in *Under Western Eyes*." In Sherry, ed., *Joseph Conrad: A Commemoration*, 119–28.

Fogel, Aaron. *Coercion to Speak: Conrad's Poetics of Dialogue*. Cambridge: Harvard Univ. Press, 1985.

Ford, Ford Madox. *The English Novel: From the Earliest Days to the Death of Joseph Conrad*. 1930. Reprint. Manchester, Eng.: Carcanet Press, 1983.

———. *Joseph Conrad: A Personal Remembrance*. London: Duckworth, 1924.

Forster, E. M. "Joseph Conrad: A Note." In *Abinger Harvest*, 136–41. New York: Harcourt, Brace, and World, 1936.

Foucault, Michel. *Discipline and Punish: The Birth of the Prison*. Trans. Alan Sheridan. New York: Vintage, 1979.

———. "The Discourse on Language." An appendix to *The Archaeology of Knowledge*. Trans. A. M. Sheridan Smith. New York: Harper and Row, 1972.

Freedman, Ralph. *The Lyrical Novel: Studies in Hermann Hesse, André Gide, and Virginia Woolf*. Princeton: Princeton Univ. Press, 1963.

Freud, Sigmund. "On the History of the Psychoanalytic Movement." In *The Standard Edition of the Complete Psychological Works of Sigmund Freud*, XIV: 7–66. Trans. and ed. James Strachey. London: Hogarth Press, 1955.

———. "On the Psychical Mechanism of Hysterical Phenomena: A Preliminary Communication." In Strachey, trans. and ed., *The Standard Edition*, II: 3–17.

———. "Remembering, Repeating and Working-Through." In Strachey, trans. and ed., *The Standard Edition*, XII: 147–56.

Friedman, Alan Warren. "Conrad's Picaresque Narrator: Marlow's Journey from 'Youth' through *Chance*." In Wolodymyr T. Zyla and Wendell M. Aycock, eds., *Joseph Conrad: Theory and World Fiction*. Lubbock: Texas Tech Univ. Press, 1974.

———. *The Turn of the Novel: The Transition to Modern Fiction*. New York: Oxford Univ. Press, 1966.

Frug, Jerry. "Henry James, Lee Marvin, and the Law." *New York Times Book Review*, February 16, 1986.

Galsworthy, John. *Castles in Spain and Other Screeds*. London: Heinemann, 1927.

Gardiner, Patrick. *Schopenhauer*. Harmondsworth, Eng.: Penguin, 1967.

Garrett, Peter K. *The Victorian Multiplot Novel: Studies in Dialogical Form*. New Haven, Conn.: Yale Univ. Press, 1980.

Geddes, Gary. *Conrad's Later Novels*. Montreal: McGill-Queen's Univ. Press, 1980.

Gekoski, R. A. *Conrad: The Moral World of the Novelist*. London: Paul Elek, 1978.

Gilbert, Katharine, and Helmut Kuhn. *A History of Esthetics*. Rev. ed. Bloomington: Indiana Univ. Press, 1953.

Gilliam, Harriet. "Undeciphered Hieroglyphs: The Paleography of Conrad's Russian Characters." *Conradiana* 12, no. 1 (1980): 37–50.

Gillon, Adam. "Conrad and Sartre." *Dalhousie Review* 40 (1960–61): 61–71.

――――. *The Eternal Solitary: A Study of Joseph Conrad.* New York: Bookman Associates, 1960.

Gordan, John Dozier. *Joseph Conrad: The Making of a Novelist.* Cambridge: Harvard Univ. Press, 1940.

Graver, Lawrence. "Conrad's First Story." *Studies in Short Fiction* 2 (1965): 164–69.

――――. *Conrad's Short Fiction.* Berkeley: Univ. of California Press, 1969.

Green, Jesse D. "Diabolism, Pessimism, and Democracy: Notes on Melville and Conrad." *Modern Fiction Studies* 8 (1962): 287–305.

Guerard, Albert. *Conrad the Novelist.* Cambridge, 1958. Reprint. New York: Atheneum, 1967.

Guetti, James. *The Limits of Metaphor: A Study of Melville, Conrad, and Faulkner.* Ithaca, N.Y.: Cornell Univ. Press, 1967.

Haight, Gordon S. *George Eliot: A Biography.* New York: Oxford Univ. Press, 1968.

Hardy, Thomas. *Tess of the D'Urbervilles.* 1891. Reprint. Harmondsworth, Eng.: Penguin, 1978.

Harries, Karsten. Yale lecture. February 20, 1983.

Hawkes, Terence. *Metaphor.* London: Methuen, 1972.

Hawthorn, Jeremy. *Joseph Conrad: Language and Fictional Self-Consciousness.* Lincoln: Univ. of Nebraska Press, 1979.

Hay, Eloise Knapp. *The Political Novels of Joseph Conrad: A Critical Study.* Chicago: Univ. of Chicago Press, 1963.

Hewitt, Douglas. *Conrad: A Reassessment.* 3d ed. Totowa, N.J.: Rowman and Littlefield, 1975.

Holquist, Michael. "Answering as Authoring: Mikhail Bakhtin's Trans-Linguistics." In Morson, ed., *Bakhtin: Essays and Dialogues on His Work,* 59–71.

Houghton, Walter E. *The Victorian Frame of Mind, 1830–1870.* New Haven, Conn.: Yale Univ. Press, 1957.

Howe, Irving. *Politics and the Novel.* 1957. Reprint. New York: Discus-Avon, 1970.

Hulme, T. E. "Romanticism and Classicism." In *Speculations: Essays on Humanism and the Philosophy of Art.* London: Routledge and Kegan Paul, 1924.

Hume, David. *A Treatise of Human Nature.* Ed. L. A. Selby-Bigge. Oxford: Clarendon, 1978.

Hunter, Allan. *Joseph Conrad and the Ethics of Darwinism: The Challenges of Science.* London: Croom Helm, 1983.

Huxley, Thomas H. *Man's Place in Nature and Other Anthropological Essays.* London: Macmillan, 1894.

————. *Methods and Results: Essays*. New York: Appleton, 1894.

Inman, Billie A. "The Organic Structure of *Marius the Epicurean*." *Philological Quarterly* 41 (1962): 475–91.

James, Henry. *Notes on Novelists: With Some Other Notes*. New York: Scribner's, 1914.

Jameson, Fredric. *The Political Unconscious: Narrative as a Socially Symbolic Act*. Ithaca, N.Y.: Cornell Univ. Press, 1981.

Jay, Martin. "In the Empire of the Gaze: Foucault and the Denigration of Vision in Twentieth-century French Thought." In David Couzens Hoy, ed., *Foucault: A Critical Reader*. Oxford: Blackwell, 1986.

Jean-Aubry, G., ed. "The Inner History of Conrad's *Suspense*: Notes and Extracts from Letters." *Bookman's Journal* 13, no. 49 (October 1925).

————. *Twenty Letters to Joseph Conrad*. London: The First Edition Club, 1926.

Johnson, Bruce. "Conrad's 'Karain' and *Lord Jim*." *Modern Language Quarterly* 24 (1963): 13–20.

Jonas, Hans. *The Gnostic Religion: The Message of the Alien God and the Beginnings of Christianity*. Rev. ed. Boston: Beacon, 1963.

Joyce, James. *A Portrait of the Artist as a Young Man*. New York, 1916. Reprint. Harmondsworth, Eng.: Penguin, 1976.

————. *Ulysses: The Corrected Text*. Ed. Hans Walter Gabler. New York: Random House, 1986.

Karl, Frederick R. *Joseph Conrad: The Three Lives*. New York: Farrar, Straus and Giroux, 1979.

————. "Three Problematical Areas in Conrad Biography." In Ross C. Murfin, ed., *Conrad Revisited*, 13–30.

Keating, George T., ed. *A Conrad Memorial Library: The Collection of George T. Keating*. Garden City, N.Y.: Doubleday, Doran, 1929.

Kenner, Hugh. *The Mechanic Muse*. New York: Oxford Univ. Press, 1987.

————. *Ulysses*. Rev. ed. Baltimore, Md.: Johns Hopkins Univ. Press, 1987.

Kermode, Frank. "Secrets and Narrative Sequence." *Critical Inquiry* 7 (1980): 83–101. Reprinted in Kermode, *The Art of Telling: Essays on Fiction*. Cambridge: Harvard Univ. Press, 1983.

Kertzer, J. M. " 'The bitterness of our wisdom': Cynicism, Skepticism and Joseph Conrad." *Novel* 16 (1982–83): 121–40.

Kirschner, Paul. *Conrad: The Psychologist as Artist*. Edinburgh: Oliver and Boyd, 1968.

Krieger, Murray. *The Tragic Vision: Variations on a Theme in Literary Interpretation*. New York: Holt, Rinehart and Winston, 1960.

Kripke, Saul A. *Wittgenstein on Rules and Private Language: An Elementary Exposition*. Cambridge: Harvard Univ. Press, 1982.

Lawrence, D. H. "Surgery for the Novel—Or a Bomb." In *Phoenix*, 517–20. New York: Viking, 1936.

———. *Women in Love*. 1921. Reprint. Harmondsworth, Eng.: Penguin, 1976.

Leavis, F. R. *The Great Tradition*. New York: New York Univ. Press, 1969.

Lester, John. *Conrad and Religion*. New York: St. Martin's, 1988.

Lester, John A. *Journey Through Despair, 1880–1914: Transformations in British Literary Culture*. Princeton: Princeton Univ. Press, 1968.

Levenson, Michael. *A Genealogy of Modernism: A Study of English Literary Doctrine, 1908–1922*. Cambridge: Cambridge Univ. Press, 1979.

Levine, George. *The Realistic Imagination: English Fiction from Frankenstein to Lady Chatterly*. Chicago: Univ. of Chicago Press, 1981.

Lewis, R. W. B. "The Current of Conrad's *Victory*." In Charles Shapiro, ed., *Twelve Original Essays on Great English Novels*, 203–31. Detroit: Wayne State Univ. Press, 1960.

Lewitter, L. R. "Conrad, Dostoyevsky, and the Russo-Polish Antagonism." *Modern Language Review* 79 (1984): 653–63.

Luftig, Victor E. " 'Intensities and Avoidances': Representing Friendship Between the Sexes in England, 1850–1940." Ph.D. diss., Stanford University, 1987.

Lukács, Georg. *History and Class Consciousness: Studies in Marxist Dialectics*. Trans. Rodney Livingstone. Cambridge: MIT Press, 1971.

Magee, Bryan. *The Philosophy of Schopenhauer*. New York: Oxford Univ. Press, 1983.

"Maimonides." In *The Encyclopedia of Philosophy*, V: 129–34. Gen. ed. Paul Edwards. New York: Macmillan, 1967.

Marcus, Steven. *Dickens: From Pickwick to Dombey*. London: Chatto and Windus, 1965.

Marten, Harry. "Conrad's Skeptic Reconsidered: A Study of Martin Decoud." *Nineteenth-Century Fiction* 27 (1972–73): 81–94.

Martin, David M. "The Function of the Intended in Conrad's *Heart of Darkness*." *Studies in Short Fiction* 11 (1974): 27–33.

McCarthy, Patrick A. "*Heart of Darkness* and the Early Novels of H. G. Wells: Evolution, Anarchy, Entropy." *Journal of Modern Literature* 13 (1986): 37–60.

McClure, John A. *Kipling and Conrad: The Colonial Fiction*. Cambridge: Harvard Univ. Press, 1981.

Mégroz, R. L. *Joseph Conrad's Mind and Method: A Study of Personality in Art*. London: Faber and Faber, 1931.

Meyer, Bernard C. *Joseph Conrad: A Psychoanalytic Biography*. Princeton: Princeton Univ. Press, 1967.

Miller, J. Hillis. *The Disappearance of God: Five Nineteenth-Century Writers*. Cambridge: Harvard Univ. Press, 1963.

———. *Fiction and Repetition: Seven English Novels*. Cambridge: Harvard Univ. Press, 1982.

———. "*Heart of Darkness* Revisited." In Ross C. Murfin, ed., *Conrad Revisited*, 31–50.

———. Introduction to *Bleak House*. Harmondsworth, Eng.: Penguin, 1971.

———. *Poets of Reality: Six Twentieth-Century Writers*. Cambridge: Harvard Univ. Press, 1965.

Morf, Gustav. *The Polish Heritage of Joseph Conrad*. London: Sampson Low, Marston, 1929.

Morson, Gary Saul, ed. *Bakhtin: Essays and Dialogues on His Work*. Chicago: Univ. of Chicago Press, 1986.

Moser, Thomas. *Joseph Conrad: Achievement and Decline*. 1957. Reprint. Hamden, Conn.: Archon, 1966.

Murdoch, Iris. "The Sublime and the Beautiful Revisited." *Yale Review*, n.s. 49 (1959–60): 247–71.

Murfin, Ross C., ed. *Conrad Revisited: Essays for the Eighties*. University, Ala.: Univ. of Alabama Press, 1985.

Najder, Zdzisław. "Conrad and the Idea of Honor." In Zyla and Aycock, eds., *Joseph Conrad: Theory and World Fiction*, 103–14. Lubbock: Texas Tech Univ. Press, 1974.

———, ed. *Conrad Under Familial Eyes: Texts*. Cambridge: Cambridge Univ. Press, 1983.

———, ed. *Conrad's Polish Background: Letters to and from Polish Friends*. Trans. Halina Carroll. London: Oxford Univ. Press, 1964.

———. *Joseph Conrad: A Chronicle*. New Brunswick, N.J.: Rutgers Univ. Press, 1983.

Newell, Kenneth B. "The Destructive Element and Related 'Dream' Passages in the *Lord Jim* Manuscript." *Journal of Modern Literature* 1 (1970): 31–44.

Nicoll, David. "Stanley's Exploits: Or, Civilizing Africa." Aberdeen: James Leatham, 1891.

Nietzsche, Friedrich. *Beyond Good and Evil: Prelude to a Philosophy of the Future*. Trans. R. J. Hollingdale. Harmondsworth, Eng.: Penguin, 1973.

———. "On Truth and Lies in a Nonmoral Sense." In Daniel Breazeale, trans. and ed., *Philosophy and Truth: Selections from Nietzsche's Notebooks of the Early 1870's*. Atlantic Highlands, N.J.: Humanities Press, 1979.

O'Connor, Flannery. *Mystery and Manners*. Ed. Sally Fitzgerald and Robert Fitzgerald. New York: Farrar, Straus and Giroux, 1969.

O'Hanlon, Redmond. *Joseph Conrad and Charles Darwin: The Influence of Scientific Thought on Conrad's Fiction*. Edinburgh: Salamander Press, 1984.

Otto, Rudolf. *The Idea of the Holy: An Inquiry in the Nonrational Factor in the Idea of the Divine and Its Relation to the Rational.* Trans. John W. Harvey. London: Oxford Univ. Press, 1950.

Palmer, John A. *Joseph Conrad's Fiction: A Study in Literary Growth.* Ithaca, N.Y.: Cornell Univ. Press, 1968.

Park, Douglas B. "Conrad's *Victory*: The Anatomy of a Pose." *Nineteenth-Century Fiction* 31 (1976–77): 150–69.

Parry, Benita. *Conrad and Imperialism: Ideological Boundaries and Visionary Frontiers.* London: Macmillan, 1983.

Pascal, Roy. *The Dual Voice: Free Indirect Speech and Its Functioning in the Nineteenth-Century European Novel.* Manchester, Eng.: Manchester Univ. Press, 1977.

Pater, Walter. *The Renaissance.* London, 1873. Reprint. New York: Boni and Liveright, 1919.

Paterson, John. *The Novel as Faith: The Gospel According to James, Hardy, Conrad, Joyce, Lawrence, and Virginia Woolf.* Boston: Gambit, 1973.

Perry, John Oliver. "Action, Vision, or Voice: The Moral Dilemmas in Conrad's Tale-Telling." *Modern Fiction Studies* 10 (1964): 3–14.

Popkin, Richard H. *The History of Scepticism from Erasmus to Spinoza.* Berkeley: Univ. of California Press, 1979.

Porte, Joel. "In the Hands of an Angry God: Religious Terror in Gothic Fiction." In G. R. Thompson, ed., *The Gothic Imagination: Essays in Dark Romanticism,* 42–64. Pullman: Washington State Univ. Press, 1974.

Price, Martin. "Conrad: Satire and Fiction." *Yearbook of English Studies* 14 (1984): 226–42.

———. *Forms of Life: Character and Moral Imagination in the Novel.* New Haven, Conn.: Yale Univ. Press, 1983.

Purdy, Dwight H. *Joseph Conrad's Bible.* Norman: Univ. of Oklahoma Press, 1984.

Putnam, Hilary. *Reason, Truth, and History.* Cambridge: Cambridge Univ. Press, 1981.

———. "Robots: Machines or Artificially Created Life?" *Journal of Philosophy* 61 (1964): 668–91.

Quigley, Austin E. "Wittgenstein's Philosophizing and Literary Philosophizing." *New Literary History* 19 (1988): 209–37.

Railo, Eino. *The Haunted Castle: A Study of the Elements of English Romanticism.* Atlantic Highlands, N.J.: Humanities Press, 1964.

Raval, Suresh. *The Art of Failure: Conrad's Fiction.* Boston: Allen and Unwin, 1986.

———. "Conrad's *Victory*: Skepticism and Experience." *Nineteenth-Century Fiction* 34 (1979–80): 414–33.

———. "Narrative and Authority in *Lord Jim*: Conrad's Art of Failure." *English Literary History* 48 (1981): 387–410.

Ray, Martin. "Conrad, Nordau, and Other Degenerates: The Psychology of *The Secret Agent*." *Conradiana* 16, no. 2 (1984): 125–40.

Reid, Stephen A. "The 'Unspeakable Rites' in *Heart of Darkness*." *Modern Fiction Studies* 9 (1963–64): 347–56.

Rorty, Richard. "The Philosophy of the Oddball." *The New Republic*, June 19, 1989, 38–41.

Roussel, Royal. *The Metaphysics of Darkness: A Study in the Unity and Development of Conrad's Fiction*. Baltimore, Md.: Johns Hopkins Univ. Press, 1971.

Royce, Josiah. *The Spirit of Modern Philosophy: An Essay in the Form of Lectures*. New York: George Braziller, 1955.

Russell, Bertrand. "A Free Man's Worship." 1892. Reprinted in Robert E. Eigner and Lester E. Denonn, eds., *The Basic Writings of Bertrand Russell, 1903–1959*. New York: Simon and Schuster, 1961.

Ruthven, K. K. "The Savage God: Conrad and Lawrence." In C. B. Cox and A. E. Dyson, eds., *Word in the Desert*. London: Oxford Univ. Press, 1968.

Said, Edward. *Beginnings: Intention and Method*. New York: Columbia Univ. Press, 1975.

———. "Conrad and Nietzsche." In Sherry, ed., *Joseph Conrad: A Commemoration*, 65–76.

———. "Conrad: The Presentation of Narrative." *Novel* 7 (1974): 116–32.

———. *Joseph Conrad and the Fiction of Autobiography*. Cambridge: Harvard Univ. Press, 1966.

———. "The Problem of Textuality: Two Exemplary Positions." *Critical Inquiry* 4 (1978): 673–714.

Schopenhauer, Arthur. *The World as Will and Idea*. Trans. R. B. Haldane and J. Kemp. Vol. I. London: Trubner, 1883.

———. *The World as Will and Representation*. Trans. E. F. J. Payne. 2 vols. New York: Dover, 1966.

Schwab, Arnold T. "Joseph Conrad's American Friend: Correspondence with James Huneker." *Modern Philology* 52 (1955): 222–32.

Schwarz, Daniel R. *Conrad: The Later Fiction*. London: Macmillan, 1982.

Seidel, Michael. *Exile and the Narrative Imagination*. New Haven, Conn.: Yale Univ. Press, 1986.

Sherry, Norman, ed. *Conrad: The Critical Heritage*. London: Routledge and Kegan Paul, 1973.

———. *Conrad's Eastern World*. Cambridge: Cambridge Univ. Press, 1966.

———. *Conrad's Western World*. Cambridge: Cambridge Univ. Press, 1971.

————, ed. *Joseph Conrad: A Commemoration*. London: Macmillan, 1976.

Shweder, Richard. "Menstrual Pollution, Soul Loss, and the Comparative Study of Emotions." In Arthur Kleinman and Byron Good, eds., *Culture and Depression: Studies in the Anthropology and Cross-Cultural Psychiatry of Affect and Disorder*. Berkeley: Univ. of California Press, 1985.

Simmel, Georg. *Schopenhauer and Nietzsche*. 1907. Trans. Helmut Loiskandl et al. Amherst: Univ. of Massachusetts Press, 1986.

Simpson, David. *Fetishism and Imagination: Dickens, Melville, Conrad*. Baltimore, Md.: Johns Hopkins Univ. Press, 1982.

Stallman, Robert W. "Time and *The Secret Agent*." In Robert W. Stallman, ed., *The Art of Joseph Conrad: A Critical Symposium*, 234–54. East Lansing: Michigan State Univ. Press, 1960.

Stark, Bruce R. "Kurtz's Intended: The Heart of *Heart of Darkness*." *Texas Studies in Literature and Language* 16 (1974–75): 535–55.

Steegmuller, Francis, ed. *The Letters of Gustave Flaubert, 1830–1857*. Vol. I. Cambridge: Harvard Univ. Press, 1980.

Stewart, Garrett. *Death Sentences: Styles of Dying in British Fiction*. Cambridge: Harvard Univ. Press, 1984.

————. "Lying as Dying in *Heart of Darkness*." *Publications of the Modern Language Association* 95 (1980): 319–31.

Strawson, P. F. *Skepticism and Naturalism: Some Varieties*. New York: Columbia Univ. Press, 1985.

Sullivan, Jack. *Elegant Nightmares: The English Ghost Story from Le Fanu to Blackwood*. Athens: Ohio Univ. Press, 1978.

Sully, James. *Pessimism: A History and a Criticism*. London: Henry S. King, 1877.

Swift, Jonathan. *Gulliver's Travels and Other Writings*. Ed. Louis Landa. Boston: Houghton Mifflin, 1960.

Tanner, Tony. "Butterflies and Beetles—Conrad's Two Truths." *Chicago Review* 16 (1963): 123–40. Reprinted in Thomas C. Moser, ed., the Norton Critical Edition of *Lord Jim*, 447–62.

————. "'Gnawed Bones' and 'Artless Tales'—Eating and Narrative in Conrad." In Sherry, ed., *Joseph Conrad: A Commemoration*, 17–36.

————. "Joseph Conrad and the Last Gentleman." *Critical Quarterly* 28, no. 1 (1986): 109–42.

Thomas, Brooke. "Preserving and Keeping Order by Killing Time in *Heart of Darkness*." In Ross C. Murfin, ed., *Joseph Conrad: "Heart of Darkness": A Case Study in Contemporary Criticism*. New York: St. Martin's, 1989.

Thomas, Keith. *Man and the Natural World: A History of the Modern Sensibility*. New York: Pantheon, 1983.

Thompson, G. R., ed. *The Gothic Imagination: Essays in Dark Romanticism.* Pullman: Washington State Univ. Press, 1974.

Thompson, John B. *Studies in the Theory of Ideology.* Cambridge: Polity Press, 1984.

Thorburn, David. *Conrad's Romanticism.* New Haven, Conn.: Yale Univ. Press, 1974.

Tillyard, E. M. W. *The Epic Strain in the English Novel.* London: Chatto and Windus, 1967.

Tindall, William York. "Apology for Marlow." In Robert C. Rathburn and Martin Steinmann, Jr., eds., *From Jane Austen to Conrad: Essays Collected in the Memory of James T. Hillhouse,* 274–85. Minneapolis: Univ. of Minnesota Press, 1958.

Todorov, Tzvetan. *The Fantastic: A Structural Approach to a Literary Genre.* Trans. Richard Howard. Cleveland: Case Western Reserve Univ. Press, 1973.

Trilling, Lionel. "On the Teaching of Modern Literature." In *Beyond Culture: Essays on Literature and Learning.* New York: Viking, 1965.

————. *Sincerity and Authenticity.* Cambridge: Harvard Univ. Press, 1972.

Van Ghent, Dorothy. *The English Novel: Form and Function.* New York: Holt, Rinehart and Winston, 1953.

Varma, Devendra. *The Gothic Flame.* London: Arthur Barker, 1957.

Varnado, S. L. "The Idea of the Numinous in Gothic Literature." In G. R. Thompson, ed., *The Gothic Imagination: Essays in Dark Romanticism,* 11–21.

Vartanian, Aram. "Man-Machine from the Greeks to the Computer." In Philip P. Weiner, ed., *Dictionary of the History of Ideas.* Vol. III. New York: Scribner's, 1973–74.

Warren, Robert Penn. "'The Great Mirage': Conrad and *Nostromo,*" 31–58. In *Selected Essays.* New York: Random House, 1951.

Watt, Ian P. *Conrad in the Nineteenth Century.* Berkeley: Univ. of California Press, 1979.

————, ed. *Conrad: The Secret Agent. A Casebook.* London: Macmillan, 1973.

————. "Joseph Conrad: Alienation and Commitment." In Hugh Sykes Davies and George Watson, eds., *The English Mind,* 257–78. Cambridge: Cambridge Univ. Press, 1964.

————. *Joseph Conrad: "Nostromo."* Landmarks of World Literature. Cambridge: Cambridge Univ. Press, 1988.

————. *The Rise of the Novel: Studies in Defoe, Richardson and Fielding.* Berkeley: Univ. of California Press, 1957.

————. "Story and Idea in Conrad's *The Shadow-Line.*" In Mark Schorer, ed., *Modern British Fiction.* New York: Oxford Univ. Press, 1961.

Watts, Cedric. *Joseph Conrad: A Literary Life*. London: Macmillan, 1989.

———. *A Preface to Conrad*. London: Longman, 1982.

Wellek, René. *A History of Modern Criticism: 1750–1950*. Vol. II. New Haven, Conn.: Yale Univ. Press, 1955.

Wells, H. G. *Works of H. G. Wells*. Ed. George Gesner. New York: Avenel, 1982.

Welsh, Alexander. "The Allegory of Truth in English Fiction." *Victorian Studies* 9 (1965–66): 7–28.

Whitehead, A. N. *Science and the Modern World*. 1925. Reprint. New York: Free Press, 1967.

Whitehead, Lee M. "Conrad's 'Pessimism' Re-examined." *Conradiana* 2, no. 3 (1969–70): 25–38.

Widmer, Kingsley. "Conrad's Pyrrhonistic Conservativism: Ideological Melodrama Around 'Simple Ideas.'" *Novel* 7 (1974): 133–42.

Williams, Raymond. *The English Novel: From Dickens to Lawrence*. London: Chatto and Windus, 1970.

———. *The Long Revolution*. New York: Columbia Univ. Press, 1961.

Wilt, Judith. *Ghosts of the Gothic: Austen, Eliot, and Lawrence*. Princeton: Princeton Univ. Press, 1980.

Wohl, Robert. *The Generation of 1914*. Cambridge: Harvard Univ. Press, 1979.

Woolf, Virginia. "Mr. Conrad: A Conversation." In *The Captain's Death Bed and Other Essays*. 1923. Reprint. New York: Harcourt, Brace, 1978.

———. *To the Lighthouse*. 1927. Reprint. New York: Harcourt, Brace & World, 1955.

Yelton, Donald C. *Mimesis and Metaphor: An Inquiry into the Genesis and Scope of Conrad's Symbolic Imagery*. The Hague: Mouton, 1967.

Young, Helen H. *The Writings of Walter Pater: A Reflection of British Philosophical Opinion from 1860–1890*. Lancaster, Pa.: Lancaster Press, 1933.

Zyla, Wolodymyr T., and Wendell M. Aycock, eds. *Joseph Conrad: Theory and World Fiction*. Comparative Literature Symposium. Proceedings of the Comparative Literature Symposium, v. 7. Lubbock: Texas Tech Univ. Press, 1974.

Index

Index

Library of Congress Cataloging-in-Publication Data

Wollaeger, Mark A., 1957–
    Joseph Conrad and the fictions of skepticism / Mark A. Wollaeger.
        p.   cm.
    Includes bibliographical references and index.
    ISBN 0-8047-1833-4 (alk. paper)
        1. Conrad, Joseph, 1857–1924—Criticism and interpretation.
2. Conrad, Joseph, 1857–1924—Philosophy. 3. Skepticism in
literature. I. Title.
PR6005.04Z936   1990
823'.912—dc20   90-36477
                                                                     CIP

⊗ This book is printed on acid-free paper.